COMPLICATED LIVES

THE RUTGERS SERIES IN CHILDHOOD STUDIES

The Rutgers Series in Childhood Studies is dedicated to increasing our understanding of children and childhoods throughout the world, reflecting a perspective that highlights cultural dimensions of the human experience. The books in this series are intended for students, scholars, practitioners, and those who formulate policies that affect children's everyday lives and futures.

Edited by

Jill E. Korbin, Associate Dean, College of Arts and Sciences; Professor, Department of Anthropology; Director, Schubert Center for Child Studies; Co-Director, Childhood Studies Program, Case Western Reserve University

Elisa (EJ) Sobo, Professor of Anthropology, San Diego State University

Editorial Board

Mara Buchbinder, Assistant Professor, Department of Social Medicine, University of North Carolina, Chapel Hill

Meghan Halley, Assistant Scientist, Palo Alto Medical Foundation

David Lancy, Emeritus Professor of Anthropology, Utah State University

Heather Montgomery, Reader, Anthropology of Childhood, Open University (UK)

David Rosen, Professor of Anthropology and Sociology, Fairleigh Dickinson University

Rachael Stryker, Assistant Professor of Department of Human Development and Women's Studies, California State University, East Bay

Tom Weisner, Professor of Anthropology, University of California, Los Angeles

Founding Editor: Myra Bluebond-Langner, University College London, Institute of Child Health

For a list of all the titles in the series, please see the last page of the book.

COMPLICATED LIVES

Girls, Parents, Drugs, and Juvenile Justice

VERA LOPEZ

RUTGERS UNIVERSITY PRESS
New Brunswick, Camden, and Newark, New Jersey, and London

Library of Congress Cataloging-in-Publication Data
Names: Lopez, Vera, 1971– author.
Title: Complicated lives : girls, parents, drugs, and juvenile justice / Vera Lopez.
Description: New Brunswick : Rutgers University Press, [2017] | Series:
    The Rutgers series in childhood studies | Includes bibliographical references
    and index.
Identifiers: LCCN 2016038036| ISBN 9780813586557 (hardcover : alk. paper) |
    ISBN 9780813586540 (pbk. : alk. paper) | ISBN 9780813586564 (e-book (epub)) |
    ISBN 9780813586571 (e-book (web pdf))
Subjects: LCSH: Female juvenile delinquents—United States—Social
    conditions—Case studies. | Teenage girls—Drug use—United States—Case
    studies. | Children of drug abusers—Family relationships—United States—
    Case studies. | Abused children—United States—Case studies. | Dysfunctional
    families—United States—Case studies. | Juvenile justice, Administration of—
    United States—Case studies.
Classification: LCC HV9104 .L66 2017 | DDC 364.36082/0973—dc23
LC record available at https://lccn.loc.gov/2016038036

A British Cataloging-in-Publication record for this book is available from the
British Library.

∞ The paper used in this publication meets the requirements of the American
National Standard for Information Sciences—Permanence of Paper for Printed
Library Materials, ANSI Z39.48–1992.

www.rutgersuniversitypress.org

Manufactured in the United States of America

In Loving Memory

Severa Luz Lopez
1931–1984

Joe S. Lopez
1950–2009

Fidencio Lopez
1923–2012

CONTENTS

COMPLICATED LIVES

INTRODUCTION

I met 17-year-old Quinn on a clear fall day. We sat outside at a picnic table during visiting hours at the Arroyo Verde state juvenile correctional facility. We were the only ones sitting outside as the other girls preferred to meet with their family members in the loud visiting room, perhaps because that's where the snack and vending machines were located. Quinn, like many of the young women at the state juvenile correctional facility, did not see her family on a regular basis. They lived in another county and were rarely able to make the trip to visit Quinn at Arroyo Verde, which meant that she was willing to meet with me during visiting time. My first impression of Quinn was that she was timid and soft-spoken. As we talked it became clear that she had endured quite a lot in her young life. At the time of our interview, she had been locked up at Arroyo Verde for three months. A striking redhead, Quinn did not believe that she was worthy of being loved. This became clear as we sat and talked on that clear fall day, surrounded by a chain-linked fence topped by razor wire.

Quinn grew up in a mid-sized city in the southwestern United States. She lived with her mother and stepfather, both of whom used methamphetamine and had served time in prison for drug-related offenses. Quinn had never met her biological father and referred to her stepfather as the only father figure she had ever known. Quinn's stepfather sexually abused her when she was 7 years old. When I asked if she had told her mother about her stepfather, Quinn said, "Yes, my mom knew, but she didn't want to break up with him, so she said I had it wrong, and she stayed with him." As she approached adolescence, Quinn began to skip school, run away, and do drugs. When she was 14, she tried methamphetamine. Eventually, Quinn's meth use began to spiral out of control. Out on the streets, she began to engage in unprotected, anonymous sexual encounters as indicated by the following story she shared: "I was waiting for the bus at the corner of Lark Lane and 25th Street when this guy sat next to me. He was older, but not too old . . . maybe early 20s. We started talking. And then it just went from there. We ended up having sex behind a Big Lots." When I asked Quinn if she had ever feared contracting a sexually transmitted infection such as HIV, she matter of factly said, "No. I didn't care if I got AIDS or if I died. Nothing mattered. I didn't care about anything. Whether I lived or died. It made no difference to me." Eventually, Quinn met a much older man who began to "pimp" her out. "I was a prostitute. I didn't care. I did whatever I could to get money, get high. I didn't care who I was with or what I had to do." After she started engaging in prostitution, Quinn was raped. She struggled with making sense of the assault and asked me: "I'm not sure if you could call it a rape? I mean I didn't want to do it, but can a prostitute be raped?" I asked if Quinn had talked about these traumatic experiences during individual therapy sessions at the correctional facility. While Quinn indicated that she had talked about her experiences, and believed that therapy was helping her, she did not feel as if she could successfully stop using meth when she left Arroyo Verde even though she wanted to stay clean and sober.

Quinn's story is not unique. The vast majority of young women in the juvenile justice system have grown up in families characterized by parental drug use, domestic violence, parental incarceration, high rates of residential mobility, and poverty (Acoca, 1998; Gaarder & Belknap, 2002; Lederman, Dakof, Larrea, & Li, 2004). Growing up in troubled families places girls at significant risk for being neglected, physically abused, and sexually victimized (Chesney-Lind & Shelden, 2013; Gaarder & Belknap, 2002; Salisbury & Van Voorhis, 2009). While boys and girls experience similar rates of neglect and physical abuse, girls are more likely to be sexually abused than boys (Hennessey, Ford, Mahoney, Ko, & Siegfried, 2004). According to gendered pathways theories, childhood trauma and victimization often lead to depression and other internalizing disorders among girls, which frequently lead to running away and self-medicating behaviors such as drug use (Chesney-Lind & Shelden, 2013; Gaarder & Belknap, 2002; Kempf-Leonard & Johansson, 2007; Salisbury & Van Voorhis, 2009). The underlying premise of this theoretical perspective is that girls run away from home and use drugs to escape and cope with victimization and trauma, which often leads to their involvement in the juvenile justice system. Implicit in this perspective is that families—usually parents—are at the root of girls' problems. In this book, I wish to expand upon this typical framing of girls' drug use and delinquency by also considering how larger sociocultural contexts and structures influence girls, their relationships with parents, and their eventual involvement in the juvenile justice system.

INTRODUCING THE STUDY PARTICIPANTS

This book presents the life experiences of 65 system-involved girls growing up in multistressed families characterized by parental drug use, domestic violence, and child abuse/neglect. *System-involved* refers to girls who are involved in the juvenile justice system. All of the girls in this study had used drugs and had been court ordered to live outside their home in a group home, residential treatment center, or correctional facility. Many of the girls interviewed for this book were also involved in the child protective and behavioral health systems. Although the 65 interviews with system-involved girls form the backbone of this book, I also draw upon focus group data with 19 drug-involved Latina girls and 8 clinicians who work with them. These interview and focus group data along with my observations and experiences derived from a 12-month clinical internship at the Arroyo Verde state correctional facility for girls informed the writing of this book.

To be included in this study, all girls had to be between the ages of 14 and 18 and have a history of using drugs other than marijuana or alcohol. In the majority of cases, girls used hard drugs with methamphetamine being by far the most popular drug of choice. As indicated in Table 1, this study was composed mostly of Latina girls (65%) of Mexican origin and White girls. While the study also included biracial girls, no African American girls participated in this study, perhaps due to the relatively small African American population in the state of Arizona.

The fact that 65% of the interviewed girls were Latinas is worth emphasizing given that Latina/o youth are disproportionately overrepresented at all levels of the Arizona juvenile justice system. While Latinas/os made up 38.8%

TABLE 1 Study Participants' Background Characteristics and Circumstances

	Number	%
Age		
14	11	17%
15	14	21%
16	19	29%
17	20	31%
18	1	2%
Race/Ethnicity		
Latina	42	65%
White	17	26%
Biracial	6	9%
Living Arrangement while Growing Up*		
With Mother Only	30	46%
With Father Only	1	2%
With Mother + Father	3	5%
With Mother + Mother's Boyfriend/Stepfather	17	26%
With Relatives	8	12%
Foster Care Parents/Group Homes	6	9%
Pregnancy History		
Never Pregnant	38	58%
Ever Pregnant	15	23%
Currently Pregnant	9	14%
Already a Parent	3	5%
Drug Use		
Drug Use Beyond Marijuana[†]	54	83%

*Living arrangements were constantly shifting for many of the girls. The living arrangement while growing up reflects the type of living arrangement they most often lived in while growing up.
†I was interested in interviewing girls with histories of drug involvement. If girls reported drug use other than marijuana or alcohol, they were eligible to participate in the study. Most girls reported using heavy drugs that went beyond marijuana use.

of the state's youth population in 2006, they made up 49.3% of youth assigned to intensive probation, 55% of youth remanded to juvenile corrections, and 59.2% of youth prosecuted as adults (Children's Action Alliance, 2008).

Another striking characteristic of the sample is that most of the girls interviewed for this book had lived in many different settings and with many different people over the course of their young lives. At the time of the interviews, all girls were living in a group home, residential treatment

TABLE 2 Race/Ethnicity by Placement Type

Race/Ethnicity	Arroyo Verde Correctional Facility		Desert Star Residential Treatment Center*		Moonlight, Green River, and Oak Canyon Group Homes	
	Number	%	Number	%	Number	%
Latina	13	52%	18	100%	11	50%
White	8	32%			9	41%
Biracial	4	16%			2	9%

*Only Latina girls were recruited at this site.

TABLE 3 Girls' Family Problems

	Number	%
Parental Drug Use	46	70%
Parent Ever in Prison/Jail	44	68%
Saw Domestic Violence between Mother–Partner	43	66%

center, or the state correctional facility for girls. A breakdown of where the girls were living at the time of the interviews is presented in Table 2.

Girls also reported a high rate of residential mobility as their parents moved often or they were shuttled back and forth between various relatives. The high rate of residential mobility among this sample is not surprising given that residential mobility has been linked with drug use and delinquency in adolescence (DeWit, 1998; Gasper, Deluca, & Estacion, 2010).

Many of the young women interviewed for this book also grew up in families characterized by parental drug abuse, domestic violence, and parental incarceration. In short, their early lives were characterized by an extreme degree of chaos, change, and uncertainty. As can be seen in Table 3, a large percentage (70%) of girls reported that either their mother or father had used drugs at some point during their childhood. Sixty-eight percent of the girls also reported that at least one of their parents had been in prison/jail, and 66% reported having witnessed a physical altercation (domestic violence) between their mothers and at least one of her male partners. (For more information about the study participants and research methodology, see Appendices A and B in the back of the book.)

PURPOSE OF THIS BOOK

The focus of this book is on understanding how system-involved girls view their relationships with parents, many of whom used drugs, had been in jail/prison, and had been involved in violent relationships. Consistent with the overarching gendered pathways to delinquency perspective (Chesney-Lind & Shelden, 2013; Kempf-Leonard & Johansson, 2007; Salisbury & Van Voorhis, 2009), this book discusses how girls' early experiences growing up in so-called troubled or dysfunctional families influenced their later decisions to run away, use drugs, and commit delinquent acts. Girls' stories are presented in full even when doing so presents their parents and families in a negative light. On the other hand, alternative views of system-involved girls' parents that are often not seen in the social science literature, on the late night news, or in other forms of popular media are also presented, including girls' happy childhood memories of parents. Central questions that are addressed throughout this book include: How do system-involved girls make sense of their relationships with parents? How do their relationships with parents influence their decisions to run away, use drugs, and commit delinquent acts? Once girls are in the system, how does the system respond to them and their parents? How are these responses gendered, racialized, and classed? And, finally, how can we better address the needs of both system-involved girls and their parents without further pathologizing, stigmatizing, and blaming them for their problems?

Although the primary focus of this book was to better understand system-involved girls' relationships with parents, it is important to recognize that these relationships are embedded within larger sociocultural contexts and shaped by larger social structures such as socioeconomic status, race, and gender. Thus, system-involved girls' relationships with parents were situated within these larger contexts and structures. Doing so required using a variety of lenses and angles to conceptualize and analyze the girls' narratives. First, a narrow focus was used to examine girls' interactions with parents as they related to girls' decisions to run away, use drugs, and engage in other delinquent behaviors. This approach required focusing primarily on girls' narratives as the basis of understanding their relationships with parents over time. A wide-angle lens was then used to examine how larger sociocultural contexts and structures influenced girls' relationships with parents, partners, and juvenile justice professionals. These goals were accomplished by relying on a critical approach to family studies that was grounded in an ecodevelopmental framework and an intersectional approach to consider how context, processes, and structures shaped young women's identities and interactions over time and placed them at risk for drug use and involvement in the juvenile justice system.

A CRITICAL APPROACH TO FAMILY STUDIES

The ecodevelopmental framework represents a useful starting point for thinking about how various contexts influence individuals' development over time from early childhood to adolescence (Szapocznik & Coatsworth, 1999). This framework is based on social-ecological theory (Bronfenbrenner, 1986) and incorporates an emphasis on child development and social interactions. In brief, the ecodevelopmental framework recognizes that a child's development is shaped by her social interactions with others, which in turn are influenced by other relationships and contexts beyond her direct experience, as well as larger social institutions, structures, and cultural ideals (Szapocznik & Coatsworth, 1999). These interdependent influences on a child's development are usually depicted as concentric circles with the individual child being at the center of this ring of circles. The innermost circle is called the microsystem and is characterized by the child's direct relationships with other individuals (e.g., parents, peers, teachers, probation officers, clinicians, social workers), settings (e.g., home, neighborhood), and institutions (e.g., school, group homes, juvenile correctional facilities, residential treatment centers). The next circle represents the mesosystem and relates to the interactions that people in the microsystems have with each other (e.g., parent–peers, parent–teachers, parent–probation officers, parent–caseworkers). The exosystem, which is represented by the third circle, is the wider context that relates to the broader community in which the child lives, but does not directly participate in. The exosystem can include parents' social support networks, legal services, welfare services, parents' work environment, prisons, local government, and the mass media. Although the child may not directly participate in or interact within these contexts, they still impact her development because they impact other people in her life. The final layer of the child's social ecology is the macrosystem and is represented by the outermost circle. This layer contains the attitudes, ideologies, laws, and norms of a particular culture. Examples of macrosystems include political laws and rhetoric (e.g., minimum sentencing drug laws, anti-immigration legislation), cultural ideals (e.g., about what constitutes "normal" families and good parenting, beliefs about meritocracy and personal responsibility), norms (e.g., drug use norms), and attitudes (e.g., attitudes that support violence against girls and women).

While the ecodevelopmental framework is a classic theory that is quite popular in family studies and child development research, it has not been used to better understand the lives of system-involved girls. Furthermore, most researchers who rely on this framework continue to focus only on

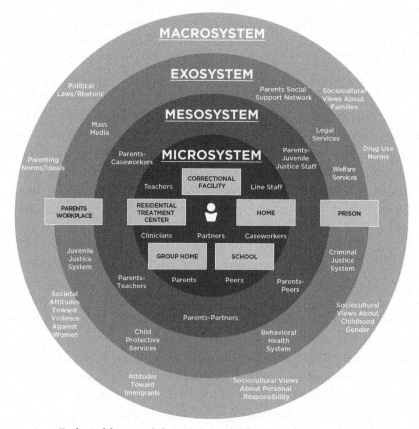

FIGURE 1 Ecological framework for system-involved girls. Created by Tyson Koerper of TK Creative, LLC.

the micro- and meso-systems with scant attention given to the exo- and macro-systems. Perhaps most importantly, while the ecodevelopmental framework stresses the importance of understanding how larger macrosystems influence individual development; no mention is made of how these systems variously impact individuals with intersecting identities and social locations. Finally, the ecodevelopmental framework is not critical nor does it benefit from a social justice perspective. For all these reasons, I advocate pairing the ecodevelopmental framework with an intersectional approach.

Rooted in traditions of Black feminist criminology, intersectionality is an approach that "recognizes that systems of power such as race, class, and gender do not act alone to shape our experiences but rather, are multiplicative, inextricably linked, and simultaneously experienced" (Burgess-Proctor, 2006, p. 31; Potter, 2015). Intersectionality acknowledges the importance of considering multiple intersecting identities while also considering how these identities are related to individuals' views of themselves and others in relation to their unique social, cultural, and contextual locations. Although most of the young women interviewed for this book shared a similar class background, they differed with regard to ethnicity and generation status. Thus, this book considers how gender, ethnicity, class, and nationality shaped young women's views of themselves, their relationships, and their experiences across a number of contexts and systems over time.

SYSTEM-INVOLVED GIRLS: CONTEXTS, RELATIONSHIPS, AND INTERSECTIONALITY

This section presents a more detailed discussion of how an interdisciplinary and critical approach to family studies can be used to better understand system-involved girls' experiences and relationships across a number of ecological contexts from childhood through adolescence. These experiences and relationships are situated within a broader sociocultural context while simultaneously considering how girls' experiences are gendered, racialized, and classed.

Microsystems

The three microsystems that were examined for the young women interviewed for this book were their homes, the streets they ran to, and the youth facilities they lived in. Girls' homes were usually characterized by their relationships with mothers, mothers' partners, and siblings. Other relatives, family friends, and parents' drug-using acquaintances were also sometimes present. The focus was primarily on girls' relationships with parents (including nonresident fathers) given that the quality of the parent–child relationship plays a critical role in children's development.

Parenting characterized by a high degree of warmth, support, monitoring, involvement, and consistent but not overly harsh disciplinary practices has been found to be predictive of positive youth outcomes across a variety of cultures and contexts (Kotchick & Forehand, 2002). Harsh, neglectful, and abusive parenting, on the other hand, has been associated with adverse emotional and behavioral youth outcomes (Becoña et al., 2012). One thing is certain: Parents play a powerful role in their children's development and when the quality of the parent–child relationship is compromised, children suffer. For the girls interviewed for this book, parental substance use definitely compromised the quality of their relationships with parents.[1] Previous research indicates that mothers with histories of substance abuse/ dependence often demonstrate "poor sensitivity, unresponsiveness to children's emotional cues, and heightened physical provocation and intrusiveness" (Suchman, Pajulo, DeCoste, & Mayes, 2006, p. 211). Furthermore, parents with substance use issues frequently flit in and out of their children's lives as a result of jail, prison, drug binges, and/or drug and mental health treatment and this was certainly the case in the current study (Kroll & Taylor, 2003; National Center on Addiction and Substance Abuse, 1999). Parental substance abuse has also been found to be associated with child abuse and neglect, and this was also true for the girls interviewed for this book whose parents sometimes neglected and/or inadvertently placed them in harm's way as a result of their drug use (Kroll & Taylor, 2003; National Center on Addiction and Substance Abuse, 1999).

The nature of girls' relationships with parents changed over time from childhood to adolescence. During childhood, many of the young women assumed adultified roles and helped their mothers care for younger siblings along with serving as their mothers' relationship advisors and attempting to protect them from violence. They assumed a high degree of control and responsibility in their homes, and as a result of these responsibilities, they were exposed to adult problems (e.g., domestic violence) and contexts (e.g., drug houses), which forced them to "grow up fast." By late childhood and early adolescence, many of these young women were already skipping school, drinking alcohol, using drugs, having sex, and hanging out with older peers. Like many adolescents, they bickered and argued with their parents when their parents attempted to discipline and monitor their behaviors. Conflicts with mothers about boyfriends, staying out late, and drug use were common. While such conflicts are not uncommon in adolescence, they do not typically threaten the fabric or integrity of the parent–adolescent relationship (Smetana, Campione-Barr, & Metzger, 2006). This was not the case for many of the young women interviewed for this book. Their problems with parents, which were rooted in childhood, came to the forefront during adolescence.

During adolescence, as posited by the gendered pathways to delinquency perspectives, many of the young women began to run away from home. While some ran away to escape abuse and victimization, others were also attracted to the "street life" that they saw all around them in the neighborhoods where they lived. The streets represented a gender salient context that was particularly dangerous for young women given their age and gender, as most of the young women lived in areas characterized by drug use, violence, and in some instances, gangs. When they ran away, they often ended up interacting with older adult drug users and becoming romantically involved with men who used and/or sold drugs.

Due to their "out of control" behaviors, the young women interviewed for this book eventually came under the scrutiny of outside officials including concerned school officials, law enforcement, social workers, and juvenile justice professionals. Eventually the state removed these young women from their homes and remanded them to an out-of-home youth placement, which is where I interviewed them. The girls interviewed for this study lived in either a group home (Moonlight, Green River, Oak Canyon), a residential treatment center (Desert Star) or a juvenile correctional facility (Arroyo Verde). These facilities and the relationships embedded within them represented important microsystemic influences on the girls' development. The facilities differed in terms of how secure they were as well as how they framed and responded to girls' problems. Not surprisingly, many of the young women struggled with following rules in these settings, because they often placed them in the conventional role of "child" or "adolescent" despite their adultified experiences. Similar to research on adult women prisoners, many of the young women interviewed for this book felt isolated from their friends, families, and communities (Arditti, 2012; McCorkel, 2013; Siegel, 2011).

Mesosystems

System-involved youth are typically involved with a number of youth professionals across a variety of systems including the juvenile justice, behavioral health, and child protective services systems, which means their parents must also interact with these professionals as well. This book focuses primarily on the mesosystem that involved parents' relationships with youth professionals across these various youth systems and contexts. Parents of system-involved youth often feel as if their contributions on behalf of their children are not valued (Aldridge, Shute, Ralphs, & Medina, 2011). For example, in their interviews and focus groups with parents of gang-involved youth, Judith Aldridge, Jon Shute, Robert Ralphs, and Juanjo Medina (2011) found that parents often felt like the juvenile justice staff belittled, patronized, and blamed them for being "bad" parents. Joanne Belknap and colleagues found that some juvenile justice professionals blame parents for their daughters' problems (Belknap, Holsinger, & Dunn, 1997; Belknap, Winter, & Cady, 2003). I certainly found this to be the case when I conducted focus groups with clinicians at the residential treatment center about the Latina girls in their care. While these educated, middle-class, mostly White women seemed to genuinely care about the young women in their care, they often relied on cultural deficit thinking rooted in stereotypes to explain why Latina girls end up in the "system" and seemed to blame Latina mothers most of all (Lopez & Chesney-Lind, 2014). Lisa Pasko and I (2015) found that juvenile justice professionals in Colorado operated under a similar premise and tended to blame the "Latina/o culture" for girls' problems and viewed both girls and their parents as being reluctant to comply with state rules and regulations as opposed to considering the possibility of language barriers, transportation issues, and a general distrust of the system as reasons for Latina girls' parents' seeming indifference and reticence to advocate on behalf of their daughters.

Exosystems

When thinking about system-involved girls, it is important to also consider how other interactions and contexts beyond their direct experiences impact them. Unlike most other youth, system-involved girls' parents are often entangled within a complex web of ever-changing interlocking institutions and systems. As previously mentioned, many of the young women interviewed for this study had parents who were either current or former drug users, were violent and/or victims of violence, or had been in jail/prison. Like their daughters, many of these parents were involved in a number of systems including the criminal justice system. Parents' involvement in the criminal justice system no doubt had a tremendous impact on their daughters given that parental incarceration often results in the breakup of the family, which leaves many children feeling sad, stunned, and shaken, particularly if they were living with the parent who has been incarcerated (Siegel, 2011). Joyce Arditti (2012) framed parental incarceration as an "ambiguous loss" where the incarcerated parent is physically absent, but may or may not be emotionally present. Either way, the children of incarcerated parents often do not know when their parents will be released, which can further contribute to this ambiguous loss. They also must contend with the stigma of having an incarcerated parent, which can preclude them from the same types of social supports that might be available to other children whose parents are absent as a result of death or divorce. Furthermore, children's parents are often incarcerated in prisons that are far away, which makes it unlikely that children will be able to visit them, which can further contribute to their feelings of confusion and abandonment (Siegel, 2011).

Parental incarceration also has many "collateral consequences" for children and families (Chin, 2002; Hagan & Coleman, 2001; Lapidus et al., 2005). Gabriel Chin (2002) defined collateral consequences as "penalties, disabilities, or disadvantages that occur automatically because of a criminal conviction, other than the sentence itself." Examples of such consequences include "disenfranchisement, loss of business or professional licenses, felon registration requirements, and ineligibility for public benefits" (p. 257). As a consequence of these overbearing restrictions and stigmatization, many children and families continue to struggle even when the parent is released from prison. Such financial stressors can also impact parenting and the quality of the parent–child relationship particularly when few social supports exist (Arditti, Burton, & Neeves-Botelho, 2010).

Macrosystem

When talking about system-involved youth such as the girls interviewed for this study it is also important to analyze the state's role vis-à-vis drug laws and rhetoric which contribute to family problems. Doing so does not negate either the youths' or parents' agency, but rather contextualizes their decisions, interactions, and behaviors, which is a critical endeavor given that U.S. culture tends to blame youth, parents, and families for their problems without considering the role of the state in exacerbating these problems, and this is particularly true for people of color. Consider the War on Drugs, for example, which began in the late 1960s and continues to this day (Díaz-Cotto, 2006). At the height of the War on Drugs, the federal and state governments initiated a number of mandatory sentencing guidelines designed to punish drug users, particularly those who used crack (Provine, 2008). As a result of these punitive guidelines, the prison population skyrocketed with poor people of color accounting for a disproportionate share of this increase (Diaz-Cotto, 2006; Provine, 2008). Harsher sentencing laws for crack possession as opposed to cocaine possession coupled with racial profiling and sentencing biases ushered in an era of mass incarceration based on criminalizing drug use that many poor families of color and communities are still dealing with today (Chin, 2002; Diaz-Cotto, 2006; Lapidus et al., 2005; Provine, 2008).

For Latinas/os, the War on Drugs has also been conflated with strong anti-immigrant rhetoric and this is especially true in Arizona where I collected data for this study. In 2010, the Arizona state legislature passed SB 1070, a bill that allows police officers to "ascertain the legal status of anyone stopped if the officer suspects that person might be undocumented" (Provine & Sanchez, 2011, p. 468). In order to bolster support for their anti-immigrant (and by extension anti-Latina/o) policies, local politicians relied on rhetoric that used a broad brush to paint Latina/o immigrants as stealing U.S. jobs, crossing the border to have "anchor babies," and being drug traffickers. Such anti-immigrant rhetoric and laws contribute to an anti-Latina/o climate rooted in distrust, fear, and derision.

Growing up in such a hostile climate can negatively impact Latina/o youth and their families. Media accounts suggest that in the aftermath of SB 1070, both immigrant and nonimmigrant Latinas/os in Arizona reported not wanting to report "crimes to the police in order to avoid contacting authorities, not visiting physicians or hospitals even in emergency situations so as to avoid detection, changing driving habits and staying home more often, and weighing the pros and cons of sending children to school" (see Santos & Menjivar, 2014, p. 7). Against this backdrop, undocumented parents in need of social services for their U.S.-born children might be afraid to seek assistance even though their children are eligible for a number of federal benefits, such as Children's Health Insurance Program, Supplemental Nutrition Assistance, and Temporary Assistance for Needy Families (Yoshikawa, Kholoptseva, & Suárez-Orozco, 2013). Research also indicates that Latina/o children fear their undocumented parents will be detained, arrested, and deported (Brabeck, Lykes, & Hershberg, 2011; Dreby, 2012). In hostile states like Arizona, these fears can become overwhelming when nightly news coverage shows the local sheriff's workplace raids targeting unsuspecting "cleaning ladies" suspected of being undocumented. The message of such sweeps is clear: We don't want you here.

Not surprisingly both undocumented parents and their children suffer from the psychological stress of being stigmatized and criminalized (Dreby, 2012). Having an undocumented parent has been associated with higher levels of anxiety, depression, attention problems, and rule breaking behaviors among Latina/o youth (Delva et al., 2013; Potochnick & Perreira, 2010). Fearful of legal repercussions, the families most in need of social services and support may be the most likely to avoid interacting with government systems and authorities, and this may be especially true for those families who are also struggling with parental substance use, intimate partner violence, and other stressors such as extreme poverty, high rates of residential mobility, and a lack of social support. Language and transportation barriers may also prevent Latina/o families from seeking support.

Given that most of the young women interviewed for this book did not explicitly link their experiences to their ethnic, national, or cultural backgrounds, I also conducted a series of focus groups with 19 drug-involved Latina girls. During these focus groups, I directly asked them how growing up as a Mexican-origin girl in the United States impacted their views of themselves in relation to how others viewed them. While most of the young women expressed pride in being Latina, they acknowledged that "others" (generally defined as White people) view "Mexicans" as "lazy," "dirty," unable to speak English, "criminals," and construction workers. When I redirected them to focus on their identities as both young women and Latinas, they all agreed that others view them as "gang bangers," "cholas," and "always pregnant." Unfortunately my focus group with clinicians indicated that their views of Latina girls conformed to the girls' perceptions. In general, the clinicians viewed drug-involved Latina girls as gang-involved, submissive to male partners, and more likely to become pregnant than other girls (Lopez & Chesney-Lind, 2014). These findings are consistent with other research, which indicates that clinicians and other juvenile justice professionals often rely on gendered and ethnic stereotypes when assessing and making decisions about Latinas in their care (Pasko & Lopez, 2015; Schaffner, 2008).

In line with the cult of personal responsibility that is so prevalent in the United States, the War on Drugs relied on stigmatizing, shaming, and blaming poor people—especially people of color—for their own problems rather than contextualizing their problems and attempting to address the very real social structures that keep certain people and families at the bottom of the power hierarchy. Indeed, most interventions targeting system-involved youth and adults typically focus on the individual rather than the structural conditions and policies—such as poverty, biased sentencing, sexism, institutional racism—that place individuals at risk for drug use. Such interventions rely on casting some people as the denigrated "other" (e.g., the drug user, the bad mother) whereas other people (e.g., middle-class White people) are held up as the standard of normality. In *Breaking Women: Gender, Race, and the New Politics of Imprisonment*, Jill McCorkel (2013) presents an extreme example of how ineffective such interventions can be at addressing women's drug use. In her book, McCorkel describes Project Habilitate Women (PHW), a drug treatment program designed to break incarcerated women down and make them accept responsibility for their personal failures. Part of this breaking-down process involved the project staff calling the program participants "drug hos" and "crack heads," contributing further to these women's stigmatized sense of self. While some women wholeheartedly rejected these systematic efforts to break them down, others succumbed to the underlying message that something was intrinsically wrong with them. Like these women, many of the young women interviewed for this book attributed their drug use to their own personal failures and shortcomings. Most notably, Quinn, whose story I opened this chapter with, referred to herself as "morally corrupt" and deviant as evidenced by her words, "I'm not normal. Something is morally wrong with me." Like the women whose stories were highlighted in Susan Starr Sered and Maureen Norton-Hawk's (2014) *Can't Catch a Break: Gender, Jail, Drugs, and the*

Limits of Personal Responsibility, the majority of the young women inter-viewed for this book believed it was their responsibility to stop using drugs and their inability to do so hinted at a personal deficiency.

Reflecting upon Context, Relationships, and Intersectionality

Although this book focuses primarily on system-involved girls' relation-ships with parents, it is important to situate these relationships within a larger set of interlocking contexts and systems that can negatively impact the quality of the parent–child relationship over time in accordance with girls' development as well as major shifts in family structure and dynam-ics. Like many system-involved youth, the young women interviewed for this book often had histories of victimization and were often exposed to a multitude of adverse childhood events (ACEs) such as parental drug use, parental incarceration, and violence. Their parents, especially mothers, struggled with raising them under these adverse conditions. Joyce Arditti, Linda Burton, and Sara Neeves-Botelho (2010) refer to such conditions as "contextual risk factors" that can accumulate over time to diminish parents' ability to effectively care for their children. When this happens, children can be placed under the care of the juvenile justice and/or child protective services system. Thus, it is also important to emphasize the role that meso-systems in the form of parents' relationships with youth professionals and contexts play in their children's lives. Understanding how exosystems (e.g., prisons if parents are incarcerated, parents' work places) and macrosystems (e.g., cultural ideals about "normal" families and good parenting, drug use norms, local drug policies, immigration laws, attitudes condoning violence against girls and women, and cultural norms touting personal responsibil-ity) impact children and their relationships with parents is also critical. Finally, a critical need exists to consider how gender, race, ethnicity, nation-ality, and class relate to system-involved girls' perceptions, experiences, and interactions not only with parents, but partners and juvenile justice profes-sionals as well. Thus, as originally noted, scholars, practitioners, and policy makers must become adept at zooming in and zooming out when seeking to understand why and how girls end up in the juvenile justice system. Blaming them, their parents, and their cultures is inadequate. We must also consider their social identities and locations within a larger web of inter-locking contexts and systems.

ORGANIZATION OF THE BOOK

Chapter 1, Growing Up in a "Dysfunctional" Family, presents girls' early childhood memories with parents and examines how they fit into larger social constructions of "normal families" and "good parenting." Girls' early "best" memories of their parents are shared in the first part of the chapter. These shared memories provide an important glimpse into girls' early relationships with parents in a way that humanizes them. The second part of the chapter presents girls' early childhood memories specific to parental drug use. Through girls' shared narratives, we can see how many of them initially viewed their parents' drug use as "normal," but gradually began to realize that their parents were "different" from other parents once they started school, interacted with child protective services, and began to comprehend negative messages about their drug-using parents from other family members.

Chapter 2, Mothers' Little Helpers, focuses primarily on girls' early childhood and adolescent experiences growing up with mothers who have been repeatedly victimized and/or have substance use problems. The chapter highlights how system-involved girls viewed mothers' victimization and substance use and how they adapted to meet the needs of their mothers by becoming "little helpers" who played a number of critical roles to support not only their mothers, but their siblings as well. While some of these supportive roles were instrumental in nature, such as taking care of younger siblings, many were specifically related to their mothers' drug use and involvement in violent relationships. In the vast majority of cases, girls sought to help their mothers by covering for their drug use, serving as relationship advisors and confidants, and attempting to protect their mothers from being victimized by intimate partners. As they entered adolescence, many of the young women viewed their mothers' "decisions" to stay in abusive relationships as a personal choice as opposed to also considering how larger social forces and economic constraints might have limited their mothers' "choices." Still, even in adolescence, many girls did their best to assist their mothers by helping out to the best of their abilities. Unfortunately, doing so took a tremendous toll on their educational and emotional development.

Growing up in troubled families can have serious emotional repercussions for young girls who often feel unloved, unwanted, abandoned, and like a burden to their parents and other extended family members. Chapter 3,

Daddy's Little Girl: Feeling Rejected, Abandoned, and Unloved, highlights girls' complicated relationships with either largely uninvolved or abusive biological fathers. Most of the girls did not live with their biological fathers for a variety of reasons, ranging from never having lived with their fathers, dissolution of the mother–father relationship resulting in their fathers moving out of the home, paternal incarceration, and paternal death. Understanding how larger cultural ideals about fathering shape girls' perceptions of and relationships with biological fathers is a critical part of this chapter. While most girls expressed feeling unloved, unwanted, and unimportant to their biological fathers, many struggled to understand why their once seemingly involved fathers had abandoned them. A refrain that I heard often was "I don't know what happened. I was Daddy's little girl." While some girls became angry and rejected their fathers in turn, other girls longed for their fathers, mythologized them, rationalized their lack of involvement, and went to great lengths to forge a relationship with their fathers even if it meant doing drugs and placing themselves at risk.

Chapter 4, Looking for Love in All the Wrong Places, examines how exposure to family violence—defined as domestic violence and child maltreatment in the home—can place young girls at risk for teen dating violence. Most of the young women interviewed for this book grew up in homes that were characterized by domestic violence and/or child maltreatment. Their narratives further suggest that many of them grew up in dangerous communities characterized by crime, violence, and drug use. Against this backdrop, they struggled to develop healthy relationships with romantic partners as they entered adolescence. Despite wanting to avoid the types of abusive relationships they saw all around them—including their mothers' relationships with male partners—many ended up with controlling, jealous, and abusive partners. This chapter focuses exclusively on how these young women navigated their relationships with their partners with an emphasis on understanding how power, control, and violence played out in these relationships. The stories of three young women—Lydia, Savannah, and Catalina—are presented to give the reader a sense of how entrenched young women can be in their relationships with boyfriends and how these relationship dynamics can in turn influence girls' decisions to engage in delinquency, drug use, unprotected sex, and prostitution.

Chapter 5, Doing Drugs: The Good, the Bad, and the Ugly, chronicles how girls' relationships with parents influence their decisions to run away and use drugs. Included in this chapter is a discussion of why some young women are attracted to street life. For some young women, living life "on the run" is fun and exciting. To illustrate this phenomenon, the stories of Christina, Samantha, and Lindsay are presented. Other young women run away from home to escape a troubled home life characterized by neglect and/or abuse. The stories of Paige, Deanna, and Alana illustrate how running away and using drugs represent a way out for some young women. Irrespective of why young women run away, many soon find themselves addicted to the so-called "hard" drugs of methamphetamine, cocaine, crack, and heroin. Some will shoot up, experience bad trips, and overdose. A few will begin to lose their youthful good looks as their skin becomes pasty, their teeth rot, and their bodies grow emaciated. Many will end up in the juvenile justice system where they will receive treatment for the first time, but most likely not the last time.

As girls begin to "act out" or become increasingly dependent on drugs, their parents and other family members often attempt to intervene on their behalf. Chapter 6, Parents' Attempts to Intervene on Behalf of Drug-Using Daughters, flips the commonly touted idea that families of youth in the juvenile justice system do not care about them. This is simply not true. Most parents, despite their own personal problems, attempt to intervene on behalf of their daughters. Several girls, for example, shared stories about how their drug-using parents warned them against using drugs. Other parents call upon law enforcement, probation officers, and other youth professionals to help them deal with "out of control" daughters. Grandparents, aunts, and older siblings often assume care of girls to prevent them from being placed in the child protective services system. The problem is that most parents are not consistent and their parenting efforts are often in vain as teen girls resent their involvement and intrusions. Parents' efforts to advocate on behalf of their daughters are further constrained by their interactions with institutional actors who frequently blame parents—especially mothers—for their daughters' problems.

Being court ordered to an out-of-home placement represents the final step for many young women in the juvenile justice system. For many of these young women, especially those who are poor and members of racial/ethnic minority groups, this treatment is often inadequate and comes with a high price tag that all too often includes the symbolic, and sometimes literal, severance of parental rights and ties. Chapter 7, Property of the State: Locked Up, Locked Out, and in Need of Treatment, draws upon my personal experiences working as a clinical intern at Arroyo Verde as well as interviews with girls to discuss how the juvenile justice system responds to girls and their parents and how these responses in turn shape girls' treatment experiences once remanded to an out-of-home placement facility such as Arroyo Verde.

Chapter 8, Moving beyond the Individual toward Programmatic, Systemic, and Policy Solutions, is divided into two parts. The first part of the chapter presents a detailed look at system-involved girls' fears, hopes, and dreams. While most were hopeful, others expressed ambivalence about leaving the youth facility and were concerned that they would relapse or fall back into the same lifestyle without support. Pregnant and parenting teens, on the other hand, wanted to do better for their children's sake. Still, other girls recognized that in order to prevent coming back into the system, they would have to cut important people—such as drug-using parents—out of their lives. Release from out-of-home placement represented a second chance, but one that was fraught with challenges and obstacles. For the most part, young women believed that the onus to change was on them and failure to do so represented a personal deficit. Thus, the second part of this chapter discusses the importance of looking beyond the individual toward programmatic, systemic, and policy solutions and emphasizes the importance of developing culturally tailored, gender-specific prevention and intervention programs as well as developing coordinated collaborations across various youth and adult agencies and systems (e.g., juvenile justice, behavioral health system, child protective services system, domestic violence, substance abuse treatment). The chapter concludes with an argument in favor of incorporating a "family perspective" when developing and implementing criminal justice policies.

Taken together, each chapter in this book contributes to our understanding of how girls' complicated relationships with parents within the context of multiple-challenged families and communities lead to their eventual involvement in the juvenile justice system, a system that despite its best intentions, often fails these girls and their families. Despite this grim outlook, there is cause for hope. Like the young women who shared their hopes and dreams, I am optimistic that we can do better to address the needs of system-involved girls who, despite their trials and tribulations, have managed to survive against seemingly insurmountable odds.

1 · GROWING UP IN A "DYSFUNCTIONAL" FAMILY

Olivia, a 16-year-old Mexican American girl living at the Desert Star residential treatment center, smiled when I asked her to share a favorite memory of her mother. She said, "A lot of the time . . . I think, like, 50% of the time, like, when she's clean, she's a great mom, and when she's not, she's a really bad mom. So when she was clean, she did a lot of good things. Like, when I was in kindergarten, I remember there was a Dr. Seuss day at my school, and she made green eggs and ham for me and for all the kids in my neighborhood. They were at my house, and we were eating green eggs and ham, and she was reading us the story. It was really fun." Like many system-involved young women whose stories I present in this book, Olivia seemed to relish the opportunity to share her favorite memories involving her parents. Like Olivia, nearly all of the young women were able to recall at least one positive memory of their mother or father, and it did not matter whether their parents used drugs, had spent time in prison, engaged in sex work, abused their partners, or had neglected their children.[1] Furthermore, many of these memories were typical of what we might expect to hear from most young people if we asked them to share their favorite childhood memories of their parents. Other young women shared stories that were not so typical because they took place in jails or prisons. Paige, a 15-year-old White girl, shared the following story about her father who was in prison, "When I would go visit him and stuff, he was just so funny. There was this one time, in the prison he was at, there were vending machines with food in it, and I would bring a big thing of quarters and get him food, and there was this egg burrito he really wanted, and it looked so gross, but I tried getting it for him and it got stuck, and he was making jokes about how much he really wanted that gross burrito. It was so funny." I share Olivia's and Paige's stories because they present a more nuanced view of system-involved girls' parents who are all too often blamed for their daughters' problems (Belknap, Winter, & Cady, 2003; Lopez & Chesney-Lind, 2014; Pasko & Lopez, 2015). While girls shared many painful memories involving their parents, it is important to note that the majority also remembered good times. The intent in sharing these memories is not to deny the harm that many of these parents inflicted on their daughters at other times, but rather to present a more nuanced view of these parents as viewed through the eyes of their daughters.

SOCIOCULTURAL VIEWS ABOUT FAMILIES: NORMAL VERSUS DYSFUNCTIONAL

Different cultural groups define family and family membership differently. Even in the United States, variability exists with regard to how individuals, legal systems, politicians, news media, and other social institutions define families, and these definitions usually include who should be in families, how family members should act, and how families should be structured. Nevertheless, in the United States, dominant socially constructed ideas about what is a normal family exist. The media, and television in particular, play a big role in defining what normal families should look like and images of the "typical normal family and the ideal healthy family both shape and reflect dominant social norms for how families are supposed to be" (Walsh, 2012, p. 9). Historically, media representations of normal or typical families have included two main depictions: the traditional family of the preindustrialized past and the nuclear family of the 1950s (Chambers, 2001). Until relatively recently, these representations of families have almost exclusively been White, middle-class, and headed by a breadwinner father and homemaker mother (Chambers, 2001; Walsh, 2012). In these media representations of families, mothers and fathers care for and cherish their children in socially acceptable ways: They eat dinner with their children, monitor their children's activities, and lovingly talk to their children when problems arise. Families that do not meet the socially constructed criteria for what constitutes a normal or typical family have historically been erased from popular media altogether or presented in a negative light. Fortunately, although limited in number, more recent sitcom depictions of families have centered on class and/or race (Robinson & Skill, 2001). Although these sitcoms have all pushed the boundaries of what constitutes a normal or typical family, they all continue to reify the nuclear, intact family that is headed by two heterosexual parents. Very few family sitcoms present the stories of single mothers, and when single mothers are presented, they are usually White woman with strong support systems (Rabinovitz, 1989). Latino families, families headed by gay and lesbian parents, and families struggling with drug addition, domestic violence, and abuse continue to be underrepresented.

Politicians also contribute to idealized notions of what constitutes a normal or good family. Like dominant media representations, politicians often reify the idea of the traditional family that is made up of two heterosexual parents and their biological children (Fineman, 1995). The 2008 Republican Platform, for example, reinforced the notion of the "traditional family" and its importance to the success of not only children and families, but the entire nation. In support of their position, Republican leaders referred to "endless social science studies," which indicate that "children raised in intact married families are more likely to attend college, are physically and emotionally healthier, are less likely to use drugs or alcohol, engage in crime, or get pregnant outside of marriage." They then linked the nation's economic problems and the need for government intrusion to single-parent families (a thinly veiled attack on poor single mothers), when they argued that the "lack of family formation not only leads to more government costs, but also to more government control over the lives of its citizens in all aspects." Their message was clear: Single parents, many of whom are mothers of color, are responsible for draining the nation's coffers as a result of their nonconforming lifestyles (e.g., single parenthood), inadequate parenting, and dependence on welfare.

Social scientists have also contributed to our understanding of idealized normal families, but rather than relying primarily on family structure to define normal families, they have instead adopted the medical/psychiatric model to distinguish between normal and abnormal or dysfunctional families. According to this model, normal families are asymptomatic and do not exhibit any symptoms or characteristics that negatively compromise the family's functioning (Walsh, 2012). This perspective is "limited by its deficit-based skew, focused on symptoms of distress and severity of problems, and inattention to positive attributes of family well-being" (Walsh, 2012, p. 5). There is a long history of referring to symptomatic families as "dysfunctional." While social scientists originally used this term to refer to families who were exhibiting symptoms of distress, it has since evolved to "connote serious disturbance and causal attributions that tend to pathologize families" (Walsh, 2012, p. 8).

WHEN BLAMING LEADS TO ANTI-FAMILY POLICIES AND PRACTICES

We live in a society that routinely blames parents, families, and cultures for the misbehavior of youth (Harris, 2006; Hutchinson, Parada, & Smandych, 2009). Doing so allows us to talk about other people's children without having to assume responsibility for the social and structural conditions— poverty, social inequalities, institutional racism, and sexism—that contribute to youth and family problems. Certain policies rooted in idealized notions of the normal or traditional family have negatively impacted families, particularly single-mother families of color. One of the most egregious examples of such a policy is the Personal Responsibility and Work Opportunity Reconciliation Act (PRWORA), which Congress passed and President Bill Clinton signed in 1996. Under this new legislation, Temporary Assistance for Needy Families (TANF) replaced Aid to Families with Dependent Children (AFDC). TANF required welfare participants, many of whom were single mothers, to find employment and limited their welfare benefits to five years maximum. This Work First Approach was "based on the idea that welfare recipients should be pushed into paid employment as quickly as possible regardless of the quality of the job offer." The underlying premise of the Work First Approach was that poverty was due to "personal inadequacies as opposed to structural societal factors such as a lack of suitable decently paid jobs in the formal labour market" (Daguerre, 2008, p. 367). This emphasis on blaming poor people for their predicament continued in the 2000s under President George Bush. During this era, President Bush and other conservative politicians championed the Healthy Marriage Initiative, which was predicated on the belief that the "collapse of traditional family values" among the poor was at the root of child poverty and all its associated problems.

As attempts to reform the U.S. welfare system illustrate, the reification of so-called normal or traditional families affects the way we perceive and attempt to solve issues of poverty and welfare. As noted by Martha Fineman (1995, p. 2192): "Intimate groups that do not conform to this model historically have been labeled 'deviant' and subjected to explicit state regulation and control justified by their nonconformity." Single mothers bear the brunt of such political rhetoric. Conservative politicians and their supporters often blame single mothers for their children's problems. Although never explicitly stated in political speeches or propaganda, these accusations tend to be racialized and classed. When conservative politicians accuse mothers, they are not talking about White mothers, but rather African American and Latina mothers who are poor. To a lesser extent, poor fathers of color have also been demonized. The most obvious example is the common usage of the term "deadbeat dad," which serves as a code for poor African American and Latino fathers who do not pay child support on a regular basis (Mincy & Sorensen, 1998). The reasons for parents' apparent lack of involvement in their children's lives are rarely linked to larger social inequalities, but instead attributed to parents' individual deficits (Lee, 2016).

At this point, it is important to distinguish between poor families living with economic stressors and families who are struggling with serious issues such as parental drug use, violence, abuse, and neglect. This is not to say that the latter families do not also struggle with poverty, but rather that they are also grappling with other issues that are often exacerbated by living in impoverished conditions (Lee, 2016). Although poor parents are often blamed for their children's problems, even more derision is heaped upon poor parents who struggle with addiction, have committed crimes, and are dealing with mental health issues. News pundits, politicians, youth professionals, and the general public often reserve the most scathing judgments for parents whose perceived shortcomings compromise their ability to effectively parent their children. The general consensus is that these damaged and troubled individuals cannot adequately care for their children. Thus, the state must intervene (Lee, 2016).

PARENT–YOUTH PROFESSIONAL INTERACTIONS

Beliefs about bad parents also influence how juvenile justice and child welfare professionals think about and interact with system-involved youth and their families (Lee, 2016). The tendency to pathologize families and blame them for their children's problems has trickled down into the juvenile justice and other youth service systems where juvenile justice professionals, clinicians, case workers, and others routinely label young people's families as dysfunctional (Belknap, Winter, & Cady, 2003; Gaarder, Rodriguez, & Zatz, 2004; Lee, 2016; Lopez & Chesney-Lind, 2014; Pasko & Lopez, 2015; Rodriguez, Smith, & Zatz, 2009). Thus, youth professionals such as caseworkers often end up "policing" the very families they are trying to help, and this is especially true for poor families of color (Lee, 2016; Silver, 2015).

Judgments about which parents are bad and which families are dysfunctional are often classed, gendered, and/or racialized (Lee, 2016; Lopez & Chesney-Lind, 2014; Odem, 1995; Pasko & Lopez, 2015). Margaret Bortner (1982), for example, found that juvenile court officials tend to perceive lower-class families as "unstable" and "inadequate" in providing appropriate monitoring and supervision of youth (p. 81). Other studies indicate that mothers—especially poor mothers, mothers of color, and those who use drugs—often receive the brunt of the blame for their children's problems and are labeled "bad mothers" and "poor role models" (Lee, 2016; Lopez & Chesney-Lind, 2014; Pasko & Lopez, 2015). In contrast, and as previously mentioned, fathers are often labeled "deadbeat dads" who have little interest in their children's welfare, and this is true even when they want to be involved in their children's lives (L. Brown, Callahan, Strega, Walmsley, & Dominelli, 2009). The blame for young people's problems often extends to their entire families, and sometimes even their cultures (Lee, 2016; Lopez & Chesney-Lind, 2014). The underlying message is that bad parents and bad families are responsible for system-involved youths' problems. Such attributions rarely take into account the barriers (i.e., lack of reliable transportation, inability to take off work without losing pay) that poor parents and parents grappling with other challenges (i.e., addiction, mental health problems) face when trying to advocate on behalf of their children.

Such judgments can have significant repercussions for youth, especially youth of color who are caught up in various youth systems such as the child protective and juvenile justice systems, which often serve an overlapping population of youth and families (Herz & Ryan, 2008). Tina Lee's recent ethnography on the child welfare system in New York is a case in point. Lee found that well-meaning case managers routinely relied on middle-class standards of parenting to make decisions about what constituted neglect, and when neglect was found, they often attributed it to parenting deficits as opposed to poverty. She argued that these professionals judge "parents to be 'fit' or 'unfit' and have used the power of the state to remove children to the care of others and/or to enforce compliance with various forms of counseling to help unfit parents learn prevailing social norms" (p. 10). Blaming youth and families also occurs in the juvenile justice system. Past research, for example, indicates that juvenile justice judges are more likely to sentence youth to out-of-home placements when their families have been officially assessed as "dysfunctional" with the underlying assumption being that these families are unable or incapable of supporting and controlling wayward youth (Rodriguez, Smith, & Zatz, 2009). Not surprisingly, parents often feel stigmatized, ostracized, and marginalized when interacting with juvenile justice and other youth services professionals (Aldridge, Shute, Ralphs, & Medina, 2011; Cleaver, Nicholson, Tarr, & Cleaver, 2007; Kroll & Taylor, 2003; Lee, 2016).

UNDERSTANDING NORMALITY WITHIN THE CONTEXT OF "DYSFUNCTIONAL" FAMILIES

System-involved girls' positive reflections are presented in the remainder of this chapter in an attempt to humanize girls' drug-using parents. Like Olivia and Paige, whose reflections were shared at the beginning of this chapter, almost all of the young women were able to recall positive memories of their parents. Such snapshots of girls' parents are rarely presented in the social science literature and media representations of drug-involved parents; however, it should be emphasized that the intent is not to minimize the harm that growing up with drug-using parents can confer on children. Past research indicates that parents' preoccupation with procuring and using drugs leaves little time to care for the basic and physical needs of their children (Sedlak & Broadhurst, 1996). Furthermore, a grow-ing body of research indicates that parents who are addicted to drugs can be emotionally absent, expose their children to dangerous conditions and influences, and often draw upon limited financial resources to support their drug use (National Center on Addiction and Substance Abuse, 1999). Despite these problems, many children care deeply about their parents irre-spective of their drug use and parents care about their children in turn (Lee, 2016). As demonstrated in past qualitative research with drug-involved parents, they often feel guilty for their perceived parenting shortcomings and employ strategies (e.g., hiding drug use, abstaining from drug use dur-ing pregnancy) to minimize harm to their children (Richter & Bammer, 2000). Unfortunately, they also feel shamed, blamed, and stigmatized by well-meaning youth professionals for being unable to adequately parent their children and often struggle to demonstrate that they are good parents who care for their children (Lee, 2016). Thus, in presenting system-involved girls' positive reflections of parents, the intent is to present an alternative view of drug-using parents whose behaviors are consistent with what soci-ety would expect from so-called normal parents. These alternative rep-resentations provide insight into why so many of the girls remain deeply attached to their parents even when their parents fail to consistently keep them safe, provide for their basic emotional and physical needs, and be present and involved in their lives. The chapter also includes a discussion of how girls' conceptions of their parents changed as they began to realize their parents were different from other parents due to their drug use, and how these changing perceptions altered their relationships over time.

JUST LIKE ANY OTHER PARENTS: EARLY CHILDHOOD MEMORIES

Like many young people, most of the girls interviewed for this book enjoyed sharing early childhood memories of their parents. For the most part, their memories were typical of what we might expect to hear from any other young person. They spoke about father–daughter dances, camping with family members, and watching movies together. Liza, a 16-year-old White girl, for example, shared the following story about her father, an active cocaine user: "My best memory of my dad? I would say it was when I was seven and my dad set up these little plastic tubs filled with water in the back-yard for my friend and me. We put toys in them and threw cups of water back and forth at each other and then my dad took both of us to Walmart in our bathing suits, and we got some drinks and snacks and stuff, and we just hung out outside, and then we watched some movies and took a nap."

Jordan, a 14-year-old Mexican American girl who was living at Desert Star at the time of our interview, also shared a fairly normal memory of her father, who "drank a lot and smoked weed on occasion." She said, "My dad is a very funny, talented guy. He loves to play the drums. He and I played golf together on the Wii so we bonded a lot. We also bonded through football.... My dad's favorite sport is football because every single Sunday he is up early just to watch the first game. I watch it with my dad. I don't understand most of it, but I watch it with him." As we spoke, it became clear that Jordan relished the time she spent with her father and managed to retain a close relationship with him even after her parents' divorce and in spite of his drinking and marijuana use. The fact that alcohol and mar-ijuana use are less stigmatized in U.S. society than harder drug use may have provided Jordan's father a socially acceptable space to simultaneously use alcohol/marijuana while raising Jordan.

Parents' periods of abstention also coincided with good times and memories. During these periods, parents attempted to care for their chil-dren by spending time with them, buying them things, and "spoiling" them, perhaps in an attempt to make up for other times when they were not emotionally or physically present in their children's lives. Melissa, a 14-year-old Mexican American girl whose mother was in "recovery" for an addiction to cocaine, shared a fairly typical memory that involved spending time with her mother. She said, "Every weekend my mom would take me to anywhere I wanted. Most of the time it was just me and her and some-times she would bring my sisters, and we would just go, and she would just spoil us. She would take us to the mall or we'd watch a movie—whatever movie we wanted—and she would take us to the store and buy us clothes [and] whatever we needed. And then we would either go to the park or [the restaurant] Peter Piper and just spend time together."

Even daughters who had been outright rejected by their parents—usually fathers—were able to share at least one positive memory of them. Sandra, a 15-year-old Mexican American girl, whose father later denied paternity (see Chapter 3), was only able to come up with one positive memory, but it was one that meant a lot to her. Sandra's narrative is also significant because it illustrates how many girls defined parents on the basis of biology. Like many other young women interviewed for this book, Sandra viewed her biological father as her real father.

> I wanted to see my real dad, so [my mother] took me down to Arizona to go see my dad's side of the family. And I remember everything about that day, except I don't remember anything that he said to me. When I got there, every-one was so happy to see me. And I saw my little cousins, and I played with them. And I saw my grandma and my aunts and uncles and they all live in the same area, so it was pretty cool, like, the same apartment complex. Yeah. They were really happy 'cause I was my dad's first born. And I remember sitting on one of those ponies that rock back and forth, and my dad was next to me, and he had his arm around me. And I remember they were taking pictures of me. I still have pictures at home.

Sandra's perception of her biological father as her "real" father was not unique. Many of the young women had stepfathers (often more than one), but most referred to their biological fathers as their real fathers irrespective of how involved these men were in their lives. This tendency to not consider stepparents as full parents has been demonstrated in other research (Gross, 1987; Schmeeckle, Giarrusso, Feng, & Bengston, 2006) Understanding how young people define parents (i.e., biological, "blood is thicker than water") provides insight into their beliefs about how parents should act toward them.[2] Sandra, for example, believed that her biological father was her real father, and the fact that her biological father denied paternity did not alter this perception. Despite her biological father not being involved in her life, she still viewed him as her father, and this view caused her considerable anguish, as we shall see in Chapter 3.

MY PARENTS ARE NOT NORMAL

Young people are not immune to sociocultural messages about what con-stitutes a normal family. More than ever before, young people are exposed to an astonishing array of popular media via cable television, film, and the Internet. They also receive messages about what constitutes a normal family from other people—relatives, peers, and teachers—in their lives. Against this backdrop, they gradually form their own impressions about what constitutes a normal family. Good parents who are loving, caring, and involved in their children's lives represent a necessary ingredient for normal families. As indicated in the Introduction, the majority of girls interviewed for this book grew up in families characterized by parental drug use and domestic violence. Yet, it was their parents' drug use that first clued girls into the possibility that their parents were different from other parents (Cleaver et al., 2007; Kroll & Taylor, 2003).

Many of the young women whose stories are shared in this book did not initially view their parents' drug use as abnormal; however, as they grew older, they began to realize that their parents did not always behave in ways that were consistent with good parenting norms. This realization usually came when the girls began school. Exposed to other children's parents, they gradually began to question why their own parents acted in ways that were inconsistent with how other children's parents acted. As they grew older, girls also began to question their parents' behaviors at home. Why did their mothers sometimes disappear behind closed doors? Why did their fathers sometimes shower them with lavish amounts of affection and ignore them at other times? An additional clue that their parents and families were somehow not normal stemmed from constantly shifting living arrangements, which made it difficult for the girls to establish roots in their families, schools, and larger communities. Some girls who ended up under the care of the child protective services system also realized from an early age that their parents were not normal, but framed their parents "decisions" to give them up as acts of love.

My Parents Are Different from Other Parents

I interviewed 16-year-old Elana at Arroyo Verde. She was a slight girl of Puerto Rican descent who was dressed in the standard uniform of tan pants and a light blue shirt. Like many of the other girls that I interviewed at this facility, Elana was battling an addiction to methamphetamine and grew up in a family characterized by parental substance use and violence. Unlike some of the other girls, who were initially hesitant to open up, Elana jumped right in and answered my questions with gusto. She talked quickly, pausing only occasionally to take a breath, as she shared her thoughts on why she was locked up for the second time in as many years. Looking back, she attributed her own drug use to growing up with a mother who used drugs. Elana described these early experiences as normal because she did not know anything different until later in her childhood. She said, "I was very little—like 5 or so. My mom would ask us to go get something for her. I remember going to get her the bong when I was in Head Start. My mom always smoked weed. It was no big deal—like, 'go get me a glass of water.'"

Elana's story was not unique. For many young women, growing up with parents who use drugs was initially "no big deal," because they often failed to fully realize what was going on; however, once they started school, they began to compare their parents to other children's parents. This was especially true of Isabel, a 16-year-old Mexican American girl, whose mother used methamphetamine. Isabel's inkling that her mother was somehow different was reinforced when she went to school and began to interact with other children. Isabel was struck by how other parents seemed to care about their children. She said, "When I started going to school, and I would go to my friends' houses, and I saw their parents . . . and their moms and dads would be into what they were doing, like, caring more, and then I would go back home, and my mom would be, like, 'Go to your room' or she would ignore me. I knew she really didn't want to spend time with me or even know how my day went like other kids' mothers."

Despite parental attempts to maintain an appearance of normalcy, children eventually began to sense that something was amiss. Savannah, a soft-spoken 17-year-old Mexican American girl at the Arroyo Verde facility had been abusing methamphetamine and alcohol since she was 15. At the time of our interview, Savannah was receiving help for her methamphetamine addiction, attending Narcotics Anonymous (NA) meetings, and seeing a counselor to help her deal with ongoing Post-Traumatic Stress Disorder (PTSD) symptoms. Seeking to understand why Savannah had become involved with drugs, I asked her to share a bit about her early life. Like many other girls that I interviewed, Savannah's parents used drugs, and she was exposed to her parents' drug use from a very early age. She said, "When I was little, my parents used to do a lot of drugs . . . . My dad was, like, in his own world when he did that. He didn't even know how to spell our names. He even held my sister back a grade 'cause when he enrolled her, he put her in the wrong grade." Initially Savannah viewed her father's drug use as normal.

He wasn't physically abusive, but he was inattentive and uninvolved in Savannah's life. He was never there for her "when it counted" and could not be relied upon "to follow through."

Other young women said they always knew their parents were using drugs, but did not realize the full impact until they were much older. Richelle, a 14-year-old Mexican American girl living in the Moonlight group home, shared this story about first realizing the impact of her mother's drug use on her life: "Well, I knew she was using before I can even imagine, but I realized how bad it was and how I didn't want her to do it, and how it affected me about three years ago." She then went on to explain: "When I was in school, kids would never want to play with me. It was mostly because my mom would never buy me clothes, and I would always be wearing the same clothes and wearing ugly shoes, because she would always be spending her money on crack and never me." Richelle's narrative is reminiscent of what other studies on young people growing up with substance-using parents have found: Faced with their parents' escalating substance abuse, children often feel like they are second best to their parents' drugs because of their parents' failure to provide for their basic physical and emotional needs (Backett-Milburn, Wilson, Bancroft, & Cunningham-Burley, 2008; Barnard & Barlow, 2003).

Whispers, Secrets, and Forbidden Spaces

Parents' sudden disappearances, whispered conversations, and secrecy provided additional hints that parents were not normal. Xochitl, a 14-year-old Mexican American girl, talked at length about growing up with parents who abused cocaine and alcohol. According to Xochitl, her parents sold cocaine out of their suburban home to family members and friends. She did not know about her parents' drug use and drug dealing until she grew older and began to ask why her mother frequently disappeared into the bedroom with her aunts during family get-togethers. She said, "I had no idea what my parents were up to. My aunts and uncles and other friends would always stop by our house, but I thought it was because they just wanted to hang out, barbeque and stuff like that. I had no idea they were all doing drugs behind closed doors, in the bathroom, wherever . . . . I had no idea until my cousin told me. Then I started to notice things after my cousin told me, and it all began to make sense."

Janee, a slender 16-year-old Mexican American girl who was living at the Green River group home at the time of our interview, also became aware at a very young age that her mother used drugs. She said, "I was about 5 or 6, and it was Easter. I remember walking into her room and seeing her sitting and, like, smoking something, but I wanted to know what it was, but every time I tried getting close, my family would pull me away and close the door." In Janee's case, other hints of her mother's drug use began to emerge. Around the age of seven, Janee began to notice that her mother spent a lot of time in her bedroom with "strange men." Although, she didn't quite know what was going on, she knew "something was up."

VERA: When did you first know your mother was engaging in prostitution?
JANEE: I don't know, but I knew something was up because all me and my siblings have different dads, so I was, like, 'Okay, my mom can't settle in a relationship,' and then it got to the point where she would kick us out of our room and then be in there for, like, an hour at a time and go in there with different guys. I didn't exactly know what she was doing, but later I figured it out.

As the previous narratives illustrate, children notice when their parents are secretive, acting different, and unable to meet the basic demands of parenting. Other people can also clue them in about their parents' drug use. Eventually, though, most children figure out that their parents are using drugs despite parental efforts to hide drug use from them (Barnard & Barlow, 2003; Kroll, 2004; Rhodes, Bernays, & Houmoller, 2010). Furthermore, as will be shown in the next chapter, some young women learn to help their mothers hide their drug use in an attempt to help them appear "normal" in front of child welfare and other state agents. In these instances, performing normality was a strategy that mothers and daughters used to keep case managers at bay.

Constant Moving and Instability

Being shuttled back and forth between parents and relatives is another sign that drug-using parents and family home lives are different. Many of the girls described childhoods punctuated by constant moving and change. In fact, while interviewing the girls, I often had to pause and ask them to walk me through their living arrangements, as many of them had lived with a variety of relatives in addition to out-of-home placements in a variety of group homes, detention, correctional facilities, drug treatment centers, and residential treatment centers. For example, Melanie, a 17-year-old White girl, tried to "break it down" for me when I became confused about her living arrangement timeline. According to Melanie, both of her parents used heroin and had an on and off again relationship throughout Melanie's early life. This meant that Melanie variously lived with her mother, both parents, relatives, and eventually in a group home.

> Okay, I'm just going to give you a little bit of a breakdown so it's easier to understand. When I was a year old, I lived in Van Nuys, California. My parents were still together, then around my first birthday, they split up and then me and my mom lived in California, and when I was four, me and my mom moved to Colorado, and then when I was seven, my mom told me she and my dad were getting back together, so we moved back to California, and then when I was 12, they split up again. We still lived in California for another year and then when I was, like, 13 or 14, I lived in Colorado and that's when I told my mom I was leaving, and I went back to California, and I lived with my dad until I was 16, and then I lived with my aunt and uncle, and then I moved back with my mom. It was a stupid idea. I should have just stayed with my dad.

Eventually, Melanie ended up under the care of the child protective services system and Oak Canyon group home where she resided at the time of our interview. Melanie's story was not atypical. For many of the young women interviewed for this book, shifting living arrangements became a routine, predictable part of life. Grandmothers played a key role in helping out with child rearing when mothers were unavailable to do so. This finding is not surprising given that kinship care is on the rise as extended family members—usually grandmothers—struggle to support children whose parents are unable to parent on a full-time basis due to parental drug use, incarceration, and other stressors (National Center on Addiction and Substance Abuse, 1999; Siegel, 2011). Olivia, whose story I presented at the beginning of this chapter, described how her mother and grandmother shared parenting duties that spanned across two separate residences. According to Olivia, she lived with her grandmother when her mother was incarcerated or on drug binges, and with her mother at other times. In fact,

Olivia referred to both her mother's and her grandmother's residences as her home.

OLIVIA: My mom had me when she was, like, 14, 15 years old. She was on drugs, and she couldn't take care of me, so my *nana* [grandmother] stepped in. I was too young to know, and when I got older, my mom eventually got off drugs, so she came back in my life.

VERA: How old were you when your mom came back in your life?

OLIVIA: I was still a baby. My nana took me away when I was 3 months old. I wanna say my mom got me and my brother back when I was, like, 1 year old.

VERA: Have you lived with her ever since?

OLIVIA: I have . . . . Yeah, we live together, but I also live with my nana because my mom sometimes messes up and uses [drugs]. I have a place to sleep at both of their houses. They both raise me, but it's just different environments.

Fifteen-year-old Annette, a White girl who was living at Green River at the time of our interview, reported that her mother often moved out of their home due to severe mental health, physical health, and substance abuse problems. Like Olivia, Annette's grandmother played a critical role in her upbringing when her mother was on drug binges or in drug/mental health treatment. While Annette believed that her grandmother loved her, she felt like "a burden" to her grandmother who was living on a fixed income and struggling to make ends meet.

My mom would sometimes go away to St. Theresa's for a couple of months for her drinking, her bipolar, and her Hep C. When she was gone, I'd stay with Grandma because my mom was always gone. A lot of time she was gone because when she was drinking and stuff like that, she'd be gone and out with people. I guess you could say she's absent a lot. She's always gone, and she always has relationships with guys and stuff like that, and never likes to be home with us. I don't really like it. I want her home. She has responsibilities to do. But when she's gone, my grandma usually takes care of us. My mom married my stepdad, and then he took care of us for a minute, but mostly my grandma.

Annie, a 17-year-old Mexican American girl living at the Desert Star residential treatment center, also spent a lot of time at her grandparents' house as a result of her mother taking off on drug binges and going in and out of prison. As a young child, Annie and her siblings spent the majority of their time at her grandparents' home. Like Annette, Annie emphasized that her mother was not taking care of her parenting responsibilities. She said, "Growing up, my mother was always going in and out of prison, so I was always living with my grandparents when I was younger and my mother just never really, I guess took responsibility for any of her kids. Like me, my sister, or my brothers, and she was always out doing her own thing, and so when she wasn't in prison, she was out doing drugs. I was always with my grandparents until a couple of years ago when I moved in with my sister."

Paige also stayed with her grandmother when her mother "went off to use drugs and party." Like Annie and Annette, Paige and her siblings often moved into her grandparents' house for weeks at a time while her mother was otherwise occupied with "doing drugs and staying out with her latest boyfriend." Paige said, "Well, my mom did meth, and she was an alcoholic. She had periods of being clean and sober, but when she wasn't, my grandma would take me in because sometimes she [Paige's mother] would leave me alone for, like, weeks at a time, and we didn't have, like, food or anything, and I had a little brother and sister to take care of, and it wasn't very good, so we would go to my grandmother sometimes."

When asked to describe what it was like living with her mother, Paige reiterated that her mother was sometimes attentive, particularly when she was attempting to stay "clean and sober," but most of the time, life with her mother was chaotic. Or as Paige put it, "Yes, our house was crazy. It was, like, known for where to get drugs and where to trade it and stuff, so it was, like, everyone was coming and going." Unfortunately, Paige's mother moved from California to Arizona, which meant that Paige and her siblings no longer had extended family members to rely on when their mother was incapacitated or physically absent from their home.

The previous narratives reveal that girls' early lives were in constant motion as they were shuttled back and forth between their mothers and other relatives. In most instances, drug-using mothers either dropped their children off with a relative or a relative intervened and took care of the children when mothers were unable to do so. Grandparents, especially grandmothers, played a critical role in girls' upbringing. They stepped in and assumed the challenges of raising their grandchildren. For the most part, fathers did not assume custody when girls' mothers were emotionally and/or physically absent. In almost all instances, fathers also used drugs, were in and out of prison, or had moved on to another relationship. Although girls generally believed that their grandmothers and other extended families members cared about them, they often felt like a financial burden and resented their mothers for abdicating their parenting responsibilities to other women in the family who were often struggling with poverty and limited support systems as well. In contrast, and as will be demonstrated in Chapter 3, girls typically did not blame fathers as much as mothers for their absences, because many assumed that mothers should be the ones responsible for the lion's share of parenting duties.

Under the Care of the Child Protective Services System

In instances when grandparents and other relatives were unable to assume caretaking responsibilities, girls and their siblings were remanded to the care of the child protective services system. Approximately one third of the young women interviewed for this study were under the care of the child protective services system, which is not surprising given that children whose parents abuse drugs and alcohol are almost three times as likely to be abused and more than four times as likely to be neglected than children whose parents do not abuse drugs and alcohol (National Center on Addiction and Substance Abuse, 1999). Children growing up in households characterized by parental substance abuse are also frequently exposed to domestic and other forms of violence, which further diminishes parenting capacity and increases the likelihood that children will be placed under the care of the child protective system (Cleaver et al., 2007; Lee, 2016; National Center on Addiction in and Substance Abuse, 1999).

Entering the child protective services system was a big indicator that parents were different from so-called normal parents. Despite this, some young women framed their parents' decisions to give them up within a good parenting framework. Fifteen-year-old Christine, a White girl living at the Green River group home, for example, said her father sought help from "CPS" because he needed help taking care of her. She shared, "My mom has never been there, just my dad, from my first day of school. He's my best friend, but Dad couldn't take care of me so he looked for help and CPS was the answer. He told me, 'I need help with insurance and taking care of you, and I just can't do it' and so that's why I'm in CPS, and I believe that."

Lolo, a 15-year-old Mexican American girl who was also living at Green River, had never met her mother, but still framed her mother's decision to give her up as an act of love. She said, "I don't know anything about her. I'm actually right now having CPS try to find her, but they haven't been able to. I want to find her to tell her thank you because she could have just not given birth to me, but she did. I want to tell her thank you for giving me life." In both of these instances, young women framed their parents' decisions to give them up as acts of love.[3] While these two young women recognized that their parents and families were different by virtue of them being under the care of child protective services, they still sought to frame their parents' decisions and behaviors as loving. Many other young women who were involved in the child protective system also viewed their parents positively and most wanted to return to their mothers' care as opposed to living in a group home.

CONCLUSION

Most of the girls were able to share at least one positive memory of their parents; however, from an early age, many of them soon realized that their parents did not conform to idealized norms of how parents should act and behave. During early childhood, observations of other children's parents and overheard conversations provided hints that their parents were somehow different. Whispered conversations, secrets, and forbidden spaces provided further clues of parents' drug use despite parental attempts to keep their drug use hidden from their daughters. Constant movement and shuttling back and forth between relatives (and sometimes foster care or group homes) further convinced girls that their parents and families did not conform to mainstream idealized versions of how parents should act and families should operate.

Girls suffered as a result of parents' substance use because their lives were often chaotic and they moved often, which made it difficult for them to establish supportive networks in their schools and communities. They also felt like a burden to their relatives who cared for them, and at times believed that their parents cared more about their drug use than them. As will be explored later in the book, girls' parents sometimes left their daughters alone with drug-using acquaintances, which led to them being physically or sexually victimized. Despite these parenting failures, most of the young women interviewed for this book were deeply attached to their parents, and these attachments ran deep. The next chapter focuses on girls' relationships with mothers, many of whom used drugs, were victims of domestic violence, or struggled valiantly to support their families. Many young women went to great lengths to protect their mothers from emotional and physical harm and did their best to help them whenever possible, including "performing normality" to avoid "being taken away" from their parents. Unfortunately, while girls struggled to help and protect their mothers, doing so sometimes came at a cost to their own emotional and physical well-being.

2 · MOTHERS' LITTLE HELPERS

In September of 2014, Silvia Tijerina was caught on video in Waller County, Texas, selling cocaine out of her car. Ordinarily this would have been a nonstory except for the fact that the mother's 7-year-old daughter was in the car. As a result, this story became fodder for national media outlets. Police officers said it looked like "the girl was there to help mom out, even being the one to pass the drugs through the window" (Blakeley, 2014). Photos of the mother in orange jail garb were plastered across social media sites and flashed on the nightly news. People were outraged and condemnation was swift. How could a mother enlist the help of her daughter to sell drugs? "It angered me when I saw the video," Waller County District Attorney Elton Mathis said. "For a mother to use her child in the drug culture this way is just totally unacceptable." Captain Brian Cantrell with the Waller Counter Sheriff's Department agreed: "It's unimaginable that a mother would place a child in this situation" (Murphy, 2014). Noted blogger of mom issues Kiri Blakeley was similarly outraged, and quipped, "So maybe we want to wonder why the mom needs to do this to make a living— and have some compassion for her, but taking her kid along and essentially setting her up to do the same thing? Ugh, no excuse for that" (Blakeley, 2014). The question Blakeley asked, then quickly dismissed, is relevant. Why would a mother deal drugs to make a living? Blakeley concluded that nothing can excuse such bad mothering; such a simplistic response places the blame squarely on the mother's shoulders while failing to question the underlying social forces—gender oppression, discrimination, economic inequality—that might have contributed to her actions (Sered & Norton-Hawk, 2014). This chapter focuses on system-involved girls' relationships with their mothers. In many ways, these mothers like Silvia Tijerina fail to fit the socially constructed notion of a good mother. They sometimes used drugs, made poor choices, and stayed in violent relationships despite the risks to their children. Still, the intent of this chapter is not to blame mothers, but rather to examine the contexts in which mothers sometimes rely on their daughters for support. Against a backdrop that is often characterized by parental drug use and domestic violence, both mothers and daughters struggle to survive with few social support systems, limited financial means, and few resources.

STIGMA, BAD MOTHERING, AND SOCIAL ISOLATION

When thinking about the context of system-involved girls' relationships with mothers, it is important to once again step back and utilize a wide lens to view the societal landscape within which these relationships take place. In the United States, norms and beliefs about what it means to be a good mother dictate how society views women who fail to live in accordance with these norms. As discussed in Chapter 1, U.S. society is swift to condemn poor women, particularly poor women of color, who struggle to live in accordance with good mothering norms and deal with parenting demands in a socially appropriate way (Bloch & Taylor, 2014; Lee, 2016). Rather than assessing the context within which these women must parent, caseworkers, probation officers, and other youth professionals along with the lay public routinely blame mothers for their parenting deficits (Lee, 2016; Lopez & Chesney-Lind, 2014). As Michelle Fine and Lois Weis pointed out in *The Unknown City: The Lives of Poor and Working-Class Young Adults* (1998): "'Good mothering,' or what passes for good mothering, happens in a particular context; a context of money, time, and excess. And that in the absence of these, it is far too easy to 'discover' bad mothering. As a society, we scrutinize the least equipped and least resourced women, holding them to standards of mothering that most of us could not and do not achieve" (186–187).

This tendency to blame poor mothers of color is rooted in the larger social discourse of personal responsibility that is endemic to U.S. culture (Sered & Norton-Hawk, 2014). Politicians also rely on this personal responsibility perspective to develop and implement policies that unfairly target poor mothers of color. An example of such policies, as discussed in Chapter 1, is the Personal Responsibility and Work Reconciliation Act (PRWORA), which is based on the assumption that "welfare mothers" are lazy and need to be forced to work for the betterment of their children (Bloch & Taylor, 2014). Such representations are often racialized, as the terms "welfare mothers" and the even more pejorative "welfare queens" typically refer to poor African American mothers who are presumed to be lazy, manipulative, and selfish (Bloch & Taylor, 2014). Conservative politicians have also stigmatized poor Latina mothers. In recent years, these politicians have implied that undocumented Latina mothers immigrate to the United States solely to have "anchor babies," which will allow them access to welfare and other social goods. The underlying premise of both the "welfare queen" and "anchor baby" rhetoric is that poor mothers of color are motivated to become mothers primarily so that they can "cheat the system" and obtain welfare and other coveted social goods that they do not deserve. As a result of these stereotypes, punitive anti-family policies such as PRWORA are developed to further punish these mothers, and by extension their children, for their supposed wrongdoings, which can contribute to a lack of financial and other government support systems (Bloch & Taylor, 2014; Romero, 2011).

Mothers who struggle with other problems such as drug use are also painted as bad mothers with the assumption being that any and all drug use leads to bad parenting (Baker & Carson, 1999; Klee, 1998; Lee, 2016). This view of the bad parenting–drug use link is so pervasive that many children are removed from their parents' care if parental drug use is suspected (Lee, 2016). The media fueled "crack baby" rhetoric from the 1980s is an example of the social stigma that is often directed against mothers, especially African American mothers, who use drugs (Humphries, 1999). Nevertheless, it should be emphasized that all mothers regardless of racial/ethnic background are stigmatized and punished if they use drugs. For example, in July of 2014, 26-year-old Mallory Loyolla, a White woman, was arrested and charged with simple assault two days after giving birth to her daughter who had tested positive for methamphetamine. She was the first woman in the state of Tennessee to be arrested under a law that allows prosecutors to charge women with criminal assault if they use narcotics during pregnancy (ABC News, 2014). What is striking about this case is that the media coverage presented a more positive view of Mallory as an expectant mother. Several stories depicted photos, presumably from Mallory's baby shower, that showed her happily standing near a crib filled with baby items. One photo depicted an assortment of cupcakes spelling out the words "Welcome, Baby." Even though Mallory appeared to be excited about having a baby, as evidenced by her Facebook photos, at the time of this writing, her daughter was still under custody of child protective services (CPS). Tennessee is not unique in punishing expectant mothers if they are drug users. Eighteen other states classify substance use during pregnancy as child abuse, 15 require health care professionals to report suspected parental abuse, and 4 states require them to test for prenatal drug exposure if they suspect abuse (Guttmacher Institute, 2015).

As Tina Lee (2016) found in her ethnography of the New York City Child Welfare System, the state often removes children from their home if their parents use drugs even when it is not clear how parental drug use impacts parenting. Lee found that the "the designation 'use' could range from parents who were addicted and their use was substantially impairing their lives and their children's well-being to parents who could have been labeled a functional addict to cases in which occasional or recreational use was discovered" (p. 114). In almost 56% of the drug cases that Lee observed, parental drug use appeared to be the only issue: Parents had either admitted drug use, failed a drug test, or were not enrolled or participating in a drug treatment program. Nevertheless, in all these instances, children were removed from their homes. Lee found that parental drug use was linked to parenting (living in dirty homes, leaving children home alone, not taking children to school, or leaving the child with a relative for an extended period of time) in only a small number of cases, but even in these instances, she argued that poverty also played a role (e.g., lack of health insurance or childcare).

Mothers who are stuck in domestic violence relationships are also at risk for having their children removed by the state. In some states, parents whose children witness domestic violence can be charged with parental failure to protect or neglect (Kantor & Little, 2003; Lee, 2016). While exposure to domestic violence has been associated with adverse child outcomes, the threat of taking children away only makes it less likely that mothers will seek assistance, which means many children will continue to suffer.

Anti-family policies punish poor mothers by making it more difficult for them to qualify for much needed support such as access to welfare. Mothers who use drugs experience an additional layer of stigma, which serves to further isolate and punish them for their perceived shortcomings. Finally, even mothers who are victims of domestic violence may be charged with failure to protect and have their children removed (Kantor & Little, 2003; Lee, 2015). Not surprisingly, poor mothers who struggle with drug issues and domestic violence may be the least likely to seek out assistance from legal and social support agencies because they fear losing custody of their children (Haight, Ostler, Black, Sheridan, & Kingery, 2007; McKeganey, Barnard, & McIntosh, 2002). Mothers who are undocumented may be even more fearful of seeking assistance for drug use or domestic violence, because many of them also worry about being deported or having their partners (who are often a source of financial support) deported in addition to being afraid that the state will remove their children (Bauer, Rodriguez, Quiroga, & Flores-Ortiz, 2000).

Unfortunately, many poor mothers—especially those who struggle with drug use and/or domestic violence—also lack other positive social support systems. This social isolation coupled with a lack of resources (e.g., financial means to pay for childcare) could potentially increase the likelihood that they will rely on their children to help them with childrearing and other household tasks. Due to their need to be taken care of, which is often rooted in their own troubled childhoods, some mothers may also rely on their children for emotional support and care (Belsky, 1980). Elizabeth Tracy and Toby Martin (2007) found that most of the 86 mothers in substance abuse treatment in their study relied on their children for support. More specifically, they found that mothers relied on 46% of the children for emotional support (e.g., listening to feelings), 40% of the children for concrete support (e.g., helping with chores), and 84% of the children for sobriety support.

RELYING ON CHILDREN DURING HARD TIMES: ADULTIFICATION

Children growing up in households characterized by parental substance use and domestic violence often assume adult roles (Kroll & Taylor, 2003). Faced with parents who are often incapacitated or inconsistent in their parenting, children assume both instrumental and emotional caretaking responsibilities (Backett-Milburn, Wilson, Bancroft, & Cunningham-Burley, 2008; Jurkovic, 1997; Kroll & Taylor, 2003). This process whereby children prematurely assume adult responsibilities in families is referred to as adultification.

Linda Burton (2007), in her seminal article *Childhood Adultification in Economically Disadvantaged Families: A Conceptual Model,* describes four types of adultification: Precocious knowledge, mentored adultification, peerification/spousification, and parentification. Precocious knowledge involves "witnessing situations and acquiring knowledge that are advanced for the child's age" (p. 336). Examples of precocious knowledge include being exposed to parental drug use, intimate partner violence, and family financial problems. Mentored adultification involves an adult mentoring a child to assume partial adult responsibilities and roles. Burton argues that this type of adultification can be beneficial if clear child–adult boundaries are in place and the child gains emotional maturity as a result of being mentored. Peerification/spousification involves the child assuming the role of a spouse or peer, but only on a part-time, as needed basis. Children who assume this role often serve as confidants to adults (usually parents) or part-time parents. Finally, parentification involves the child serving as a full-time parent to younger siblings. With the exception of mentored adultification, the other types of adultification usually result in negative social and emotional outcomes for children and adolescents (Jurkovic, 1997).

Adultification played a major role in the lives of the girls in this study. The majority of girls shared stories about how they assumed adult responsibilities and roles. This appeared to be a gendered phenomenon as girls reported primarily supporting, protecting, advising, and helping mothers. Similar to the "high-risk" young women in Jean Bottcher's (2001) study of gender and delinquency, the young women interviewed for this book assumed childcare and parental responsibility at a young age. They cared for younger siblings, served as their mothers' relationship advisors, protected their mothers from violence, and served as their mothers' confidantes. On only a few occasions did they mention helping, supporting, or advising fathers, no doubt because the majority of these young women grew up in single-mother households with only sporadic contact with biological fathers.

Taking Care of Mom and Younger Siblings

Girls frequently helped their mothers with younger siblings. Unlike children growing up in low-income, single-mother households whose parents often actively enlist their help, the girls in this study were just as likely to help out when their mothers were otherwise unavailable or unable to care for their siblings due to drug use, incarceration, or mental illness. Richelle, for example, helped take care of younger siblings when her mother was unable to parent effectively due to drug use. Given the previous involvement of child protective services, Richelle was vested in helping her mother appear like a so-called normal mother when caseworkers visited. During caseworker visits, Richelle downplayed her caretaking duties in order to protect her mother and make sure "CPS didn't take us away from my mom." She said:

> I would have to serve my brother and . . . because my brother was the only one born then, I would have to wash him, you know, take him a shower because he didn't know how to wash himself, and I would put him to bed. I help, you know, because when you're in a parenting stage when you're young, you can't . . . it's hard for you to get out of it, so I've just been . . . I'm used to it. My mom doesn't even have to tell me. I'll . . . you know . . . clean his diaper, you know. Whenever his diaper needs changing, my mom doesn't have to even tell me. I'll just do it and sometimes my mom will stop me from doing it because she doesn't want to get in trouble because of CPS. She tells me, 'No, you can't do it because CPS will get on me and think you're responsible for him,' and I'm, like, 'No, just let me do it.' And then I wash the dishes. I try to do, like, more chores than what she would do. But when CPS comes around, I have to be, like, a normal daughter, you know.

As Richelle's narrative reveals, notions of normality influenced both her and her mother's actions. It was very important that child protective services view her mother as normal. Thus, Richelle and her mother performed normality in an attempt to meet the caseworkers' expectations. During our interview, Richelle also went to great lengths to describe her mother in positive terms that conformed to notions of good mothering. According to Richelle, her mother was "very loving and caring" and would spend a lot of money on her children when she was sober. However, Richelle, who was used to being in charge of her siblings, resented her mother's periodic intrusions and was especially frustrated when her mother wasted money on frivolous items such as toys and chips. Still, she appreciated her mother's efforts even though she did not agree with them, as indicated by the following narrative: "My mom is very smart. She has really good advice. She has a lot of strengths. She's a really good mom. Just sometimes she gets us whatever we want and that's kind of not what I want. She's kind of wasting her money, like, you know, my little brothers and sister are little, so they think that it's not really a waste of money to get whatever they want. If they could get whatever they want, they would have whatever they want, and we would go to the store, and my mom would buy them all these toys and a bunch of chips, and we don't need all those chips, you know."

Richelle's role as caretaker was not consistent. When her mother was sober or in "a good mood," she would assert her authority and assume caretaking responsibilities that often went against Richelle's beliefs about how the younger children should be parented. When child protective services became involved, Richelle was then expected to downplay her contributions by acting like a "normal daughter" so that her mother could appear like a good mother. While Richelle contributed to her siblings' care, her contributions were often not acknowledged, which led to frustration. Like most people, children want their caretaking efforts to be acknowledged and validated (Van Parys & Rober, 2013).

The problem with children attempting to care for younger siblings is that they are ill-equipped to do so. Adultified children have few support systems and resources to effectively protect and care for their brothers and sisters especially when they are growing up in distressed families in impoverished neighborhoods (Jurkovic, 1997). For example, Lexus, a 14-year-old White girl, ran away and took her 10-year-old brother with her in an effort to keep them both safe from an abusive grandfather. In her mind, she was helping her brother by escaping from their grandfather, as indicated by the following quote: "Yeah, I took my little brother and ran. I don't feel like a bad sister either. They always tell me 'You're a bad sister and you always set a bad example for your brother.' And I'm not. I'm not a bad sister. I took my brother with me because I wanted to protect him from my grandfather (who had physically abused Lexus). So that makes me feel good about myself, you know, because I was trying to help him."

Lexus did not consider going to a school official or other adult authority figure because she did not believe they would be able to help her nor was she comfortable disclosing the abuse. Her distrust of adults is understandable given that adults in authority roles had been unable to help her in the past. The possibility of being placed in another foster care home was not something she wanted to endure again given her previous negative experiences in such settings. Unfortunately, Lexus ended up in the juvenile justice system instead after she was charged with truancy and running away for attempting to protect herself and her brother. At the time of the study, Lexus had been incarcerated for six months and had been participating in individual and group therapy to help her deal with the trauma of her abuse.

Janee, who was first introduced in Chapter 1, also shared a disturbing story related to trying to parent a younger sibling. At a young age, child protective services removed Janee and her siblings from their mother's care as a result of maternal drug use and mental health problems and abuse. While in a foster care home, Janee attempted to care for her younger sister, but was accused of trying to molest the younger girl while doing so.

> Me and my siblings went there [foster care home]. I have two sisters and a baby brother. And being the oldest, whenever they cried, since my mom was only 16 when she had me, I was just, like, their mom, too. I had the mother instinct at a very young age; and so my sister, the one right behind me, she had a fever; and she was crying in her sleep; and we had bunk beds and we shared a room, so I got down, and I could tell she was hot and had a fever, and I was only seven, so I took off her shirt to cool her down; and I was behind her trying to rock her to calm her down; and the foster dad came and claimed that I was molesting her because it happened to me in my past, so he said that it would happen again, that I would start doing the action that had been done to me.

According to Janee, she was immediately removed from the foster care home and placed in another home. At the time of our interview, Janee had not seen her mother or siblings in almost 10 years. As with Lexus, Janee's attempts to care for a younger sibling resulted in negative consequences. Both girls' attempts to take care of their younger siblings were also shaped by their experiences and interactions with caseworkers in the child protective system. In Lexus's case, she did not trust caseworkers or other adults, as they had not been able to help her in the past, whereas Janee was young and confused when initially placed in a foster care home and was doing her best to comfort her younger sister in an unfamiliar setting.

Girls also reported being concerned for and taking care of their mothers. Some worried about their mothers' personal safety and were afraid that their mothers would "overdose" or "die as a result of drugs." Paige, for example, said that while she was used to her mother being "high or drunk," there were times when she became concerned for her mother's safety: "I remember, like, times when she wouldn't be doing good, and I would check on her to see if she was okay. I would wake myself up and make breakfast for all the kids, but I totally thought it was normal. You know, even though I was always frustrated, I thought our lives were normal. I thought it was normal for my mother to be passed out in the morning. Until I moved here [group home], I thought all the stuff I grew up with was okay." As this narrative reveals, in addition to taking care of her siblings, Paige sometimes had to care for her mother. This finding parallels what other researchers have found in studies of children growing up with mentally ill parents (Mordoch, 2010). For many years, Paige viewed her responsibilities (e.g., taking care of siblings) and her mother's behaviors (e.g., drug use, passing out) as normal, and despite feeling frustrated and overwhelmed, she did her best to support and care for both her mother and siblings. Unfortunately, there was no one left to care for Paige, who was sexually molested by one of her mother's ex-boyfriends.

Serving as Mom's Relationship Advisor

Girls also served as mothers' relationship advisors. In many instances, they tried to warn their mothers to stay away from abusive or manipulative men. Dee, a 16-year-old White girl who was living at the Oak Canyon group home at the time of the study, recalled warning her mother against Tony. While Dee admits that she was "selfish" about wanting all of her mother's attention, she still felt like Tony was a bad relationship choice.

His name was Tony, and I hated him, like, I don't know, like ever since I was little, I don't judge people—well, technically, I do—but I just never liked him, you know, and I was always selfish with my mom. I would sleep with her every night and, you know, that was my mom. I didn't want to share her even with my brother, but I just didn't like him. There was just something about him I hated. And then one day, he did my mom wrong, and I was, like, 'I told you,' and I was, like, 7 or 8 saying that. I was, like, 'I told you he was no good,' and she was like, 'Why wasn't I listening to you?'

What is notable about Dee's narrative is that she was only 7 or 8 and already providing her mother with relationship advice, a finding that is consistent with other research, which indicates that drug-dependent mothers often rely on children between the ages of 6 and 11 for emotional support (Tracy & Martin, 2007). Like Dee, other girls also tried to warn their mothers against certain men—men who sometimes reminded them of their own fathers. For example, Bianca, a 17-year-old Mexican American girl who was living at Desert Star at the time of our interview, was very upset when her mother began a relationship with a man who had just come out of prison. She could not understand why her mother would choose such a partner after her failed relationship with Bianca's father who had also been in and out of prison for drug-related charges. She said, "And that's why I hated [my mom's boyfriend] because he kinda manipulated my mom. And I started realizing the person he was, you know. Especially from coming out of prison, from being in prison for so many years. It just really made me mad, 'cause my mom came out of a really bad relationship with my dad, and then she gets into another relationship, you know. It just made me really, really mad."

When I asked her to provide an example of her mother's boyfriend's troublesome behavior, Bianca rolled her eyes as if to say, "Where do I begin?" She then shared a story about how he left her and her mother for drugs and alcohol. Bianca could not understand why her mother "took him back." She shook her head and said that she has decided for her own peace of mind not to get upset about her mother's decision to stay with her boy-friend. She said, "I don't know, I don't really worry about it anymore 'cause I'm on my own now. I told my mom, and I try to give her good advice, you know as a daughter, but I can't do nothing about it if she's not gonna take it so . . . I just try not to worry about it. I mean to tell you the truth, I'm kinda over it 'cause I have my life now, and she has hers now. Before I would kinda want to control her life, I guess you could say, so I would tell her, 'Don't do that.' And she would always tell me, 'You can't tell me what to do.' But I just felt so hurt 'cause I thought she loved me or she should love me. I thought she should love me first before anyone, but it wasn't like that." After a slight pause, Bianca continued, "Like, I just have to accept the fact that my mom is, you know, with him, because I always wanted my mom to leave him. Because after the things he put us through and my mom, you know, getting hurt by him. I just told my mom to leave him, and she never did. At one point, she did want to leave him, but I don't know . . . I don't know why my mom doesn't just leave him . . . . I don't know if she is scared to leave him, or what it is, but she just won't leave him. I don't understand that."

The previous narrative suggests that Bianca felt like she was being replaced every time her mother started dating someone new. She also did not like that her mother's current boyfriend had a history of incarceration and drug use nor did she think he was a good partner for her mother. In order to protect her mother and herself, Bianca repeatedly implored her mother to not develop a relationship with this man. Despite Bianca's pleading, her mother continued to stay with an abusive partner. Like several young women interviewed for this book, Bianca began to refrain from giving her mother relationship advice during adolescence.

Lydia, a 14-year-old Mexican American girl who was living at Desert Star at the time of our interview, also had very strong opinions about her mother's partner. In this instance, Lydia's mother was involved with a man who "sometimes beat her and had a tendency to come and go." Lydia said:

I think he feels he has power over her. He tries to put his hands on her a lot of times, and my mom, she tries to cover it with makeup, and I am, like, 'Why is your eye black?' and she's, like, 'Oh, it's just always like that,' and I'm like, 'You're tripping.' And one time he tried to threaten her with a sword that was in the house, like, a big old sword and it was real, and my little brothers were there. And they're setting a bad example for them 'cause they're little kids, and what are they gonna learn, to beat up their wife when they get older? It's abusive. I don't know, she says she's not gonna let him beat on her, she's not gonna put up with that, but obviously she does 'cause they're still together.

While Lydia acknowledged the issue of relationship power, she blamed both her mother and stepfather for fighting and setting a "bad example" for her younger brothers. Still, she seemed to blame her mother most for putting up with a man who beat her. She was further confounded by her mother's refusal to leave the relationship because her stepfather was not financially contributing to the family household, which in Lydia's eyes meant that he was clearly expendable in the sense that her mother was not bound to him for financial reasons.

They argue often. Yes, they do, because she's always talking about [how] he doesn't help her with anything. He needs to 'cause he needs to be responsible for his child [Mom's boyfriend is the biological father of one of Lydia's half-brothers]. And, he's out there spending money on prostitutes and wild women and strip clubs and stuff. So, yeah, they fight about money. 'Cause my mother has Section 8 program. You know what that is? And, she needs help because she's currently unemployed and she's going to school. Thank God she has the FAS, or something like that to go to school, I don't know what it's called, like, financial help. So, that's good. She's unemployed and she gets welfare, but that's not enough for the household. I tell her he needs to help out. She needs to put him on child support 'cause he's not doing anything for her as it is.

Like Bianca, Lydia expressed frustration with her mother's decision to stay with an abusive partner. "She makes threats to leave, but she doesn't go through [with them] because he doesn't follow what she says. She tries to say this is what you need to do financially, and this and that, but he doesn't do it. He doesn't give her money. He's not there. Basically, we say he's the man of the house, and he doesn't take charge and doesn't do what he's supposed to do to keep his family good." In Lydia's eyes, not only did her stepfather beat her mother up, but he also failed to provide any financial support to the family. She also believed that her stepfather's treatment of her mother was not right. She said, "He tripping because he doesn't do anything for her so if she ever wanted to do what she feels is right, he tries to put her down [and] that's not okay for him to do, because he doesn't have the right to do it." Like Bianca, Lydia simply could "not understand" why her mother chose to stay with such a man.

Bianca's and Lydia's difficulty understanding why their mothers stayed in abusive relationships is not surprising given that victims of domestic violence are often blamed for their own situations within a larger culture that tacitly reinforces violence against women as opposed to critically examining the role that larger social forces—that is, gender oppression, economic inequality, discrimination—play in limiting women's abilities to exit violent relationships (Sered & Norton-Hawk, 2014).

Protecting Mom from Violence

Occasionally girls attempted to protect their mothers from being physically victimized by either trying to physically intervene, yelling at the abuser to stop, obtaining help, or begging their mothers to leave the relationship. Connie, a 16-year-old Mexican American girl who was living at the Desert Star residential treatment center at the time of our interview, shared one such story: "Yeah, one time . . . oh, my God. We went to my mom's friend's house and we got home by 9:13. And my mom went in the room, and I heard her crying, and I opened the door. And it was locked, but that was not gonna stop me. And I opened it, and he had her like a little kid bent over his knees, like, spanking her. I'm, like, 'No!' That's not cool, you know. I jumped on top of her, I'm, like, I'm a little girl still, but I jumped on my mom to protect her." Connie was only 5 when this happened. Although she did not quite understand what was happening, she understood enough to know that her mother was being victimized. Unfortunately, her father continued to physically abuse her mother for another five years until "she [mother] finally opened her eyes and realized she didn't need that."

Claudia, a 17-year-old Mexican American girl who was incarcerated at Arroyo Verde at the time of our interview, also tried to intervene on her mother's behalf when she was younger. Claudia felt like her mother always took her boyfriend's side and could not understand why her mother would side with her boyfriend instead of her children. She did not consider the possibility that her mother might have been afraid to disagree with her boyfriend. She said, "He was trying to tell us what to do, and my mom always took his side, and I just didn't like that. The guy she was dating thought he could just come over and tell us what to do because he was dating my mom. I just couldn't take that. He would hurt my mom all the time. He would hit my mom, and she still went back to him. And one night, I heard him hitting her, so I hit the door, like, three times, and the door broke down. I was going to stab him and after that I couldn't be there anymore."

Girls sometimes attempted to protect other mother figures in their lives. For example, Ophelia, a 15-year-old Mexican American girl living at the Moonlight group home, shared a harrowing account of how she attempted to intervene on behalf of her stepmother who was being beaten by her father who had recently been released from prison. Amazed that her aunts could hear what was going on, but refused to intervene, Ophelia decided to call her own mother, who also had a history of being in prison for selling drugs, to come over and intervene.

My dad doesn't allow my stepmom to work or leave the house or anything. He pushes her around a lot 'cause he beats her. She's really pretty, too. But she doesn't stand up to him. One time . . . when I went to visit him, my *tia* [aunt] got mad because I told my mom. I was, like, 'Well, I saw him!' What was I gonna do? Just go home all happy? No! I was scared out of my life. 'Cause I was there, and I was playing with my little sister, and I heard them fighting, but it was nothing 'cause I was used to it already. Yeah. And then I was play-ing with my little sister, and then they come out in the kitchen, and the living room is right there next to the kitchen, and he just punched her in the face. And she hit the table with her head! She was gushing blood, and I'm, like, 'How is my tia *not* going to get mad?' I could have saved her life. 'Cause he could have done a lot worse 'cause he's really strong, you know. He's short and fat, but he's strong. It's just crazy how [my aunts] protect him. My aunt was in the next room. She didn't do nothing. I was, like, 'Oh. My. God.' And I'm, like, 'Who are you protecting?' Somebody is gonna end up dying! At first I ran to [my aunt]. I was, like, 'Oh my god, he just hit her!' and she's, like, 'Shut up! Don't say nothing.' And I'm, like, 'What?!' and then I'm, like, 'Uh-uh . . . I'm calling my mom.' And I called her and she came right away, and then she yelled at [my dad], and she put him in his place and everything. And he got mad and just stormed off, and my stepmom was just so grateful.

When I asked if her stepmother and father were still together, Ophelia said they were still together even though her father is still abusive. Like many of the girls, especially the Latina girls, Ophelia strongly rejected the notion that women should be controlled and abused by their partners. Yet, like the other girls, Ophelia also blamed her stepmother for staying in the abusive relationship. She said, "He still takes a lot of advantage of her, a lot, but he does that to everyone. Personally, if it was me, I would tell her to leave him. I mean I've told her, but she can take my advice or leave it. I can't make her. But I think it's her bad, but then she sees it as okay, so what can I do?"

Ophelia acknowledged that her presence in her father's house mini-mized the abuse at least when she was there. As illustrated next, Ophelia assumed the role of protecting her stepmother from being victimized by her father by simply being present to act as a deterrent. She threatened to "call CPS" on her father. The threat of state intervention was enough to get her father to back down, because in addition to being a drug user, he was undocumented.

He would be more lenient with her when I was there, so I think that's probably the reason why she would like me to go over a lot 'cause you know he would be, like, okay. I don't really care about him, you know, but he can't take me away from my brothers and sisters. 'Cause I have a lot of dirt on him and I could go to CPS right now and get those kids taken away from him. But the only reason I don't is because I know that they need a dad. And him, to them, he's, like, a good dad to them, and I don't want to take that away from them. So, that's the only reason why, but that's the reason why [my stepmom] wants me to go see him.

RESISTING ADULTIFICATION IN ADOLESCENCE

Girls assumed adultified roles early in their childhoods and these roles often persisted into adolescence. Nevertheless, some girls did attempt to reject these roles during adolescence. This was particularly true when they felt trapped between fighting parents, but only when they had close relationships with both parents. In these instances, girls felt conflicted and often tried to extricate themselves by saying they did not want to be involved. Delia, a fast talking 15-year-old Mexican American girl, resisted being put in the middle of her parents' relationship problems. Unlike some of the other young women, Delia was quite resolute about not wanting to be "mixed up in" her parents' "drama." She had her own problems to take care of and steadfastly resisted being drawn into her parents' relationship problems.

My mom is a tough person to get along with, so she kinda makes it hard for him to get along with her. He just doesn't feel loved from her, like, he don't feel that connection anymore like they used to have. . . . He don't feel like she's in love with him anymore. It's pretty good, but whenever it comes to their relationship and their love life and stuff like that, it's kinda bad. 'Cause then they kinda put me in the middle of it and he, like, drags me in it, and talks to me, like, 'You really understand me when I say this and that about your mom. I'm not saying I don't love your mom, but look at what she's doing. She's tearing us apart' so, like I said, he kinda drags me in the middle of it, and I'm, like, 'Yo, why am I in the middle of your guys' love life? This is yours, not mine, I got my own love life to take care of.'

Fourteen-year-old Jordan also resisted being put in the middle because it upset her when her parents talked about each other. Like Delia, Jordan cared for both her mother and father and did not want to choose sides.

> Well, when they were together, it was always constant fighting, and you know, it was name-calling and stuff, and like . . . I felt, well, I was really young, so I don't really know, but I just kind of felt, like, oh no, they are going to break up. You know, and it was always scary. I felt really bad for my dad because my mom would always go out with men and stuff, and like, you know, they would talk to each other behind their backs with me. They would say bad things about each other to me. And, like, I loved both of them, so I didn't really wanna hear that stuff, you know. I think it's better for me, because I don't like to see them fight, you know, it hurts my feelings.

Other girls, such as Bianca, whose story I shared earlier, refrained from giving their mothers additional relationship advice out of frustration, whereas other girls, as a result of therapy directives, tried to disentangle themselves from being overly involved in their mothers' relationships in an attempt to focus on their "own mental health" instead.

BLAMING MOTHERS

Although girls helped and supported mothers, many of them also blamed their mothers for their problems. Some girls viewed their mothers as "weak" for repeatedly dating violent men, as "selfish" for putting their drug use before their children, and as "not very smart" for being unable to extricate themselves from lives plagued by violence, substance abuse, and poverty. For example, Shannon, a 17-year-old White girl, referred to her mother as "weak and dumb" with the insinuation being that her mother was not strong or smart enough to solve her own problems. She said, "Before I used to think she was really weak and dumb. I just thought she was really stupid, and I don't know, lost. And now she's . . . I feel, like, she's kinda strong now. 'Cause she's finally realizing, you know, what it means to be dumb. I don't know. She's just different now. I think she's kinda a little bit stronger now. I really don't talk to her that much about, like, my personal issues, because she's messed up her own life, but she's a little stronger now so maybe she can make better choices." Although Shannon had seen growth in her mother, she still did not feel as if she could go to her for advice or talk to her about personal problems. It was clear from our conversation that she was there for her mother, but did not feel like her mother had a lot to offer her in turn. Like other young women in this study, Shannon adopted the parental role, and saw it as her duty to take care of her mother.

Debbie, a 16-year-old Mexican American girl at Arroyo Verde, also spoke about taking care of her mother. She spoke about her mother in much the same way a parent might speak about a disobedient child in need of a time out. For example, she shared what happened after she and her mother got into an argument about her mother staying out late using drugs: "At the time, I can tell it got to her, you know. And at the time she just went into her room, and the next day, when we woke up, she made breakfast and we had a whole heart to heart. Like I said, if she tells me something, like if it's my fault, I'm gonna tell her if it's my fault. I have to own up to that. But you know, if it's not my fault, I'm gonna tell her, you're mad at whoever she's mad at. Don't take it out on me. I will tell her straight out, and she knows it, too. So she'll just go into her room, and watch TV and calm down, or whatever. Then we'll talk about it later after she's not trippin'."

As the oldest child of four, Dulce, a 14-year-old Mexican American girl, also assumed the role of primary decision maker. In fact, as indicated by the following exchange, she viewed her mother as unassertive, the type of person who lets other people tell her what to do.

DULCE: I think she's beautiful. She looks like me just older. She's really nice and everything. She just lets people make decisions for her. I'm more, like . . . how to put it . . . like when there's a problem I give her solutions so we can work on it together. Or I help her . . . know what I mean?

VERA: Can you give me an example?

DULCE: Kinda, like, lets say we're getting evicted, we're gonna get kicked out or something. I tell her that everything is gonna be okay and . . . I dunno, she's the most important person in my life. If there was a bus coming, and it was just us two standing there, I would push her out of the way and get hit, you know? She's everything to me. She gets sad and stuff, and sometimes she's not grateful for things that I do, but, you know, when it's your mom, you love them.

As we continued to talk, it became clear that Dulce's mother struggled with bouts of depression in addition to drinking. As such, Dulce had learned early on to take care of her mother's emotional needs as well as attend to the emotional and physical needs of her younger brother and sisters even though she attributed her mother's problems to being unassertive and not very strong.

Some young women were also critical of mothers whom they believed to be "lazy," "inadequate," and "slutty." They attributed their mothers' behaviors solely to their mothers' character deficits, as illustrated by Melanie:

> When I was little, she was a stripper, and then she was a bartender. And then when I was in my tweens, like, elementary school-ish, until, like, high school, she worked in retail in different stores—Bath and Body Works, Foot Locker, the Body Shop, and a couple other ones—oh, Wells Fargo. She's perfectly capable of getting a regular job, like, she has people skills. She could work. She's very good at working in retail. She's just lazy. She doesn't want to go to a regular job, so she decides to open up her legs for money. It would be different, like, I know some girls who have no other options, but she's perfectly capable of, getting a regular job, but she just doesn't want to because she is lazy.

As the previous narratives illustrate, while girls cared deeply about their mothers and sought to support and protect them, many of them also held their mothers to a higher parenting standard than their fathers (as will be demonstrated in the next chapter). They subscribed to overarching views of individual responsibility and held their mothers accountable when they violated these standards. Of course, girls also suffered as a direct consequence of their mothers' decisions and these experiences also colored their views of their mothers' actions. They also were often frustrated with their mothers and worried about them, which no doubt impacted their own emotional well-being.

CONCLUSION

This chapter began by using a wide-angle lens to examine girls' relationships with their mothers within a larger sociocultural context that often punishes poor mothers, especially poor mothers of color who use drugs and are in relationships characterized by violence. Anti-(poor)family laws based on the presumption that poor mothers need to be heavily regulated and policed set the stage for these mothers to feel like they have few options (Bloch & Taylor, 2014; Lee, 2016). The illicit nature and stigma associated with drug use makes it less likely that drug-using mothers will seek support from social service agencies. Mothers with felony drug records may even be cut off from much needed welfare and housing benefits (Allard, 2002; Hirsch, 2001; Van Olphen, Eliason, Freudenberg, & Barnes, 2009). Latina mothers who are undocumented experience an additional layer of stigma, which further contributes to their social isolation (Bauer, Rodriguez, Quiroga, & Flores-Ortiz, 2000). Against this backdrop, poor mothers who are already struggling with other issues such as substance abuse and domestic violence may rely on their children to meet their emotional and social needs.

Despite growing up in multistressed families, the young women in this study demonstrated remarkable agency. They did not present themselves as victims, but rather as active problem-solvers and caretakers within their families. They assumed the role of quasi parent, spouse, and peer in their interactions with siblings and mothers. Even when they themselves were abused, as was the case with Lexus, they sought to protect their younger siblings. Alternatively, as was the case with Connie, Claudia, and Ophelia, they also tried to protect the adult women in their lives—most notably their mothers—from physical victimization. They did this by employing both direct (physically putting themselves between their mothers and male partners) and indirect (threatening to notify child protective services or law enforcement, calling on other adults for support) strategies. Unfortunately, girls' attempts to protect younger siblings and mothers were often constrained by their physical, emotional, and developmental limitations. Furthermore, their contributions were rarely acknowledged or validated by either their mothers or state actors (e.g., child welfare workers). Mothers, for example, sometimes asked their daughters to minimize their caretaking roles within the presence of child protective services staff so as not to make them look like bad mothers. At other times, as was the case with Lexus and Janee, girls attempted to care for or protect younger siblings only to be punished for their efforts. As they grew older, some of the girls attempted to provide relationship advice to their mothers, only to have their advice ignored. For the most part, girls' attempts to actively assist with family problems were met with limited success and only rarely or inconsistently acknowledged by the adults in their lives.

3 · DADDY'S LITTLE GIRL

Feeling Rejected, Abandoned, and Unloved

As I sat down to write this chapter, I was reminded of a conversation I once had with Lizbeth, a young woman I met early on in my career. I remember Lizbeth saying that her father used to sing a special song to her when she was little, and even though things were different now, she would always be "daddy's little girl." Although I am not proud to admit it, my first thought was, "How could Lizbeth possibly think she was 'daddy's little girl' when her father had never been consistently involved in her life?" As a result of his stint in prison and subsequent breakup with Lizbeth's mother, he had only lived with Lizbeth for the first year of her life. Upon his release from prison, Lizbeth's father immediately became involved with another woman who became pregnant shortly thereafter. He did not retain custody of his five other children nor did he pay child support or see them on a consistent basis. Despite this, Lizbeth mythologized her father and referred to herself as "daddy's little girl" even though he had only been minimally involved in her life. I remember struggling with understanding how Lizbeth could possess these feelings about a man who had not been there for her, a man who failed to pay child support, a man who had spent significant amounts of time in prison, and otherwise failed to be consistently involved in her life. My gut reaction back then was to blame Lizbeth's father for his perceived failures, but I was soon humbled by Lizbeth's response when I asked her how she could feel like "daddy's little girl" when her father was only intermittently involved in her life. She said, "I know he has done some bad things in his life, but there's another side of him that not everyone sees, but I've seen it." This simple but powerful exchange with Lizbeth reminded me that young people can have powerful attachments to their fathers, even when their fathers are not consistently involved in their lives. Over the years I have interviewed and worked with many young women from similar backgrounds as Lizbeth. Like Lizbeth, many of these young women steadfastly refer to themselves as "daddy's little girl" or "daddy's little princess" even though their childhoods were anything but fairytales. This chapter is about these young women and their complicated relationships with fathers.[1]

SOCIOCULTURAL IDEALS ABOUT FATHERING

Fathers have historically been ignored in the social science literature (Goldberg, Tan, & Thorsen, 2009; Nielsen, 2012). The emphasis has been on mothers, and fathers have largely been an afterthought in research and practice. When fathers' contributions have been acknowledged, they have been largely reduced to financial contributions: Fathers are important because they contribute financially to the household, which benefits children. Despite shifting gender norms and expectations around parenting, most Americans still "believe that breadwinning is primarily the father's job" (Nielsen, 2012, p. 44). In 1999, an *American Psychologist* article asked, "Are fathers essential to children's wellbeing?" Upon reviewing the literature, the authors concluded that, "parenting roles are interchangeable, that neither mothers nor fathers are unique or essential, and that the significant variables in predicting father involvement are economic, rather than marital" (Silverstein & Auerbach, 1999, p. 399).

The popular media also reinforces the view that fathers are not essential or even all that important to children's development. A study of 29 popular TV shows from the 1950s to the 1990s, found that the father is usually presented as the "target of a growing number of jokes and is portrayed in situations that make him look foolish" (Scharrer, 2001, p. 23). In a more recent analysis of 12 sitcoms, fathers were still being depicted as being more foolish than mothers (Pehlke, Hennon, Radina, & Kuvalanka, 2009). Race and class also color TV and film representations of fathers. In recent years, evidence suggests that positive representations of minority fathers exist (Goldberg et al., 2009). Unfortunately, representations of minority fathers, especially Latino fathers, continue to be rare in mainstream TV programs and film.

Popular news media also shape how society views fathers. Nowhere is this more evident than the depiction of "deadbeat" dads who are usually presented as young African American and Latino men (Hamer, 2001). Such stereotypical depictions exist despite evidence to the contrary. One study found that over half of the "deadbeats" (defined as fathers who can afford to pay child support, but do not) were White men in comparison to two-thirds of "turnips" (defined as men who cannot afford to pay child support without further impoverishing themselves) who were young African American and Latino men. The turnips were younger, less educated, less likely to be employed, and more likely to be living with relatives than deadbeats (Mincy & Sorensen, 1998). These findings call into question the enduring stereotype that minority fathers are deadbeats who do not care about their children.

While social science research on fathers has increased dramatically over the past several decades along with more positive representations of fathers in TV and film, negative stereotypes still exist, and this is especially true for poor African American and Latino fathers. In a society that blames individuals for their problems, it is easy to blame poor and minority fathers without taking into account the larger structural forces and institutional practices that shape and constrain their abilities to parent children. African American and Latino boys and men continue to be disproportionately disciplined in school, arrested by the police, and incarcerated in our nation's prisons (Rios, 2011). Until we plug this school-to-prison pipeline, African American and Latino men will continue to be disproportionately impacted by limited opportunities and time with their children will be severely curtailed as a result of time spent in jails and prisons. This is especially true for African American and Latino men who use drugs, as the War on Drugs has proven itself to be not a war on drugs, but a war on people of color (Chin, 2002; Nunn, 2002; Provine, 2008).

FATHERING ON THE MARGINS

Many of the girls interviewed for this book had fathers who had spent time in jail or prison. As Joyce Arditti (2012) noted in her book on the effects of parental incarceration on children, prisons are not family friendly and are often located far away from prisoners' homes and communities, which makes it challenging for children to visit their incarcerated fathers, and even when they are able to make the visit, children are often subject to long waits, crowded visiting rooms, and limited opportunities to engage in child-friendly activities at the prison (Nurse, 2002). Prison rules also impact fathers' ability to parent their children while incarcerated. Anne Nurse, in her study of incarcerated adolescent fathers, found that the "one girlfriend rule" prevented many of these young men from listing multiple women on their visitation list. This meant they were only able to receive visits from children from the girlfriend on their visiting list even if they had children from other women. In this way, the prison context served as a barrier that impacted incarcerated fathers' ability to parent children from multiple women.

As briefly touched upon in the introduction, formerly incarcerated parents face a number of barriers upon release from prison. They are ineligible to receive certain types of welfare or engage in certain types of work and must often continue to meet with parole officers if they are on parole (Chin, 2002; Hagan & Coleman, 2001; Lapidus et al., 2005). In addition, they face an enormous societal stigma if they have a drug or other felony conviction on their record, which makes it even more difficult for formerly incarcerated parents, irrespective of gender, to find a good job that will allow them to support their children. The end result is that many formerly incarcerated parents face significant social stigma, limited employment opportunities, and continued challenges upon their release from prison.

Latino fathers who are undocumented face an additional layer of stigma and surveillance. Several of the young women reported that their fathers had been deported or had fled Arizona to find more immigrant-friendly work opportunities in other areas of the country. Within a climate of fear, undocumented Latina/o parents irrespective of gender worry about being detained, deported, and ultimately separated from their children (Santos & Menjívar, 2014). Their fears are not unfounded. A recent study, *Shattered Families: The Perilous Intersection of Immigration Enforcement and the Child*

Welfare System, conducted by the Applied Research Center (ARC) estimates that approximately 5,100 children in foster care have a parent who has been either detained or deported. When parents are detained, they are usually sent to jail-like facilities far away from their families (Hidalgo, 2013; Wessler, 2011). Even more disturbing, as illustrated in the ARC report, undocumented parents do not have to commit a criminal offense in order to be detained and deported as several mechanisms such as the 287(g) program allow local police to act as Immigration and Customs Enforcement (ICE) agents.[2] In Maricopa County, where the interviews for this study took place, the ARC estimated that approximately 4.5% (n = 274) of youth in foster care have a parent who has been detained or deported. Furthermore, undocumented parents often have difficulty meeting the demands of the child welfare system due to a number of barriers including limited English proficiency, lack of transportation, and a lack of access to public services such as Medicaid, public housing, and TANF (Wessler, 2011). Although federal immigration policies implemented by local authorities impact both mothers and fathers, the girls interviewed for this book only discussed fathers' deportations. Although only a handful of them cited deportation as a reason for their fathers' absences, their narratives are important because they illustrate how the state can actively work to break up families and weaken parent–child relationships.

MATERNAL GATEKEEPING AND FATHERING

The relationship between fathers and mothers can also impact the quality of the father–child relationship. A growing body of research indicates that mothers often serve as gatekeepers and their views of children's nonresident fathers can either facilitate or hamper children's relationships with their fathers (Trinder, 2008). While mothers cite a number of reasons for limiting children's relationships with fathers (Trinder, 2008), fathers often feel like mothers are purposely punishing them by restricting access to children (Arditti, Smock, & Parkman, 2005; Roy & Dyson, 2005). This was certainly the case for a few of the young women interviewed for this book whose mothers played a pivotal role in limiting their daughters' access to fathers usually in an attempt to protect daughters from fathers who they considered irresponsible and/or "bad influences." In two instances, girls reported that their mothers were angry with fathers who had left them for other women. In these instances, mothers spoke negatively about fathers to their daughters. Although maternal gatekeeping appeared to play a role in a few of the girls' lives, it should be emphasized that in most instances, girls did not report mothers restricting access to fathers. Instead, most of the girls viewed fathers' physical and emotional absences as being a direct result of their fathers' personal choices or plights. Still, many of the young women, with some notable exceptions, longed for a relationship with their nonresident fathers. For some young women, this meant meeting fathers on the margins and developing relationships through shared drug use, via sporadic prison visits and letters, and over long distances. Eventually, perhaps as a result of maturation, some of the young women began to accept fathers for what they were able to offer them as opposed to being disappointed and resentful when fathers failed to live up to their expectations.

GIRLS' PERCEPTIONS OF FATHERS

Although most research has centered on the mother–child relationship, fathers play an important role in girls' lives and they notice when fathers are not involved. How they interpret fathers' lack of involvement depends on many factors including why their father is not involved, their mother's relationship with their father, whether their father has ever been involved, and their expectations of how their fathers should feel, act, and behave. Furthermore, how young people—such as the girls in this study— experience fathers' lack of involvement can impact how they feel about themselves as well as their ability to trust others, feel loved, and take part in healthy relationships (Rohner & Veneziano, 2001). Some fathers were like phantoms in the lives of their daughters. They floated in and out of their daughters' lives, but rarely stayed for extended periods of time. Even though most of the young women interviewed for this book did not live with their fathers or even spend significant amounts of time with them, they had a lot to say about their relationships with fathers. They spoke of being overtly rejected by fathers who denied paternity, of being replaced by their fathers' new families, and feeling like they were "not an important enough reason" for their fathers to stop using drugs or engaging in criminal behaviors. They spoke about losing fathers who died, were deported, or simply moved away.

While some spoke with great longing and mythologized their fathers, others were quite angry with their fathers and refused to have anything to do with them. Others barely knew their fathers or knew them only through their mothers' recollections. Irrespective of how girls talked about fathers, one thing was clear: Most girls had at one time or another wanted a meaningful relationship with their fathers built on love and support. For many, this desire continued to go unmet despite girls' often repeated attempts to forge loving and supportive relationships with their fathers. How girls responded to fathers' inconsistent involvement varied greatly depending on context (Lopez & Corona, 2012).[3]

Mythologizing Fathers

Many girls longed to have a stronger relationship with their fathers and expressed sadness about not being closer to them. They reminisced about how good their lives used to be when their fathers were present and shared memories of when they were "daddy's little girl." In these instances, girls reported that their fathers disappeared suddenly as a result of them abruptly moving out after breaking up with girls' mothers, jail/imprisonment, or deportation. For example, 15-year-old Jessica, a Mexican American girl who was living at Desert Star, talked about how much she missed her biological father who had moved out of her home when Jessica was 10 years old: "My dad and I used to be close. He would take me and my brothers to the park and buy us ice cream, but then he moved out. Got locked up. And I hardly ever hear from him now, but he used to be a good dad, and I miss him." Jessica's sadness at losing her father might have been compounded by her mothers' subsequent incarceration. As a young child, Jessica was shuttled back and forth between various relatives and ultimately ended up in foster care when both of her parents went to prison. Although she has since reunited with her mother, her father remains incarcerated. Jessica's only contact with her father is an occasional letter. When asked what her father writes about, Jessica said, "He always says that he loves me and my brothers and that he wants us to be a family again when he gets out." Although Jessica expressed an interest in wanting to visit her father in prison, like many children of incarcerated parents, she is dependent on the adults in her life to facilitate this process (Arditti, 2012; Siegel, 2011). At the time of our interview, she had not seen her father in several years, but looked forward to reuniting with him upon his release from prison.

Annie, a 17-year-old Mexican American girl, also longed for her father who was deported to Mexico when she was very young. Like Jessica, Annie reminisced about spending time with her father as a young child. Although Annie only lived with her father for two years, she said he was a "good man" and that he tried to be a father to her.

> My father . . . I would describe him as a good man. He definitely tried to be a father to me. I could tell that he had good intentions; obviously him being illegal was a problem, but other than that he was a good guy. He, you know, he always tried to do the right thing, even with my mom being the way she was; he always wanted her to go down the right road and he tried helping her. I guess, you know, obviously, the kinda things that he wanted for her, she didn't want but that never stopped him from trying to reach his goals and the things that he wanted to do. I think he is a very successful guy and even though, you know, he had to deal with the whole immigration thing. Other than that I see him as a really good guy.

Being separated from her father was "painful" because Annie had always felt like her father cared about her, unlike her mother who was addicted to drugs and frequently in and out of prison. (Annie's grandparents ended up raising her and her siblings.) Yet, she realized that her father had genuinely tried to be a good man, which meant being a good father and husband. His sudden absence as a result of him being detained and deported was a tremendous loss for Annie and she longed to have him back in her life as indicated by the following narrative.

> When I was little, I spent more time with my father than I did with my mother. But, you know, because he is not from the United States, and he was caught here illegally, he was deported back, so you know, it sucks that I am not allowed to see him as much. So, I don't have any anger towards him, but I'd like to spend more time with him. Well, like I said, it hurts. I can truly see that he cares about me. He has helped me by sending money and things like that, but I just think that, you know, those kinds of things aren't that important to me. I would rather have him be around so that I can get to know him better . . . . That would be better.

The fact that her father was deported against his will contributed to Annie not interpreting her father's absence as a personal abandonment. This allowed her to hold on to early childhood memories of a loving and caring father. The fact that Annie felt like her mother did not care about her made the separation from her father even more painful. Annie's story represents what can happen to families when parents are deported. Immigration policies that separate children from parents can rip families apart, which can further impoverish struggling families and place children at risk for future emotional and behavioral problems as well as involvement in the child welfare system (Brabeck & Xu, 2010; Dreby, 2012; Hidalgo, 2013; Lonegan, 2007; Wessler, 2011).

Some girls idolized their fathers even though they barely knew them. Fifteen-year-old Paige, for example, talked at length about how her life would have been different if her father had been there to protect her from the people who had abused and trafficked her. Although she recognized that her father had done some "bad things" and been accused of hurting another girl, she minimized his actions. The fact that he was in prison (and later died in prison) for these acts did not daunt her.

> He was very funny, bright and optimistic. He was a really good guy. I could just tell by the letters and stuff that if he hadn't been in prison and got messed up and stuff, like, he would have been one of those fathers that was, like, a huge part of your life, like, he would have been the kind of father that said all the right things to you, and like, met your first boyfriend, and like, was very protective and just a great dad. I got to talk to him a lot about a lot of stuff that was going on in his life. I feel like if they would have gotten him help with a therapist or helped him before things got really bad, things would have turned out really differently. He wasn't really a big drinker. He was respectful towards women and overall just a really great guy from what everyone has told me and just knowing him . . . he would not have let my life . . . He would not have let anybody hurt me. He would have been a really good father.

Paige's idea of how a good father should act centered on traditional conceptions of fathers as protectors (see Nielsen, 2012). She believed that her father's personal problems related to drug abuse and mental health problems precluded him from being a good father. Since she viewed her father as a victim of circumstance, she did not hold him accountable for his actions. The fact that Paige had never spent time with her father outside of prison also meant that her relationship with him was largely based on prison visits, letters, and her mother's stories. Limited contact with her father may have allowed her to develop an idealized version of him based on the man he could have been had it not been for his drug use and mental health problems. This was evident when I asked why her father was in prison.

PAIGE: I don't really know the details of why he was in prison, but I guess, well what I heard was that my mom gave him my older sister's Ritalin and it mixed with his depression medication so he went kind of haywire, and he started doing cocaine, and my mom babysat a few kids at that time, and I guess he hurt the girl my mom was babysitting, and he hit her a few times pretty bad, and he put something inside her.

VERA: Did he sexually abuse her?

PAIGE: Yes, but that's the part that no one thinks really happened, but he physically hurt her. I don't know. I mean if he really did that . . . I don't look at my dad any differently I mean it's really messed up, and I'm really sad if he did that, but it happened, and I don't try to say too much about that. I just try to focus on how I know my dad.

Paige clung to early childhood memories as evidence that her father cared about her. She idolized her father despite the fact that he had been accused of sexually abusing and physically beating a little girl. She felt like he was misunderstood and emphatically stated that if he had not gotten into trouble, he would have been a good father who would have protected her from other men.

As the previous narratives illustrate, girls who longed for their fathers generally had fond childhood memories of them. In some instances, girls longed for fathers who were no longer in their lives due to external circumstances (e.g., deportation, incarceration). Girls who mythologized their fathers did not mention histories of physical abuse or domestic violence. Instead, they emphasized happy early childhood memories that centered on their relationships with fathers and they continued to engage with their fathers whenever they were afforded the opportunity (e.g., via phone calls, responding to letters). Most importantly, the girls did not feel personally rejected by their fathers, which allowed them to continue to long for a stronger connection with them.

Rejecting Fathers

Some girls were very angry with their fathers, variously referring to them as "self-centered," "mean," "unimportant," "immature," "selfish," and "dead."

In almost all instances, girls recalled a pivotal event that unequivocally demonstrated their fathers' rejection. Sandra, a 15-year-old Mexican American girl living at Desert Star, described an incident that happened when she was 6 years old:

> When I was little, I used to go see him, and I used to be the happiest little girl in the world 'cause I was, like, 'I'm gonna go see my dad.' So one day [mom] dropped me off at his house and the house was empty. He wasn't there yet, [but] the door was unlocked. He left it unlocked for me. And so I sat there and I was watching TV, and about three hours later, he comes in through the door. He is, like, high or drunk or whatever he was, and he walks through the door, and he stands in front of me, and looks at me, and says, 'Who are you?' And I go, 'I'm your daughter' and he says, 'No, you're not, you're too ugly.' I guess his true colors were shown that day and I cried. I was crying on the couch, and he told me 'to get the fuck out' and that I 'wasn't his daughter' and that I was a 'piece of trash' and that I was a 'big mistake.' So, I ran out the house, and I ran to the Circle K and called my mom, and I didn't see him again.

Sandra said she was "shocked" and did not understand why her father rejected her; however, she later learned from her mother that she was the "product of a one night stand." Her mother explained that Sandra's father doubted that Sandra was his child—or as Sandra put it, "My dad denied me because I was White and really light skinned and he's not." Despite this devastating rejection, Sandra continued to pursue a relationship with her biological father who lived in "the neighborhood." She repeatedly tried to connect with him, but eventually gave up when he continued to reject her. She said, "We practically have no relationship. I wanted one, but now I'm at the point where I have begun hating him, so now I just blow off any connection I have with him. When I go see my little brothers and sisters, I make sure he's not there. He's irresponsible and inconsiderate of everyone else's feelings. He's very self-centered. He's still a child even though he has six of them. He's just selfish, neglectful, just not a good person. I hate him."

Karina, a 16-year-old girl Mexican American girl living at Desert Star, also shared a story about her father denying paternity. According to Karina, her father was physically abusive toward her mother, and her parents eventually divorced. Initially Karina's father wanted to take Karina and her brother to Mexico, but her mother refused to let him. That's when Karina's father denied paternity, moved to Mexico, and severed all ties with Karina and her brother. "When I was age 8, my mom and my dad got a divorce. My mom wouldn't let us see him because he threatened to take us away. He was gonna takes us to Mexico with him and my mom didn't want that. And ever since that day, we haven't seen him. He says we're not his kids." When I asked Karina how she felt about her father denying paternity, she said, "It don't bother me. I don't know him, and I don't want to know him."

A pivotal event also shaped Julia's perception of her father. Julia, a 16-year-old Mexican American girl, lived with her father in an abusive household. She described her father as a "mean man." When I asked what she meant by "mean," Julia shared the following story: "One day, when I was about 8, he left me outside with the dogs. He left me out there all night. Yeah. He had me eat dog food, and he had me on a leash. I wanted to die. Just because I called him a dog because [of] the way he eats his bones so he goes, 'I'm not a dog. I'm gonna treat you like a dog that way you know what it feels like to be a dog.'" Julia confided that she "hated" her father and was "happy" when he moved back to Mexico. When asked how she currently feels about her father, Julia said, "He don't really matter to me. To me he's dead." She was "angry" and wanted "nothing to do with [her father]." Although Julia described one event that stuck out in her mind, it should be noted that her father was routinely physically abusive toward Julia, her mother, and her siblings.

Like Julia, Ashley, a 16-year-old Mexican American girl, grew up in an abusive home. Her father was physically abusive toward her mother. Ashley's parents broke up when she was very young. Although Ashley's father was abusive toward her mother, Ashley still missed him and looked forward to visiting him in the summers. When her father remarried and had a "new daughter," Ashley began to feel displaced. She remembered one pivotal event that—in her mind—symbolized this displacement: "And I went to go visit him one summer, and I used to be his princess and he had a wife and his wife had a kid, and she got bit by some ants, and I was standing by the doorway, and he picked up the little girl and called her his little princess. So, yeah it was rough." Unlike Julia, Ashley continued to seek out her father's attention, but he rejected her. She wrote him letters, but he did not respond. She eventually grew angry and rejected him in turn. She said, "Yeah, like, I used to be with him all the time. Now I don't want to be with him unless there is something in it for me. I just feel, like, he doesn't deserve to know. If he's not around, then it's his choice to be around or not. If he's not around, then why should I tell him, when he should already know? Like, he thought I was still 15 . . . it has been six months since my birthday."

Although Ashley recalled being "daddy's little princess," she was hard pressed to recall specific memories of her father prior to his departure— probably because he left when Ashley was only 5 years old. While Ashley initially clung to the hope of developing a strong relationship with her father, she eventually gave up that dream, and began to resent him. In Ashley's eyes, her father had failed to live up to his paternal responsibilities. As she indicated, "it was his choice to be around or not" and he had clearly chosen not to be involved in her life.

Unlike the girls who mythologized their fathers, the girls who were angry and rejected their fathers had all tried to establish a relationship with their fathers, but were repeatedly rejected. Their fathers denied paternity, never responded to phone calls, and/or humiliated and abused them. They viewed their fathers as being either uninterested or harsh and violent. They wanted nothing to do with these men and believed they were better off without them in their lives.

Feeling Conflicted about Fathers

Other girls were conflicted about their relationships with fathers. Although these girls often said they "didn't care" about their fathers, they would later contradict themselves by expressing a desire to have a better relationship with their fathers. Eva's narrative illustrates this ambivalence. When asked if she was satisfied with the amount of time she currently spends with her father, 17-year-old Eva said, "No, well . . . I just really want him to be involved, you know, and stuff like that, but then, like, as I get older, I just realize that he doesn't want to be, so when I spend time with him, I really don't care. It's not really a big deal. I just want him to take me out to dinner or something. No. Not really. I wish I had like a dad. You know? He just has the label 'dad' but he is really not anything to me." Although Eva's father lived out of state, she still expected him to maintain regular contact via phone. She was frustrated by his lack of consistent contact and resented him for not following through on his promises to call her on a regular basis. In her mind, her father was reduced only to a "label"; in other words, he was a "dad" in title only as illustrated by the following passage: "Okay, my dad is, like, you know? He acts like he wants to be involved, you know? And, like, when he talks to me, he is like, 'Oh, I love you.' And I'll call him, and he says he's gonna call me, and then he never does, and he doesn't call me, and like, he is not really involved in my life."

As the previous narratives illustrate, girls were often conflicted about their relationships with fathers. Although they expressed frustration with their fathers' mixed messages, they were not yet ready to shut them out of their lives completely. On the other hand, they were ready to protect themselves from further emotional rejection by either adopting an indifferent stance or confronting fathers about their inconsistent behaviors. Yet, they had not given up hope of having a meaningful relationship with their fathers.

Explaining Fathers' Behaviors

Similar to their explanations of their mothers' behaviors, the girls interviewed for this study often attributed their fathers' behaviors to individual deficits (e.g., "weak," "immature"), but they seemed to feel more empathy for their fathers and were less judgmental. This was especially true for girls whose fathers were not physically abusive or who had not outright rejected them. Brianna, a 17-year-old biracial girl living at Arroyo Verde, had this to say about her father: "I think he's weak . . . lonely. I dunno, he's just not really smart. I think he's just really sad I guess. Because of the crowd he hung around with back then, and how he was into drugs and alcohol and how he wasn't willing to give up all that for my mom's marriage and for us. After that, he just got worse, after the divorce he . . . that's why he's weak, he could've been stronger, kept a job or took care of us, but he wasn't working, his whole life just fell apart. He's just weak."

Yesenia, a 16-year-old Mexican American girl at Arroyo Verde, said her father was immature and had no one to raise him, and this is why he became involved in drugs and alcohol. "He's immature. He has good intentions, but he just doesn't know how to express his feelings, but overall, he's a good man, but he just . . . his parents died when he was young, and he didn't have nobody to raise him or teach him how to be a parent or a man." She then added, "He's 57, but he has the brain of a 16- or 17-year-old boy, so . . . he's not really like a real dad." Given her father's upbringing, Yesenia was willing to forgive him for not being more involved in her life.

As they did with their mothers, young women also worried about their fathers' drug use, and several expressed relief when their fathers were incarcerated, because they viewed prison as an intervention that would force their fathers to abstain from drug use. Anique, a 17-year-old biracial girl, "felt bad" for her father who was serving time in prison on drug-related charges. Yet, she was "kinda happy" that he was in prison instead of getting in trouble "in the world." She believed that prison was good for her father even if it meant she did not see him often.

> Prison is good [for my dad] 'cause he's sober, and he can't do nothing, so it's better. I don't always have time to write him 'cause I have my own life, but when I do write to him, I tell him what's going on, and he tells me that he misses me, and he wishes he was here, and he misses my mom, and stuff like that. I kinda feel bad for him 'cause I know that he could've changed, but in a way, I'm just, like, it's too late. 'Cause he had a lot of chances to change, my mom gave him so many chances.... I'm kinda happy that he's locked up 'cause he's not in the world, and he's not getting into trouble, but I feel bad 'cause he's lonely without us. He can't see us growing up, and me and my other sister had a baby, so he can't see his grandchildren grow up, so it kinda sucks.

Selena, a 17-year-old Mexican American girl at Arroyo Verde, also spoke about prison being good for her father because he stopped smoking, earned his General Equivalency Diploma (GED), became an ordained minister, and is keeping clean while locked up. She said:

> I'm proud of my dad 'cause my dad's different from what he used to be like 'cause he was always there, but he wasn't really there, you know. Now he's got his GED and he's in [name of prison] and he even quit smoking cigarettes. They have an opportunity to smoke and he doesn't, and he wants to stay clean. He looks really healthy. He took some classes or he did something, and now he's an ordained minister, so he can marry people, and he can do that now. He really did all that. He took parenting classes in there. He goes to work. He's done construction since he was, like, 16 'cause that's what he loves to do. He loves to pour concrete, so sometimes when they need him to do that, that's when they call him, and he says that he loves to do that. He even talks different now. He don't even curse anymore. My dad's changed a lot.

Both Anique and Selena viewed prison as a good thing for their fathers, a forced abstinence from drug use and its associated dangers. In their eyes, they did not have to worry about their fathers while they were in prison, and were relieved to have one less person to worry about given the often chaotic nature of their home lives.

RELATIONSHIPS WITH FATHERS
AND GIRLS' RISKY BEHAVIORS

Using Drugs with Fathers to Get Close with Them

System-involved girls had a lot to say about their relationships with fathers even though these men were rarely involved in their lives on a consistent basis. Girls often interpreted their fathers' lack of involvement as a personal rejection. Yet, many of them found it difficult to let go and continued to long for a relationship with fathers who in their eyes were supposed to love them unconditionally. For a few young women, this need to forge a close relationship with their fathers was so strong that they even used drugs with their fathers as a way to get closer with them. Christina, a 14-year-old White girl, noted: "I looked up to my dad as my idol. My relatives looked down on my dad, but I looked up to him. I don't know why I looked up to him, but I did. I was daddy's little girl and then I decided I wanted to grow up to be just like him. My dad would come around high off of crystal meth and I used to get high with him. I felt left out . . . and I wanted to be with my dad. I was daddy's little girl." Tara, a 17-year-old Mexican American girl, also used drugs with her father. In fact, her father—who had been kicked out of the house by Tara's mother—was the person who introduced Tara to methamphetamine when she was 14. She said, "Yeah . . . my dad and I would party together. He actually got me into drugs. Well, the worst kinda drug, crystal meth. Okay, it's not the worst worst, but it's really bad. I never knew about it and he got me into it. He was on it and he . . . I mean I had tried weed and coke before, and I told him, you know, but never meth. My parents split up and he was, like, 'Have you ever tried glass?' and I was, like, 'no' and he's, like, 'Wanna try it? Try it. It's better than coke.' And so I was like, 'alright' so I tried it and after that I kinda just started doing it." For Tara, her father's departure translated into an opportunity to do whatever she wanted. Because her mother had kicked her father out of the house, Tara sided with her father. She eventually began to hang out and do drugs with him on a regular basis. She viewed her permissive father as the 'cool' parent, and it wasn't until much later, after substance abuse treatment, that Tara realized their relationship was not a 'healthy' one. She said, "It kinda got closer, 'cause I didn't really understand who he was, but I saw who he was, but I didn't see him as a bad person. I thought he was kinda cool 'cause he let me do my thing, hang out with my friends when they got divorced, and it's weird 'cause when they were married he wouldn't let me. But when they got divorced I did whatever I wanted, went out with my friends, drank, did drugs.... I would tell him, and like, cuss around him, and he wouldn't really discipline me. I thought it was cool, but now that I'm older I kinda realize, your dad is supposed to be like a role model, you know? But he wasn't."

Better Off without Dad in the House

Girls' relationships with fathers were complicated. As indicated in Table 1, most of the girls in this study did not live with their fathers and many of the girls were glad their fathers were not living at home. Research indicates that it is the quality of the father–daughter relationship that matters, not the quantity of time that girls spend with fathers (Nielsen, 2012). Several of the young women interviewed for this book certainly agreed with this sentiment. While some young women wished their fathers lived in their homes, others were quite adamant that it was better for them and their families if their fathers did not live with them. Ashley, for example, originally longed for her father after her parents' divorce, but eventually began to realize that his physical absence from the home was in the best interest of her family. She said, "It's for the best, I believe. When he was around there was so much drama, there was a lot of tension. He's a negative person, so when he does come around, it's a bad visit, all the time, no matter what. When I was younger, I was daddy's little girl. I didn't really care. He was still the same person, but I didn't care that he had a quick temper, you know? I just wanted to be with my dad, but after he left I'm, like, you know this is good. There's no fighting, there's nothing really bad going on. So it's better, you know."

Girls whose fathers used drugs and alcohol and/or were physically abusive were the most likely to be relieved when their fathers moved out. They reported feeling less stressed with their fathers out of the home.

For example, Gloria, a 16-year-old Mexican American girl living at Green River, said:

> I didn't know my dad was doing that [drinking and using drugs] at the time. I just knew they would just always be arguing or my dad would never show me love, only when he would be drinking, he would want to try to be affectionate. He never really showed us affection, he would never ask us how our day was; he would never tell us that he loved us, or anything. Only when he would drink he would tell us that he loved us, or try to hug us. He would never be like that when he was sober. He was an alcoholic. And he was like . . . I don't know how to describe it. He was horrible, really abusive and stuff. I used to remember him being like a dad. You know, like we used to do a lot of family stuff together and then he just became an alcoholic and that's when everything went down. And we started, like, physically fighting and stuff like that. So yeah . . . looking back, it's much better at home without him in it. Less fighting.

Bianca also agreed that her home life was more peaceful after her mother divorced her drug-using and abusive father. Like Gloria, she reported feeling stressed when her father was living in her home because his behavior was unpredictable and often volatile. While she still wanted a relationship with her father, she preferred not to live with him.

> He was into drugs and alcohol and my mom got tired of it after 20 years of being with him. He was always, like, he lived there but every weekend, every paycheck it was always, like, 24 pack of beer, drugs, and I don't know. My mom was used to being abused. I never knew what was going on. I just remember I would always be crying or the cops would always be at my house. Or stuff like that. I remember being scared. I just never knew what was going to happen 'cause I was so little. And my dad . . . he never wanted to stop so finally my mom just decided to leave him . . . it was a better choice for us. Because I don't know, she probably didn't want us to grow up like that, but I think she should have left him a long time ago, so I didn't have to be so hurt.

As these narratives illustrate, girls wanting to forge close relationships with their fathers did not necessarily translate into wanting to live with them. In many instances, they realized their fathers represented a volatile and unpredictable element in their homes especially when fathers were physically abusive toward girls' mothers and/or were substance abusers. Most of all, they wanted peace in their households even if this meant their fathers had to move out.

CONCLUSION

This chapter began by asking if fathers are essential to children and adolescents' development. Interviews with system-involved girls indicate that fathers are very important to girls' development especially under certain conditions. Girls growing up in families characterized by multiple problems—parental drug abuse, mental illness, parental incarceration, domestic violence, physical abuse, poverty—often lack either a mother or a father who have been consistently involved in their lives in a prosocial way. Many of the girls' mothers—like their fathers—had been in jail/prison, were drug users, or struggled with the demands of parenting due to preexisting mental illness, poverty, and lack of social support. The girls in this study often lacked even one parent who was able to consistently address their emotional and physical needs. All too often, as demonstrated in Chapter 1, girls were shuttled back and forth between various relatives, and as they grew older, among various group homes, treatment centers, detention facilities, and correctional facilities. For the most part, the girls in this study grew up in extremely chaotic conditions. They struggled with feeling like their fathers did not care about or love them. For these girls, their fathers' inconsistent involvement represented another instance of an adult letting them down.

For some girls, fathers' rejection was indisputable. Some fathers denied paternity usually as a way to get back at mothers. Unfortunately, the girls were the ones hurt most by their fathers' complete denial of paternity as was demonstrated by the cases of Sandra and Karina. Like pawns in a chess match, they were the ones who were sacrificed in a game they did not even know they were playing. For other girls, their fathers' rejection was more covert. In these instances, fathers strung daughters along with promises of phone calls and visits. Unfortunately, these fathers often failed to follow through on their word, which led their daughters to feel like they were not a priority. Although it is possible that other barriers beyond the fathers' control limited their ability to be more fully involved in their daughters' lives (L. Brown, Callahan, Strega, Walmsley, & Dominelli, 2009; Roberts, Coakley, Washington, & Kelley, 2014), girls were often not privy to such knowledge or insights.

Despite fathers' perceived shortcomings, most girls at one point or another wanted a relationship with them. Paige, for example, never knew her father outside of prison. Yet, she talked at length about what a good man he was and how her life would have been different if he had been involved. Even more disturbing, Paige refused to entertain the possibility that child sexual abuse allegations against her father were true. She simply said there must have been a mistake. This tendency to mythologize fathers is not unusual. For some girls, the need to forge a relationship with their fathers can be so strong that they even use drugs with them in an attempt to develop this closeness.

Clearly fathers are important in the lives of system-involved girls. After all, traditional U.S. parenting ideals dictate that fathers should be loving, caring, and supportive (Marsiglio, Day, & Lamb, 2000). They should be protectors, breadwinners, and positive male roles. When fathers are not involved, their absence is keenly felt. Research indicates that father absence is related to a host of negative emotional, behavioral, and academic outcomes for girls (Nielsen, 2014). As will be demonstrated in the next chapter, when I asked girls how their relationships with fathers shaped their lives, many pointed to an inability to trust romantic partners, an intense craving for male attention, and a wish that their fathers had been there to protect and guide them. Even more interesting, they consistently referred to themselves as "daddy's little girl" or "daddy's little princess" despite evidence to the contrary. While some girls continued to long for the status of "daddy's little girl," others had clearly moved on. They were angry, rebellious, and rejected their fathers in turn. Irrespective of how girls interpreted fathers' inconsistent involvement, it was clear that this relationship meant a lot to them as they spent even more time talking about fathers than mothers in the interviews. Supporting these often complicated relationships means rethinking how prominent youth systems—child protective services, juvenile justice, behavioral health— engage and interact with fathers, particularly nonresident fathers as these fathers are often ignored by youth systems and their input rarely solicited. The implicit assumption is that fathers do not matter, but the girls' narratives presented in this chapter indicate they do.

4 · LOOKING FOR LOVE IN ALL THE WRONG PLACES

It was a warm spring day as 14-year-old Dulce and I sat in the staff office at the Green River group home. While sipping on a soda, Dulce had spent the better part of an hour talking about her family, particularly her mother whose story was presented in Chapter 2. When I asked Dulce if she thought her relationships with her parents had influenced her own relationships, Dulce sighed and said, "I can't really have a good relationship. In relationships, I kinda tend to not be with good guys, I look for bad relationships 'cause it's just more comfortable for me. And I don't know why, maybe it's 'cause my dad used to hit my mom a lot. Me and my mom, we're like the same with relationships, like, when somebody's nice to her, she kinda pushes him away. And, like, I'm the same way . . . with my current boyfriend, he's really nice to me, but I push away from him. And sometimes we think we love somebody, but we don't. I'm kinda, in a lot of ways, like my mom. I think it's because of how my dad treated my mom. That's kinda what I grew up seeing."

Dulce's assessment of how her parents' violent relationship impacted her own relationship is not unique. Girls in the juvenile justice system are at heightened risk for both witnessing and personally experiencing violence in the home (Abram et al., 2004; Acoca & Dedel, 1998; Cauffman, Feldman, Waterman, & Steiner, 1998; Chesney-Lind & Shelden, 2013; DeHart, 2009; Lederman, Dakof, Larrea, & Li, 2004; Lopez et al., 2011; Schaffner, 2006). Leslie Acoca and Kellie Dedel (1998), for example, found that an astonishing 92% of 193 young women in detention had experienced one or more forms of physical, sexual, or emotional abuse. While emotional abuse was the most frequently reported type of abuse (88%), 81% had also experienced one or more incidents of physical or sexual abuse. In a more recent study, DeHart (2009) found that 98% of 100 adjudicated girls in the South Carolina Department of Juvenile Justice (SCDJJ) reported either being witness to or victims of violence: Sixty-nine percent had experienced caregiver violence, 81% had experienced sexual violence, and 90% had witnessed violence. Many of the young women also witnessed and experienced violence in their homes. As indicated in the Introduction, 66% of the girls interviewed for this book had witnessed domestic violence between their mother and a male partner.

Exposure to family violence (defined as domestic violence and child victimization in the home) has been linked to teen dating violence (Jouriles, Mueller, Rosenfield, McDonald, & Dodson, 2012; Moretti, Obsuth, Odgers, & Reebye, 2006).[1] Early exposure to domestic violence increases the likelihood that young people will enter similar types of violent relationships during adolescence (Holt, Buckley, & Whelan, 2008; Jankowski, Leitenberg, Henning, & Coffey, 1999; Simons, Wu, Johnson, & Conger, 1995). Child maltreatment has also been linked to teen dating violence (Wekerle et al., 2009). Two recent studies indicate that harsh parenting and exposure to interpersonal violence have additive effects on teen dating violence (Jouriles et al., 2012; Moretti et al., 2006), and this is especially true for girls involved in the juvenile justice system (Jouriles et al., 2012).

According to social learning theory, children who observe and experience family violence learn that aggression and violence can be used to deal with conflict (see Giordano, 2010). Not only do children observe violence, but also the emotional triggers for violence, circumstances of violence, and consequences of violence (Foshee, Bauman, & Linder, 1999; Giordano, 2010). Vangie Foshee, Karl Bauman, and Fletcher Linder (1999) found that adolescent girls who had witnessed a parent hit a parent or who had been hit by a mother were more accepting of dating violence, had a more aggressive conflict style, and were more likely to be perpetrators of dating violence than girls who had not experienced either of those types of violence. Consistent with this perspective, several of the young women interviewed for this book attributed their choice of partners to what they were used to seeing growing up. They were attracted to "bad boys" who shared certain characteristics—crazy, use drugs, popular—with their fathers. Sixteen-year-old Liza, for example, said:

> I like the bad kind of guys. I like the guys with attitudes, the mean ones, not to me but to other people, I don't know. I guess I like the crazy ones, I guess, the ones that get in trouble. I have never liked the calm guys, I don't know why; I have never liked those kind of guys. I find them boring, not interesting, I don't like the guys that stay home all day. I like being out. I don't like being in a house all day. I guess you could say I like guys like my dad. In fact, some of the guys that I did go out with before used to do drugs with my dad. They were, like, drug addicts, but not real drug addicts, because they still had a job and everything, but they did the kind of drugs my dad did, so they are drug addicts in some kind of way.

While Liza and other young women professed to liking "bad" boys, they often shared heartbreaking stories about being "disrespected" and "cheated on" by these young men. Nevertheless, many of them said they were attracted to a certain type of boy/man who was crazy, violent, and lived life with abandon. This is not surprising given that such attributes are associated with masculinity among some inner-city adolescents (e.g., Valdez, 2007). Thus, not only were girls exposed to violent male role models within their families, but also in their communities where being "soft" was associated with weakness and being tough was seen as a source of strength (see N. Jones, 2009; J. Miller & White, 2003).

While social learning theory has been used to explain how violence is learned, it fails to take into account how young women's emotional psyche and desire to feel loved might also color their perceptions of their romantic partners and relationships. Girls who have been exposed to family violence often suffer from anxiety, depression, low self-esteem, and a poor sense of self (Margolin & Gordis, 2000) and are at increased risk for seeking affection and love from unhealthy relationship partners (Pawlby, Mills, & Quinton, 1997). This "overdependence on a romantic partner may lead to increased vulnerability to overlooking [a] partner's abuse, dishonesty, unfaithfulness, or abuse of drugs or alcohol" and pave the way for future victimization (Purdie & Downey, 2000, p. 346). In other words, without support, many young women who long to feel loved by someone as a result of not feeling loved or cared for by parents might be at increased risk for "looking for love in all the wrong places" (Pawlby et al., 1997).

In this study, several young women attributed their "need for male attention" to lacking an involved father. Seventeen-year-old Eva, for example, never lived with her father, but cherished the time she spent with him. She blamed her desire for male attention on not having a father around.

> I've never lived with him. We had a weird life because my mom and dad really wasn't together, but my dad would come over when I was little and maybe stay a whole week or weekend, and he would spend the night, and then he would leave, and he would come back, then he would leave. He never really lived with us, you know. He lived with his aunt, so he would come over and leave, then come over, so that's the way it was . . . but when he was around, I cherished those moments. So now since we moved to Arizona, I don't get to see him, and that month I went to Michigan—he lives in Michigan—I went to see him, and I spent 30 minutes with him and that was it, and I was there a whole month. So I haven't really spent a lot of time with him. I miss him. I think that's why I crave male attention, so sometimes, I don't respect myself, and I go out with different guys and have different boyfriends and so . . . I think if I had, like, a male . . . a daddy around I wouldn't do that, you know. I wouldn't crave that [male attention] so much and it wouldn't get me in trouble.

Paige, age 15, also attributed her desire for male attention to not having her father consistently involved in her life. She said, "I just wanted somebody to, like, love me and stuff. For me, I was trying to fill that void I had from not having my father around and stuff. I was looking for that unconditional love and trying to find it in all these things . . . like boys and sex and stuff." Eva's and Paige's perceptions and experiences are consistent with research which suggests that daughters have more satisfying relationships with men when they have good relationships with their fathers (Nielsen, 2014; Van Schaick & Stolberg, 2001). Daughters with good relationships with their fathers are more likely to rely on their boyfriends for emotional support and feel secure in their relationships (Black & Schutte, 2006); feel less anxious, less fearful, and less distrustful with their boyfriends; and are more satisfied with their physical appearance than daughters with weak father–daughter bonds (Sanftner, Ryan, & Pierce, 2009; Scharf & Mayseless, 2008).

Like Eva and Paige, some young women have a difficult time distin-guishing between healthy and unhealthy relationships (Foshee et al., 1999). Part of this is no doubt due to being an adolescent with limited relation-ship experience (Collins, Welsh, & Furman, 2009); however, even when they do recognize that a relationship is unhealthy, girls often lack sufficient power, support, or resources to disentangle themselves from violent rela-tionships (Amaro & Raj, 2000; Gutierrez, Oh, & Gillmore, 2000). This is especially true for girls who run away from home to escape their troubled home lives (Chesney-Lind & Shelden, 2013; Kempf-Leonard & Johansson, 2007). Many young women, such as the ones interviewed for this book, live in economically distressed areas characterized by high rates of drug use, violence, and crime (N. Jones, 2009; Valdez, 2007). Thus, when they run away from home, they must also navigate a terrain fraught with potential dangers. Once on the street, girls by virtue of their gender and age are easy prey for adult men who seek to use and abuse them (Gaarder & Belknap, 2002). Some girls might not initially be able to recognize the warning signs that these men might be intending to use or hurt them.

(MIS)INTERPRETING BOYFRIENDS' CONTROLLING BEHAVIORS

Most of the young women in this study had been in at least one hetero-sexual romantic relationship.[2] While most of them placed great value on these relationships and shared positive stories about their partners, many also shared stories about how their boyfriends attempted to control and monitor their behaviors (Lopez, Chesney-Lind, & Foley, 2012).[3] Common warning signs of abuse include controlling behaviors such as checking a partner's cell phone or email without permission, constantly putting one's partner down, extreme jealously or insecurity, an explosive temper, mak-ing false accusations, possessiveness, and telling one's partner what to do (K. A. Murphy & Smith, 2009). Unfortunately, many of the young women interviewed for this book failed to fully recognize warning signs of abuse and instead interpreted their boyfriends' controlling and jealous behav-iors as evidence of love, minimized their boyfriends' controlling behaviors, or rationalized their boyfriends' abusive behaviors by attributing them to drug/alcohol use. While part of the explanation for girls' difficulty in recognizing warning signs may have been rooted in their early exposure to family violence, it should be emphasized that gender norms and overarching power dynamics that privilege men over women also contribute to an environment that normalizes gendered violence and the objectification of girls and women (N. Jones, 2009; Valdez, 2007; Wesely, 2012).

Young women must constantly contend with media images that sexualize and objectify girls and women (Faulkner, 2010; Wesely, 2012). Photos of young girls with pouty lips and scanty clothing gloss the covers of magazines and sexualized images of girls and women are routinely used to sell everything from beer to shoes. Some advertisements do not even bother to include the faces and heads of young women and instead focus only on their breasts, hips, waists, and behinds. The message is clear: Girls and women are sexual objects that boys and men can use and dispose of at will. Consistent with this line of reasoning, several young women interviewed for this book indicated that their boyfriends physically marked or branded them in some way (e.g., tattoos of boyfriend's names, "hickies") to denote that girls belonged to them. Connie, for example, said her boyfriend gave her "hickies" so that other boys knew she belonged to him. She said, "He would hit me sometimes, and bite me, and give me hickies all over my neck, you know, and he'd do it on purpose, and he wouldn't let me do that to him, and that was kind of a sign he was cheating on me, because he didn't want anybody to know that he had a girlfriend, but he wanted other guys to know that I belonged to him." Although Connie did not like how her boyfriend treated her, she acknowledged that it "could have been a lot worse" and that he only hit her "sometimes." As discussed in Chapter 2, Connie's biological father regularly beat her mother. Growing up in an abusive household no doubt shaped Connie's own views about what constitutes healthy relationship behaviors (Giordano, 2010). While she found her boyfriend's controlling behaviors and occasional blows troubling, she consoled herself by saying that her relationship could have been a lot worse, meaning that her relationship could have been more like her parents' relationship, which was characterized by frequent violence.

Relationship beliefs rooted in traditional cultural gender scripts can also contribute to teen dating violence, and this may be especially true for Latina girls. Although Latina girls who participated in focus groups presented themselves as independent and powerful (see Lopez & Chesney-Lind, 2014), the girls who participated in the individual interviews indicated that while they saw themselves as having the most relationship power, they still maintained beliefs and acted in ways that were consistent with traditional gender roles and relationship expectations.[4] For example, traditional views about virginity played a significant role in how Latina girls viewed their relationships as well as why they "put up with" boyfriends' controlling behaviors. Many believed that virginity was sacred and defined "losing [their] virginity" as something special that binds two people together and signifies love (Carpenter, 2002; Garcia, 2009). Thus, it was very difficult for some of the girls to leave their "first loves" even when these young men were controlling and abusive. For example, Nora, a 17-year-old Mexican American girl, believed that losing her virginity to her boyfriend bonded them forever. She said:

> He really didn't like me wearing tight clothes or showing too much skin. 'Cause he's, like, 'They're gonna like it' or whatever, just jealous. I would do what he said, 'cause I loved him, and I cared about how he felt. I would wear t-shirts all the time and pants, like, his t-shirts, you know, to school or whatever, 'cause he didn't want guys looking at my boobs or my butt or whatever, 'cause he got jealous. It made him jealous, really mad and . . . I was young and thought that meant he loved me. I loved him, too. I never really wanted to (hang out with friends) 'cause I always wanted to spend time with him. I guess when you lose your virginity to a guy, you really fall in love with them after that, and you just always wanna be with that person.

This view of girls' virginity as being a sacred commodity that should only be "given away" to one's true love is not unique to the Latina girls interviewed for this book.[5] Mary Odem (1995), in her analysis of case reports from the 19th and early 20th centuries found that premarital sex was tightly linked to prevailing ideals about morality and femininity. Many of the Latina girls interviewed for this book still subscribed to such traditional views and linked losing their virginity with being in love and staying in a committed relationship even when their boyfriends were jealous and controlling, as illustrated by the following quote from Nora: "Yeah, he was my first love. So he was really jealous, 'cause a lot of guys liked me, and a lot of guys wanted to be with me. So he was jealous of other guys taking me away from him, me leaving him for them, whatever, also 'cause he took my virginity away, so he was really jealous about that I guess. After I lost my virginity, that's when he started being really controlling. He never hit me or anything like that. Well, he wouldn't let me talk to guys, of course. If I talked to a guy like in school or something, he'd tell that guy off or wanna beat him up. He did try to control what I did, but he never hit me." This passage reveals that Nora felt bonded to her boyfriend because he was her first love and she had lost her virginity to him. She wanted the relationship to work even if she had to act and dress in accordance with her boyfriend's demands. Looking back, Nora acknowledged that her young age and relative lack of relationship experience contributed to her desire to maintain this early relationship despite her boyfriend's controlling behaviors.

Traditional views rooted in Marianismo also contributed to girls staying in violent relationships, but this was true for only three girls.[6] All three girls who explicitly endorsed traditional gender scripts were Mexican American.[7] According to 15-year-old Angelina, she had to obtain permission from her 23-year-old boyfriend prior to doing anything. She said, "When I want something, I go to him, and I ask permission, like, I don't know . . . it's really weird. He got me trained, it sounds really weird, but he got me trained." Although Angelina's boyfriend regularly cheated on her, she rationalized his behavior by saying she was his "girlfriend" and the one he "thought about" when he was with other girls. While Angelina did not like that her boyfriend cheated on her, she was initially willing to put up with his behaviors because of her coveted girlfriend status. Angelina's views are consistent with other work on high-risk Latina girls. Valdez (2007), for example, found that being a girlfriend or wife was a socially desirable status among many gang-affiliated Mexican American girls who did not want to be associated with the sexually promiscuous "hood rats" who were often looked down upon by both the girls and the boys in their communities. Such gender scripts, rooted in traditional views of girls' sexuality, can inadvertently contribute to young women staying in unhealthy relationships because they do not want to be perceived as being a "slut," "ho," or "hoodrat."

WHEN LOVE TURNS VIOLENT

While a few girls believed that boyfriends should be in control, none believed that it was okay for boyfriends to physically or sexually assault their girlfriends under any conditions. Yet, a few girls were victims of physical and sexual violence. While they acknowledged that these relationships were unhealthy, they still tended to blame themselves while minimizing the extent of the violence and/or rationalizing their boyfriends' behaviors. Simone, a 15-year-old Mexican American girl, described an incident in which her 18-year-old boyfriend physically assaulted her: "He would just get mad sometimes, and he was, like, jealous, and he would slap me on my face. Once he punched me in my belly and it made my belly ring rip off. I didn't know what to do. I just stayed with him 'cause I was dumb. I really liked him and I didn't care. I was just, like, I don't know, go ahead." When asked if she had ever tried to stop her boyfriend from hitting her, Simone said, "Yeah, once he hit me in my face, like, punched me, but it wasn't that hard. I don't know why. I just started cussing at him when he did that, and it made him go more, so after the second time he hit me, I just stopped saying stuff so he wouldn't hit me anymore." In addition to physically assaulting her, Simone's boyfriend sexually assaulted her. "He wasn't going to stop. He wasn't hurting me. He was just holding me down. I was, like, 'Wow' and afterwards I was mad, and I just left because I wanted him to stop and he wouldn't . . . [When I left] he didn't say anything, he just said I was a 'bitch' and I just left, and then he called me, like, an hour later, and I didn't wanna talk to him then."

As the previous account reveals, Simone stayed with her boyfriend despite his abuse.[8] She also minimized her boyfriend's abuse. While she said that her boyfriend punched her in the face, she clarified that "it wasn't that hard" and that he "wasn't hurting" her when he held her down during a sexual assault. Instead of blaming her boyfriend for his actions, Simone internalized the blame for staying in the relationship by saying she was "dumb" and that she stayed because she cared about him. This tendency to minimize her boyfriend's abusive behaviors might have been partially rooted in Simone's early childhood experiences growing up in a household characterized by domestic violence. Although she did not say it, Simone may also have felt trapped in the relationship and afraid to leave.

Like Simone, 15-year-old Jessica was also involved with a physically abusive older boyfriend. In this instance, Jessica's 17-year-old boyfriend introduced her to drugs, which he "gave to [her] for free." Jessica's dependence on methamphetamine might have further contributed to her staying in this relationship, because her boyfriend supplied her with "free" drugs. In the following account, she describes how her boyfriend's drug use influenced his behaviors toward her. She blamed the drugs, not her boyfriend, for his abusive and controlling behaviors.

> He introduced me to drugs and stuff like that. And then, after a while, we started getting into drugs real bad, and he started being mean to me, and calling me bad names and stuff like that. He started getting really impatient with me. And, I don't know, he would sometimes set me straight. Slap me up. He started losing a lot of patience with me, and then I started defending myself when he would talk stuff to me, so after I defended myself, he would get mad, and he would throw stuff at me. I had a big shoe print on my face, and he would kick me all the time, and then slap me. And he would punch me in my arms, but not really in my face. But I had bruises on my arms and then on my breasts, stuff like that. Like, he would get mad when he was on drugs, and then he would get mad when he was off drugs. But he would mainly be mad because he didn't have drugs.

Magda, a 17-year-old White girl who was living at the Moonlight group home at the time of our interview, also described a relationship that was physically abusive. Her boyfriend, who was the same age as her at the time of their relationship, frequently hit her and once forced her to have sex against her will. "Something just, like, wasn't really working, you know . . . like, I would get bruises from him, but, you know, only because it's easy for me to bruise, and you know things just weren't quite right . . . . We were just better off being just friends. He was really violent. He just. . . . what he did was a little bit rougher than it should have been. After we broke up and stuff, he asked me what this one bruise was from, and I said, 'You gave it to me,' and he was like, 'I don't remember that. What the fuck are you talking about?' and I was, like, 'That's from you. Don't play.'"

In the few cases that were characterized by physical or sexual violence, the violence was extreme (e.g., punching, kicking, stomping, rape). Although girls recognized their boyfriends' behaviors as abusive, they tended to minimize the abuse or blame themselves or other external factors (e.g., boyfriend's drug use) instead. Not only did these young women grow up in families and communities characterized by violence, they also had to contend with larger societal norms that condone violence against girls and women. Thus, even when they wanted to leave the relationships, they often lacked the social support and resources to do so. Their young age relative to their boyfriends, in some instances, further constrained their ability to extricate themselves from abusive and dangerous relationships.

GIRLS' RELATIONSHIPS, DELINQUENCY, DRUG USE, AND PROSTITUTION

The stories of three young women—Lydia, Savannah, and Catalina—are presented in this section to provide a more nuanced sense of how entrenched some young women can become in relationships and how these relationships influence their decisions to engage in delinquency, drug use, and prostitution. Both Lydia and Savannah were involved with older partners who directly pressured them to drink alcohol, use drugs, and commit delinquent acts. Catalina's story is a bit different, though still relevant. Unlike Lydia and Savannah, Catalina inadvertently became involved with a man who she initially thought was "nice" and "cared about" her. She soon found out that this man was a violent "pimp" who did not care about her. In all three instances, girls' involvement with boyfriends (or potential boyfriend, in Catalina's case) resulted in decisions that had life altering consequences, or what Shari Miller, Patrick Malone, and Kenneth Dodge (2010) refer to as snares. Snares such as legal problems, early childbearing, and drug use can negatively alter girls' lives in the long run.

Lydia's Story

Lydia, who was first introduced in Chapter 2, had been romantically involved with a 19-year-old man prior to being committed to the Desert Star residential treatment center. Like many girls interviewed for this book, Lydia witnessed her mother being physically assaulted by several partners, including Lydia's biological father. Although Lydia hated seeing her mother victimized and frequently counseled her mother to leave these abusive men, Lydia also became involved with a controlling partner. Ironically, both Lydia's mother and her boyfriend's mother attempted to protect Lydia from her boyfriend's wrath.

Lydia's boyfriend was older than her, and she attributed his controlling behavior to this age difference. "He was really controlling. I think it's because he was so much older and that just never works out; it was terrible." Lydia's relationship with an older man is not uncommon for "at-risk" girls who are often romantically and/or sexually involved with older men (Marín, Coyle, Gómez, Carvajal, & Kirby, 2000; Young & d'Arcy, 2005). When I asked the young women in this study why they preferred older partners, they often said older boys/men were more "mature." It is possible that adultified girls who are used to interacting with and engaging in adult activities may prefer older partners as opposed to same-age partners because they often view the latter as "silly" and "immature." Lydia initially enjoyed spending time with her boyfriend because he was "older and more experienced." Plus, she "lost [her] virginity to him," which from her perspective, further cemented their relationship.

Despite the initial honeymoon phase of the relationship, Lydia's boyfriend soon grew more controlling by attempting to regulate her appearance so as to minimize the likelihood that other males would be attracted to her. She said, "When school started again, he was there for about two weeks, and then he got kicked out of school for drugs and stuff. So, whenever I would go to school, he would tell me how to dress. He would tell me to wear basketball shorts, or like, big stuff, I couldn't wear, like, a tight shirt like this. He would want me to have my hair up, and tell me to don't put make up on. I would tell him, 'Don't tell me what to wear!'" Eventually, Lydia's boyfriend became even more controlling. "It just got to the point where he was really tripping, like, I couldn't go nowhere. I had to go to sleep on the phone with him. I would just sit there and I have nothing to talk about . . . it's, like, 1 o'clock in the morning . . . 'Can I go to sleep?' and he would just start snoring, but I can't hang up, of course, because he'll be, like, 'Oh, why you hang up?' He'll call right back. One time I tried it, and I hung up and [he] called right back, and he's, like, 'Who's there? Oh, let me talk to your mom.' At 1 o'clock in the morning! Get for real! Trippin' . . . talk to my mom!"

Lydia's boyfriend began to stop by her house and accuse her mother of lying when she said Lydia wasn't home: "He would be at my house a lot even against my mom's will . . . . My mom was, like, 'You gotta get away from him because he's not good for you . . . Who does he think he is?' She didn't know everything that was going on. She didn't know about all the other stuff he did. But, she could see how my attitude was just changing, and that was, like, the time when I started to be more distant from my mother 'cause of him." Lydia's boyfriend's stalking behaviors began to intensify. She said:

He was crazy, like, he would totally go off. I think it's 'cause he drunk a lot of alcohol. One time he went to my house and he punched holes in the wall and broke my window 'cause my mom, she was, like, 'She's not here' and I really wasn't there . . . . I was actually in Sonora [juvenile detention facility]. And my mom was, like, 'She's not here' and he was, like, 'Yes, she is.' I think he was drunk. And then he went around and started knocking everybody's trash can down, and we live in a residential neighborhood, it's, like, old people and stuff there, and he lived around there, too, and he just went over there and he started knocking people's trash cans down, and then he went back to my house, and he broke through my room window, and he tried to get in the house and it was crazy. It was terrible, punched holes in my walls, wouldn't leave and it was crazy.

Lydia's boyfriend's controlling behaviors eventually escalated into physical violence against her, even though she minimized the violence because it only happened once. She said:

He never put his hands on me to physically hurt me except for this one time when he said I was messing with his brother, which I wasn't, and he punched me in the head back here [points to a spot on back of her head], and I had a big old bump. Yeah. And then he, like, choked me, and then pulled me up against the wall, you know what I'm saying? I think I passed out and every-thing. I don't even know for how long, and I woke up, and I was all slobbering and everything, [and] I was, like, 'Oh, my God.' And then there was that time he punched me in the head. He apologized. He was, like, 'I don't know what I'm doing.' I think he was coked up or something was wrong with him. He started crying, and I was, like, whatever, I don't care if you cry . . . . And then his mom told me to stay away from him; he's not good for me 'cause I was so much younger, too. She said stay away from him, he's only going to get you in trouble, get you locked up. He was doing bad stuff. He was going around rob-bing people, robbing houses, and all types of stuff, and she was, like, 'Are you gonna get involved with that? Are you gonna end up being in jail?' Because of him I was actually locked up one time because we were just riding around with his cousin, and there was this girl, and he was, like, go take her purse. So, I was, like, 'Oh, my god, do I do it? Do I not do it?' But I did it because I was under pressure. I did it and the police caught us and I got charged with assault and stuff like that . . . theft and all types of stuff.

At the time of our interview, Lydia had not seen her ex-boyfriend in sev-eral months. While she spoke about his controlling (and violent) behaviors, she often laughed at his "craziness" and sometimes minimized his actions (e.g., "he only put his hands on me one time"). Given that she had grown up in a family in which her stepfather routinely beat her mother, Lydia's conception of a healthy relationship might have been skewed (Giordano, 2010). While Lydia clearly did not like her boyfriend's controlling behaviors, she rationalized that at least he did not regularly beat her. Still, both Lydia's mother and her boyfriend's mother attempted to dissuade her from continuing this relationship. Unfortunately, their attempts were unsuccessful and Lydia's boyfriend continued to have a huge influence on her by encouraging her to use drugs and commit crimes.

Savannah's Story

As indicated in Chapter 1, 17-year-old Savannah grew up in a household characterized by parental drug use. Unlike many of the other girls whose stories are shared in this book, Savannah's father was not physically abusive toward her mother nor did she witness physical violence in her household. Nevertheless, Savannah noted that her parents' relationship was fraught with conflict and they "sometimes screamed and yelled at each other for no good reason." Seeking to escape the constant arguing and screaming as well as searching for freedom to do what she wanted, Savannah often ran away for short periods of time. While "on the run" she met an older man who eventually became her boyfriend. Looking back, Savanna recognized that her boyfriend was controlling, but made sure to point out that he was not abusive. "He [boyfriend] wasn't abusive, but he was real controlling, and he made me feel like I had to be with him all the time. All I knew about having a relationship was being with him 'cause I was young when I met him, and I had never had a relationship, and I would try to leave him, and he wouldn't let me, and sometimes I would have to leave his house, like sneak out to get away from him." Like Lydia, Savannah experienced less relationship power and increased vulnerability due to her relationship with an older male partner. Although Savannah said her boyfriend was not physically abusive, she admitted that her boyfriend once took "advantage" of her sexually.

> I remember one Christmas, he got me drunk, and then he took advantage of me. I think of all that stuff . . . that was the worst. My mom, I told her all that stuff, but not when it happened. I didn't tell her until later when I was in counseling. She never knew, and she was, like, 'If you would have told me a long time ago, I would have kept you away from him.' But I felt like I had to be with him sometimes, but then I also would go with him to go out if I didn't want to be home, so it kind of went both ways. I talk to my caseworker about it 'cause

when we have our board to get released, we have to think about all kinds of stuff, like, what are you going to do in the community, who's going to be your support group, and ten what ifs.... What if I ended up going to a party and all this stuff.... What if my ex-boyfriend gets out of prison and goes looking for me? 'Cause he used to stalk me, which is very weird. 'Cause I went out with this guy one time, and he didn't even know, and he called me the next day, and said, 'I saw you going out with that guy,' and he even told me what I was wearing. I freaked out and was, like, 'Man, you are weird.'

Like Lydia, Savannah did not interpret her boyfriend's behaviors as abusive even though he took "advantage of" her. Instead of viewing this assault as part of a pattern of abuse, Savannah described it as an isolated incident. Like Lydia, Savannah was a virgin when she met her boyfriend. Her young age and relative inexperience made her easier to control. Through her association with her boyfriend, Savannah began to drink and do drugs, which contributed to a fatal car crash, which resulted in Savannah being charged with vehicular manslaughter, which ultimately led to her incarceration at Arroyo Verde.

Catalina's Story

Seventeen-year-old Catalina was one of the few young women who admitted to engaging in prostitution. While she did not enjoy engaging in sex work, she felt like it was the only means for her to survive on the street. As a young girl, Catalina struggled with feeling abandoned by her biological father and getting along with her mother's current boyfriend. She also witnessed physical altercations between her mother and her mother's boyfriend who "fought on a regular basis." To escape the constant arguing and fighting at home, Catalina began to run away at a young age. She said, "They fought all the time. She couldn't do nothing without him acting all crazy. Getting in her face, and she wouldn't do nothing. Just kept taking it. I tried to get her to leave him, but she wouldn't. So I ran away. I was on the streets. I just couldn't take that. It was better to be on the streets. So I started running the streets. I was about 11. I did whatever to stay away from the house and make money. I robbed people. Stole from stores. Drug dealing ... whatever ... just moving from one friend's house to another." While on the street, Catalina began to use "coke, ecstasy, but not meth or heroin or anything like that" and became pregnant. After the birth of her daughter, she moved back in with her mother. Frustrated with having to live at home and not being able to support her daughter (and possibly drug use, but she did not explicitly state this), Catalina ended up engaging in prostitution.

At first I liked [prostitution], but at the end, I didn't like it at all 'cause I got hit. My daughter was, like, a year and a half. I was 15 when I got into [prostitution], and I got tired of my mom taking care of my daughter. I had to stay around my mom's house, and I didn't like it. I told her I didn't want to be putting up with that shit [mom's relationship with boyfriend] anymore, but my mom was buying my baby clothes and diapers 'cause I couldn't get a job . . . so one day, I met this guy, and I didn't believe my mom and my sisters saying that he was a pimp. They said, 'That's a pimp,' and I said, 'No, it's not,' so I was hanging around him. Next thing you know he came at me with it and I was one of his . . . girls I guess you could call it.

Catalina described how her pimp eventually lured her into working for him within a couple of weeks of meeting her. "He took me into the mall, and he took me and the other girls shopping. He was, like, 'I want to go shopping for you like this all the time. Don't you want to shop like this?' and that night he showed me what to do [how to meet customers], and I was interested, and then the next week I asked him to come pick me up, and I wanted to go do it. And that night I made a good $400 to $500."

Seeking to better understand Catalina's reality, I asked if she was scared the first time she engaged in prostitution. Her answer surprised me. While I expected her to say she was afraid of her customers, Catalina told me that she was more afraid of the police. She said, "At first, yeah. I was scared. I was scared for, like, 30 to 45 minutes. I was scared because I could see the police pass by. I wasn't scared [of the customers] 'cause I always had a knife on me no matter what, and I could protect myself. I was more worried about the police 'cause I had a warrant out for my arrest. I had a warrant out ever since I got pregnant. I mean the sex stuff, it was an easy thing to do because of how much money I could get, but hard because I didn't want to get caught by the police." Although Catalina said she was rarely scared of her customers while working, she did share one story that illustrates how dangerous sex work can be for young women. "I wasn't afraid of getting a disease or having sex. I used protection and sex was just for money, but I did almost get raped one time by this old guy. He's not that old, but he was, like a big guy. He looked way older, a White guy. He took me, and he held me down, and I was trying to get to my knife, and he got my hand and my purse, and he was, like, 'Throw it [knife] out!' and I was, like, 'Let me up!' and he let me go, and he slammed the door, and he took off. That was scary, but I just went back out and worked on a different street." Catalina seemed to accept the possibility of sexual victimization as a hazard of the job, but attempted to protect herself by always carrying a knife.

Despite the threat of sexual victimization, Catalina attempted to maintain some control over her sexual interactions with her customers. She laughed and said, "Plus after a couple of weeks, I really didn't have to get into it for them. I found out you could make them feel, like, they're doing something, but they're really not. They're, like, hitting on your inner thigh so I really got into it after that . . . 'cause I really don't have to get into it for them you know. 'Cause they're so small, you know what I'm saying?" In this way, Catalina was able to trick the very men who were using her, and she seemed to delight in this small measure of control and power.

Catalina eventually grew tired of working as a prostitute. She missed her daughter and was concerned that her daughter would look down on her once she grew older and realized what her mother did for a living. She wanted to quit using drugs, stop prostituting, and get her life together for her daughter. Unfortunately, Catalina's pimp did not just let her walk away from "the life." Catalina describes how difficult it was to break away from her pimp: "I got real tired 'cause I didn't want to come [to Arroyo Verde], and I was real scared, and my daughter was getting older and starting to talk, and I didn't want her to know about me, so I told him that I didn't want to be in it no more, and he beat the hell out of me. He had always told me before that . . . when we were in a relationship that he never wanted me to leave him, but I just got tired of it, and I missed my daughter 'cause my daughter wasn't with me. She was with my mom, and I just missed my daughter so much." When I asked Catalina if she was surprised that her pimp beat her, she said, "Yeah, I was shocked . . . real shocked. I still have a dent in my leg from when he trampled on it. I was coughing up blood because he kicked my stomach. I didn't think he'd do that to me even though he did it to the other girl that was living with him. He beat her up all the time. I remember he beat her with a bat, a little miniature wooden bat. He beat the hell out of her. He beat her up a lot, but he had never beat me up. Not like that. Looking back, I think he's a dickhead. And I can't believe I was doing that kind of stuff. It's crazy how I survived everything."

A few weeks after Catalina's pimp beat her, she was arrested and later sent to Arroyo Verde where she was seeing a counselor to discuss past traumas. Catalina's mother had custody of her daughter. At the time of our interview, Catalina was grateful for the respite and the opportunity to work on some of her "issues" in a relatively safe setting, but looked forward to being reunited with her daughter upon release.

GIRLS' COUNTERSTRATEGIES

Many of the young women in this study were involved with older boys or men. Their young age constrained their abilities to negotiate healthy relationship boundaries. Furthermore, they sometimes (mis)interpreted boyfriends' controlling behaviors as evidence of love and were hesitant to break up with the boys/men they loved and who they believed loved them in turn. Other girls felt trapped and did not know how to extricate themselves from toxic relationships, and this was especially true of girls who were physically and sexually assaulted or girls like Catalina who found themselves involved with violent men on the streets. However, this is not to imply that these young women were passive victims only. There were many instances when they attempted to strike back. In fact, many of these young women used a number of indirect and direct strategies to counter their boyfriends' attempts to control and abuse them. Such strategies included lying, flirting, cheating, physically fighting back, openly defying/breaking up with their boyfriends, and maintaining emotional distance.

Lying, Flirting, and Cheating

Several girls lied to their boyfriends about participating in "forbidden" behaviors, flirted with other boys, or cheated on their boyfriends. Lydia, whose story I highlighted earlier, eventually began to flirt and cheat with other boys at school as a way to get back at her boyfriend. "He would hear that I was flirting with guys a lot at school 'cause once he got kicked out I was still going to school. He didn't [like it] 'cause I was, and I never confessed that I was, but I was, and he heard it 'cause he used to go to that school [and] he knew a lot of people." She then went on to explain, "I've cheated on him, too, plenty of times, and I don't really care." She responded to her boyfriend's past infidelities, jealousy, and controlling behaviors by actively seeking out the attention of other boys at school and through "cheating."

As illustrated by Lydia's account, girls sometimes reacted to their boyfriends' controlling behaviors by flirting with other boys, and in rare instances, cheating on them. Doing so allowed girls to feel as if they were getting back at their boyfriends. In most instances, girls never told their boyfriends. Unfortunately, flirting or cheating was an ineffective strategy for dealing with boyfriends' controlling behaviors as it often intensified boyfriends' suspicions. Nevertheless, girls experienced some degree of satisfaction at "getting one over" on their boyfriends.

Physically Fighting Back

Several girls used aggressive or violent behavior as a means to respond to victimization. Melissa, age 14, described how her 16-year-old boyfriend habitually "looked at other girls" and how these episodes usually ended up in verbal and/or physical altercations: "Yeah, he hit me two or three times, no four times . . . . Like everything was for some stupid reason. We'll start fighting and stuff, and like, we'll stop and then be happy again, and then we go somewhere, and he is looking at this girl, and I tell him, 'Okay?' And he is, like, oh so this and that, and we go back to where we are supposed to be, and then he'll be after me [again], and then talking stuff, so then I just get mad, and yell back at him, and then he hits me, then I hit him back."

Jessica also described how she responded to her boyfriend's abuse by defending herself: "After a while he started losing a lot of patience with me, and then I started defending myself when he would talk stuff to me, so after I defended myself, he would get mad, and he would throw stuff at me." As illustrated by Melissa's and Jessica's accounts, girls sometimes used violence as a means of defending themselves against their boyfriends' attacks. These findings are consistent with a larger body of research on adolescent teen dating violence, which indicates that girls are just as likely as boys to be perpetrators (Hickman, Jaycox, & Aronoff, 2004). Unfortunately, girls suffer more serious forms of violence than boys (Foshee, 1996). The previous narratives highlight the importance of considering the context of teen dating violence.

Openly Defying/Breaking Up with Boyfriend

Several girls openly defied their boyfriends' attempts to control them. They either refused to do what their boyfriends wanted them to do or they eventually broke up with them. Simone, who described many instances of abuse and control, indicated that she eventually broke up with her boyfriend.

The turning point was when her boyfriend impregnated another girl: "I broke up with him before 'cause someone told me he was doing things with them, like with her, and I didn't wanna believe it, but then I asked him, and he said no, and I kinda believed him for, like, two days until they told me again, and I was, like, 'I can't deal with it,' so I just broke up with him."

Seventeen-year-old Magda also broke up with a boyfriend who was physically abusive and who had forcibly had sex with her. Although Magda broke up with her boyfriend, she still had to stand firm against his frequent implorations for them to continue to have sex for fun.

> Like, he wanted to [have sex] and stuff after we broke up. We started getting into arguments about it, and he was, like, 'We could have sex and have fun,' and I was, like, 'I'm not ready for it.' He was, like, 'No, it's not because you're not ready. It's because you're scared.' I was, like, 'No, that's not it.' To a degree, yes, I'm scared. I'm scared crapless. [Laugh] I'm afraid what happened to me before is going to happen to me again. No matter who it is, but especially him. Like, I'm always going to have that fear. Yes. I've talked to my counselor about it, but sometimes I feel that if somebody pressures you into it enough that there's no point. You're going to have to do it and face it.

Although girls often broke up with abusive and controlling boyfriends, they usually got back together with them, only to break up with them again at a later date. Thus, breaking up was usually a long drawn-out process rather than a quick one. Furthermore, girls often endured their boyfriends' controlling and abusive behaviors over an extended period of time before trying to break up with them. Reasons for staying with boyfriends included interpreting jealous and controlling behaviors as love and believing their boyfriends would change.

CONCLUSION

Family violence is linked to teen dating violence (Jouriles et al., 2012; Moretti et al., 2006). Not surprisingly, many of the young women interviewed for this book were involved with controlling boyfriends who attempted to monitor their appearance, behaviors, and social interactions. Boyfriends' behaviors were often rooted in jealousy. They viewed girlfriends as their personal possessions and wanted to make sure that other potential rivals stayed away. In order to do so, they demanded that their girlfriends adhere to traditional good girl standards that dictate how young women should dress, act, and interact with others. Boyfriends often demanded that their girlfriends dress modestly, refrain from talking with other boys, and not go out with friends. The goal was to minimize the possibility that a potential male rival would be interested in their girlfriends.

Girls differed with regard to how they interpreted their boyfriends' controlling and abusive behaviors. While most girls said they maintained the most power in their relationships, their narratives demonstrated otherwise. This was especially true of the Mexican American girls in the study. Even when these girls resented their boyfriends' attempts to control them, they still felt compelled to try and make the relationships work, particularly if they had lost their virginity to their male partners. A significant portion of these girls also initially interpreted their boyfriends' jealous and controlling behaviors as evidence that they loved them. Girls who feel rejected by parents and other adults might be more susceptible to boyfriends' proclamations of love even when such proclamations are characterized by an undercurrent of control rooted in jealousy and possessiveness (Purdie & Downey, 2000).

Although this chapter focused primarily on girls as victims of boyfriends' controlling and abusive partners, it should be emphasized that girls did attempt to fight back. They used a number of strategies to deal with controlling and abusive boyfriends, including cheating and flirting, physically retaliating, breaking up, and maintaining emotional distance. Unfortunately, girls' strategies were often ineffective and sometimes even exacerbated their boyfriends' behaviors. Girls did not use healthy conflict resolution skills to address their relationship problems most likely because they did not know how to do so. Most of them grew up in families where conflict was handled through violence. Even when young women vowed to avoid men like their mother's abusive partners, this sometimes happened anyway.

Mothers also played an important role in girls' relationships by attempting to dissuade their daughters from becoming involved with controlling or abusive boyfriends, in much the same way that daughters often tried to protect their mothers from abusive partners (see Chapter 2). In no instance did girls report that their fathers attempted to protect them from controlling and abusive partners despite the fact that they believed fathers should serve as protectors (see Chapter 3) nor did girls or mothers rely on outside sources such as schools, social services, or law enforcement to intervene on girls' behalf even when daughters were being physically and sexually victimized by abusive partners. Instead, girls and their mothers relied on each other to deal with intimate partner violence and attempted to deal with such situations via informal means (i.e., dissuasion). This is not surprising given past research on inner-city girls growing up in communities characterized by violence. In such communities, people—particularly those of color—often have long complicated relationships with law enforcement, which makes them less likely to call upon the police for help (N. Jones, 2009; Rios, 2011). Nevertheless, as will be demonstrated in Chapter 6, some mothers eventually became desperate enough to do just that when it came to their daughters' drug use. Still, calling upon law enforcement was never a first choice, and this may have been especially true for those mothers who were still actively using drugs and/or were undocumented.

Finally, it should be noted that girls' involvement with controlling and abusive partners influenced their own delinquent, drug use, and sexual risk-taking behaviors. Similar to the young women that Emily Gaarder and Joanne Belknap (2002) interviewed in their study of girls transferred to adult court, the young women in this book accepted responsibility for their drug use and delinquent behaviors; however, it should be emphasized that, in many instances, they were involved with older boys/men who had more power and control in their relationships, which limited their agency. This is not to say that boyfriends were solely responsible for corrupting girls by leading them astray, but rather that girls' involvement with controlling and abusive partners influenced their own decisions and actions. This was certainly the case with Lydia and Savannah whose stories I presented in full. These young women were already skipping school, acting out, drinking, running away, and engaging in minor forms of delinquency before meeting their partners; however, involvement with their boyfriends exacerbated these already "troublesome" behaviors.

5 · DOING DRUGS

The Good, the Bad, and the Ugly

In the opening scene of the 2003 movie *Thirteen*, two middle-school girls, Tracy and Evie, sit on Tracy's bed huffing duster surrounded by movie star posters, stuffed animals, and purple walls. "Hit me!" Tracy screams. "I'm serious. I can't feel a thing." When Evie hits her full force in the face, Tracy laughs through a mouth full of blood, and pleads, "Again. Do it harder!" When Evie complies, Tracy exclaims, "I don't feel anything. This is awesome!" Like many of the young women whose lives are chronicled in this book, 13-year-old Tracy feels frustrated and misunderstood by the adults in her life, most notably her mother, a former drug user who regularly attends 12-step meetings, and her father, who has all but abandoned Tracy. While Tracy's mother does her best to be a good mother, Tracy rebels against her. Tracy is angry that her mother has reconciled with her boyfriend, a former drug user who has been in and out of prison and halfway homes. To deal with her pain and frustration, Tracy regularly cuts her arms until they drip with blood, a welcome release. One day, Tracy meets Evie, the most popular girl in school, a classic bad girl who is sexually promiscuous, uses drugs, shoplifts at the local mall, and wears tight fitting clothes. Mesmerized by Evie, Tracy seeks to emulate her and eventually loses herself in the process. At the end of the movie, Tracy manages to break away from Evie. Unfortunately the same is not true for many girls in real life, girls whose forays into the dark world of drugs result in years of addiction, girls whose parents may not be able to help them, girls who end up in the juvenile justice system. This chapter presents the stories of girls like Tracy whose parents have a history of drug use. Like Tracy, these young women often fought with their parents (usually mothers), became involved with "deviant" peers, and began using drugs.

PARENTAL DRUG USE, CHILD MALTREATMENT, AND ADOLESCENT DRUG USE

Growing up in families characterized by parental drug use/abuse places young people at increased risk not only for neglect, but also physical and sexual abuse (National Center on Addiction and Substance Abuse, 1999). Parents who use drugs are often consumed with either getting drugs or using drugs. This preoccupation often leaves them with very little time to care for the basic physical and emotional needs of their children (Kroll & Taylor, 2003). The chaotic and uncertain lifestyle that coincides with parental drug use often makes children—especially girls—easy prey for physical and sexual abuse, as parents often leave their children unattended or with unsuitable people (Kroll & Taylor, 2003).

Early exposure to drug problems among family members also increases the risk of drug use for young women and has been found to be associated with higher rates of persistent offending (Johnson, 2004). A study of 470 incarcerated women in Australia found that alcohol and drug problems were prevalent in their families: Forty-four percent said family members had problems with alcohol, 26% had problems with drugs, and a total of 52% had either drug or alcohol problems (Johnson, 2004). The women who were classified as drug-dependent were three times as likely as those without a dependency to have grown up in families with drug problems and more likely to have grown up in families with alcohol problems. Similarly, the girls interviewed for this book reported high rates of parental and family substance use.

Drug use is also quite prevalent among adolescent female offenders. In a large-scale study, approximately 70% of adolescent female arrestees and detainees reported using at least one of seven drugs (marijuana, cocaine, crack, amphetamines, heroin, crystal methamphetamine, or Phencyclidine) in their lifetime (Kim & Fendrich, 2002). Similarly, Gary McClelland, Linda Teplin, and Karen Abram (2004) found that 77.3% of detained youth in Cook County, Illinois, reported drug use in the past six months and 90% reported lifetime use. While marijuana accounted for the majority of self-reported drug use in both studies, self-reported use for other drugs were most likely underestimates given that juvenile offenders may be less likely to self-disclose the use of harder drugs such as methamphetamine, cocaine, and heroin when responding to surveys in juvenile detention facilities (Kim & Fenrich, 2002; McClelland, Teplin, & Abram, 2004).

PATHWAYS TO DRUG USE

According to gendered pathways research, girls who have been sexually or physically abused as children are at heightened risk of running away and using drugs to cope with the abuse (Chesney-Lind & Shelden, 2013; Gaarder & Belknap, 2002; Kempf-Leonard & Johansson, 2007; Salisbury & Van Voorhis, 2009). Several scholars have built upon this model of girls' drug use by exploring why certain young women might be more prone to following this pathway. Kristin Carbone-Lopez and Jody Miller (2012) argue that the early adoption of adult roles and responsibilities can set the stage for young women's initiation into drug use. They interviewed 35 women who were addicted to methamphetamine and found that the majority of them "described how traumatic events and parental involvement in drugs led them to adopt roles such as parenthood, sibling care, independent living, and involvement with older peers or romantic partners at an early age" (p. 198). They found that this involvement in adult roles and activities provided opportunities for drug use initiation. Like the women in Carbone-Lopez and Miller's (2012) study, the majority of the girls interviewed for this book were adultified, reported that methamphetamine was their drug of choice, and had parents who used drugs. The majority of them were also attracted to older boys and men who either introduced them to or encouraged their drug use.

The young women interviewed for this book also struggled with authority and many of them shared stories about arguing with mothers. As girls approached adolescence, they began to resent their mothers' sudden intrusions and attempts to monitor and supervise their behaviors.[1] In such instances, they often went "on the run" because it provided them with the freedom that comes with being able to do what they wanted to do when they wanted to do it. The allure of life on the run is characterized by good times, drug use, relationships with older boys and men, and a respite from parental, school, and other authority figures (Bloom, Owen, Rosenbaum, & Deschenes, 2003; Schaffner, 2014). Like Tracy, whose story was shared at the beginning of this chapter, these young women may not necessarily have experienced sexual or physical abuse at home, but they did spend part of their childhoods with parents who used drugs and most also witnessed violence in their homes. Thus, to a certain extent, they were seeking a respite from a chaotic home life, but they also wanted to enjoy a life free of adult monitoring and rules. These young women appeared to be peer-oriented and enjoyed talking about their various escapades during the interviews and often smiled and laughed when sharing their stories about running away to party, do drugs, and be with boyfriends. While the allure of a party lifestyle pulled these young women toward the street, they often did not stay on the streets for long stretches at a time. Their running away was cyclical in nature, and they always had a home base to return to when they needed a respite from life on the streets (McKinney, 2014; Schaffner, 2014).

In contrast, other young women ran away to escape neglect or abuse at home. For the most part, these young women did not smile and laugh as they discussed their experiences on the streets where they were more often sexually and physically victimized in comparison to the girls who viewed their "on the run" experiences as adventures. These young women did not view life on the streets as fun and many struggled with feelings of anxiety and sadness as they sought to cope with past traumas and victimization. As Emily Gaarder and Joanne Belknap (2002) found in their study of girls transferred to adult court, young women on the streets are particularly vulnerable to further victimization due to their age, gender, and limited financial means. They are also more likely to engage in prostitution as a means to support themselves, their children, and/or their drug use.

Irrespective of why they left home, the young women interviewed for this book often ended up on the streets for varying lengths of time. Given that most of them lived in high-crime areas characterized by drug use and violence, the streets represented a "gender salient context" that was based on patriarchy, and this was particularly true of street contexts involving drugs (Javdani, Sadeh, & Verona, 2011a, p. 1326). Drug markets represent a street context that is dominated by men (Valdez, 2007). Adolescent girls who use drugs are particularly vulnerable within such male-dominated contexts due to their young age, lack of economic power, and dependence on drugs (Gaarder & Belknap, 2002).

Living life on the streets has also been associated with accelerated drug use and involvement in the juvenile justice system (Tucker, Edelen, Ellickson, & Klein, 2011). Thus, much like the adolescent-limited boys in Terrie Moffitt's (1993) study on life-course and delinquency, young women who run away and use drugs run the risk of becoming ensnared in this life-style if they drop out of school, become addicted to drugs, and/or are incarcerated. Indeed, research on adolescent girls indicates that many of them do suffer grave consequences as a result of their drug use and delinquent behaviors during adolescence (Moffitt & Caspi, 2001). Thus, what started out as a desire for independence and fun may end up costing young women in the long run.

ALL OF THEM USE DRUGS

Unfortunately, the majority of young women in the juvenile justice system have a history of drug use and this is especially true for young women who have been remanded to out-of-home placements such as those interviewed for the current study. My informal conversations with direct care staff and therapists who worked with these young women revealed that almost all of the young women in their care had a history of drug use. In fact, these staff members often chuckled when I asked how difficult it would be to limit my sample to girls who had a history of drug use. As I found out during the interviews, most of the young women had extensive histories of hard drug use. This was especially true for the young women who were incarcerated and in residential treatment. While girls reported using methamphetamine, heroin, cocaine, and ecstasy, almost all of them were poly-drug users.

This chapter examines the accounts of these young women's drug use in terms of why they initially used, continued to use, and the consequences associated with their use. These accounts revealed that while drug use was closely related to running away from home, the push and pull factors for running away differed among girls. While all of the girls ran away from home for varying periods of time, some ran away primarily to escape abusive situations and cope with their pain via drug use whereas others were attracted to the "allure of the streets" and the potential good times being on their own could offer. Irrespective of why girls initially ran away, their drug use almost always intensified while on the streets, which resulted in overdoses as well as being arrested and/or charged with drug use. These snares worked together to propel girls on a collision course with the juvenile justice system where many of them also received treatment for the first time. To better understand both the allure of drugs as well as how challenging it can be for young women to extricate themselves from those around them who use drugs, the narratives of six young women in full are presented in this chapter.

THE ALLURE OF THE STREETS

In this section, I share the stories of Christina, Samantha, and Lindsay. All three young women were incarcerated at Arroyo Verde. Both Christina and Samantha lived with their mothers. In contrast, Lindsay lived with her father because her mother was in prison. Unlike Christina and Samantha whose mothers were in recovery, Lindsay's father was still actively using methamphetamine. All three girls were White and none reported any histories of abuse. This is not to say that their relationships with parents were not fraught with conflict, but rather to point out that they did not report histories of abuse. Their stories illustrate what happens when parent–adolescent conflict pushes girls toward the street as well as how the allure of the streets draws them in.

Christina's Story

Christina, a 14-year-old White girl, was locked up at Arroyo Verde for "doing drugs and running away." Prior to being remanded to Arroyo Verde, Christina had lived with her mother, sister, and brother. Her parents were divorced and her father was still "using meth." Although Christina's mother was no longer using methamphetamine, Christina acknowledged that both parents used methamphetamine around her and her siblings when they were younger. Christina first started drinking alcohol at age 10 in the company of her parents and their friends. By age 11, she had tried methamphetamine for the first time in the company of an older male friend. She said,

"I started using meth when I was around 11. I was with this boy, Peter, hanging out at his house. He was, like, 17. I was the youngest there. I went to take a shower, and when I came out, I saw them and I said, 'What are you guys doing?' And he was, like, 'I'm smoking,' and I was, like, 'Oh, okay.' Then he asked if I wanted to use it, and I was, like, 'Alright, whatever . . .' and that's how I started using." When I asked if she was scared to use that first time, Christina said, "No. I just did it. It wasn't a big deal because I grew up with seeing people do that. It felt good." Like some of the women interviewed by Kristin Carbone-Lopez and Jody Miller (2012), Christina viewed her use of methamphetamine as normative given that both parents had used when she was younger and her father was still actively using. She grew up around methamphetamine and the people who used it, so using methamphetamine at an early age "wasn't a big deal."

Soon after using methamphetamine for the first time, Christina ran away and began living with various friends. According to Christina, she did not run away to escape a bad home life, but rather to achieve the freedom to do whatever she wanted without having to worry about following her mother's rules. She resented her mother's attempts to "control" her given that her mother had been largely uninvolved during Christina's younger years. Thus, Christina ran away after an argument or confrontation with her mother over Christina's escalating drug use or when she simply wanted to go somewhere or stay out later than her mother permitted. Like many runaways, Christina's running away was limited to short stints (McKinney, 2014; Schaffner, 2014), as she would often run away for short periods of time and then come back home only to repeat the cycle at a later date.

Life was not always "one big party" for Christina while she was on the run. She spent much of her time living with her older boyfriend or with various friends. During these times, she rarely attended school and spent most of her nights "getting high" with her boyfriend and various drug-using peers. Not surprisingly, Christina's school attendance was sporadic at best, but while she acknowledged the importance of school, she noted that it was simply not a priority at that point in her life. She also occasionally had "bad trips" and once had a very scary overdose experience after a night of using methamphetamine with her boyfriend. She said:

> I was using meth that night, the whole night I was using meth. I was at my
> boyfriend's house and I was fine, but I kept using meth, kept using until I lay

down and passed out. I woke up at 6 o'clock in the morning. I only know what time it was 'cause I was drinking, too, that night. I passed out, and I woke up at 6 o'clock, and I looked around the room, and I was cold. My body felt cold, and I was shivering, and I was laying next to him, and it was real cold to me, and he was, like, 'What's wrong, Babe?' He looked at me and my face was pale, and he was, like, 'I'm going to get you something to eat,' and I threw up, and I was, like, 'Don't talk about food,' and I threw up again. He was, like, 'I'm going to get you something to eat,' and I wasn't eating. I wasn't hungry. My body just shrunk and I looked over at him, and I was screaming, 'What's wrong with me?' I got up, and I tried to walk, and I flopped to the floor.

Unsure of what to do, Christina's boyfriend called her mother who raced over, picked up Christina, and rushed her to the hospital. At the hospital, Christina overhead the doctor say she was overdosing and might die. When I asked Christina what was going through her head when she heard the doctor say she might die, she said: "I felt my whole life flash in front of my eyes. When they told me, I cried. I was, like, 'How am I going to die? I'm only 14 and I'm going to die already!' My whole life flashed in front of me." At this point, Christina was convinced that she would never use methamphetamine again; however, within a few days of being released from the hospital, Christina began using again. She said, "I got on the bus, and I went to see Damon, and he was, like, 'Where you been?' I was, like, 'I almost overdosed. I almost died.' And he was, like, 'I'm sorry. You wanna get high?' And I was, like, 'Yeah, sure.'" When asked if she was afraid of overdosing again, Christina said, "Yeah, I was afraid, but I really didn't care." When I probed why she did not care, Christina said, "Life happens. If something bad happens, it's going to happen, ain't nothing you can do about it."

As Christina's narrative reveals, for some young women, using hard drugs such as methamphetamine was normative in much the same way that marijuana and alcohol use is normative for other teens (Gilliard-Matthews, Stevens, Nilsen, & Dunaev, 2015). While growing up, young women like Christina were exposed to drug contexts related to hard drug use and observed their parents and other adults in their families using drugs. For them, using drugs like methamphetamine was part of everyday life. What is interesting about Christina's narrative is that her mother had stopped using methamphetamine and was actively trying to prevent her daughter from "making the same mistakes" she had made. Unfortunately, Christina's mother's attempts were in vain, as other adults around Christina still used, and she was constantly exposed to drug use.

Samantha's Story

I interviewed 17-year-old Samantha on a sunny June day at Arroyo Verde. She had long auburn hair, a clear complexion, and an engaging smile. At the age of 13, Samantha ran away from home to be with her boyfriend, a 16-year-old boy named Juan. Like Christina, she initially ran away from home because she had been fighting with her mother and wanted to be on her own without having to abide by her mother's rules. She said, "My mom was mad at me. She was going to kick me out. She didn't like my boyfriend because he was bad; he didn't go to school; and I lied to her and said he was in high school. So I left to be with Juan. A few days later, I called my mom. Then I went home. And it was just a cycle. Every time that we would argue, I'd just run away again." Like Christina, Samantha cycled between running away and returning home. She described her "on the run" adventures as exciting and fun. Her eyes sparkled and she laughed as she recalled some of the good times that were associated with running away and drug use as illustrated by the following account of running away with her boyfriend Juan. She said, "And then one time I ran away for several weeks with Juan and his friend. We went to, like, four different towns, but then we got caught, and we were in a car that Juan's friend had stolen, and I was driving. That's when I got sent to juvie." Even though Samantha was caught and "sent to juvie," she described the entire escapade as "fun and exciting" and laughed while sharing this story.

Soon after this escapade, Samantha moved to Arizona with her mother and younger siblings. It was not until Samantha was 15 that she started to use methamphetamine. Like many girls that I interviewed for this book, Samantha's older boyfriend, a 30-year-old drug dealer named Oscar, introduced her to drugs. Unlike Christina, Samantha had never been exposed to methamphetamine, but she was open to trying it. She said, "My mom would actually take me to [Oscar's] house. She thought he was 19, but he wasn't. He was 30 and he was a drug dealer of meth. One day we were lying down and he asked me if I wanted to do some glass. And I was, like, 'What is glass?' And he said meth. 'Cause I didn't know. Over in Texas they call it ice or just meth. I started using with him and dealing with him. I started watching, hanging out with him, and seeing what he was doing. I'd get money and weigh it out and everything so I started smoking it, too."

Overall, Samantha described her experiences with methamphetamine as being positive. She was able to get high with her (older) friends and live a life free of adult rules; however, when I asked if she had ever experienced any negative consequences related to her methamphetamine use, she said:

> Yes. I was at my friend's house around April. I was at Mike's house, and I had been smoking, and I had been smoking every day for, like, seven days straight. And I smoked some PCP, and I had never done that before. I didn't know it had PCP in it, and I started feeling weird. I called Mike and said, 'This isn't meth.' And the next day, the cops raided his house and that is how I got caught. I was really dizzy and started seizing and then the ambulance came and I went to the hospital. They said I had PCP. I thought I was going to die. I didn't know where I was or anything for , like, a week. Then I went to juvie. They kept me there and just watched me and stuff.

Like Christina, Samantha began using methamphetamine again soon after overdosing. For the most part, she viewed methamphetamine use as positive, pleasurable, and fun. Despite some negative experiences, she did not report wanting to quit using upon being released from Arroyo Verde.

Lindsay's Story

Seventeen-year-old Lindsay was a petite girl with shiny blonde hair. She was conventionally pretty and had been a cheerleader before she became addicted to methamphetamine. On the day of our interview, she wore a light blue shirt and tan pants, the standard Arroyo Verde uniform. She seemed relaxed during our interview and freely shared that both parents had been in prison for drug-related charges. She had lived with her mother, her father, an aunt, and been in two treatment facilities prior to being incarcerated at Arroyo Verde. At the time of our interview, Lindsay was at Arroyo Verde for a probation violation. Lindsay's journey to juvenile corrections started when she was 12. That's the age she first began to use methamphetamine. She said, "I've been using meth since I was 12 years old. I was sitting on the bathroom counter at my friend's house. I don't remember their names, but I was staying at my friend's house, and I was 12, and my cousins were there, and they were, like, 'Here, you want to smoke this?' and I was, like, 'Yeah,' and I stayed up for three days. And I couldn't go to sleep and I cried and stuff. But the next day I started using it, like, regularly." When I asked if she knew what she was doing, Lindsay said, "Yeah. I knew what it was 'cause that's why my mom went to prison . . . for using and dealing and violations of probation. I wanted to know why my parents did it when I was young. I wanted to try it." Like Christina, Lindsay's parents along with other adults in her life used methamphetamine regularly. Like many young women who end up in the system, Lindsay's relationship with her parents was fraught with conflict. Only in this instance, her father ended up kicking her out of the house when she was 13 after the two of them were involved in a physical altercation. She said:

> When I was, like, 13, my dad kicked me out of the house. He said, 'Get the fuck out of my house, you're fucking crazy' 'cause I, like, tried to stab him. 'Cause he would, like, do things for his friends' kids and stuff and never take me and my brother anywhere, or like, take care of us. We had to be on welfare and stuff, and I was, like, 'You're just a piece of shit.' He was all high on stuff. I used to find dope in his drawers and razor blades, and I was, like, 'You're a fucking piece of shit.' After that, I just started getting in more trouble like ditching school and getting bad grades and being a runaway and getting in fights at school and stuff. But then I got caught as a runaway again, and I ditched school too much, and then I got arrested for truancy, like six times, and my aunt came and picked me up, and she made me live with her, and I didn't really use for the first couple days, but then after that, I didn't come home one day 'til, like, three in the morning, and she was, like, 'What the hell?' you know. I didn't care. I just told her to shut up and was a bitch to her.

Lindsay described running away, partying, and doing methamphetamine as "really fun." She supported her methamphetamine addiction by dealing drugs. "I used a lot. Every day. All day long I just got high 'cause I used to sell it for this guy . . . so I'd just go around, smoke a lot of dope, sell drugs, go home, make money, go shopping, and do it all over again." When I asked if her aunt knew what she was doing, Lindsay said, "Yeah, she knew, but she couldn't do anything about it 'cause I would tell her to 'Shut, the fuck up!' and 'Who was she to be involved in my life?'" Not soon after this incident, Lindsay began to inject methamphetamine. A 37-year-old "friend of a friend" introduced her to needles.

> I was, like, 16 at the time. And my friend . . . she was, like 23, she went over there to [the 37-year-old man's] house, and I knew she only used needles, but I usually just smoked weed with her. I went over there, and I was, like, 'Where's

the pipe at?' and she was, like, 'We don't have it here.' And then, like, [the man] came out with this tray, and it had three syringes on it, and he's, like, 'You ready to do it?' And I was, like, 'What? I never done this before.' And I was very scared and nervous. Then I just closed my eyes, and I did it, but he missed. He missed my vein. And you know what happens when you miss? A big bump comes up 'cause it's the meth that's sitting in your skin, and it needs to get out. Well, he missed my vein. I had closed my eyes. It hurt really bad, and I almost cried, and he did it again. And it felt good, but it still hurt right here [points to arm]. I was really scared, and I blamed my friend. I told her, 'You're the one that told me to do it.' And, like, I hated her after that. And then she started saying that 'I won't hit you.' She wouldn't hit my vein for me unless I did something for her. And I was, like, 'That's wrong.' She was like, 'Well, I told you, I got you hooked, but I'm not going to feed your habit,' and I told her, 'I didn't say feed my habit. I asked you to shoot me up 'cause I can't do it.' But then I learned how to do it myself. And so, like, she went to prison anyway. Then I started learning how to do it. I learned how to do it by myself. I could do it by myself every day, so I was doing it a lot more than I should have been 'cause I was really bad. . . . I was scared, like . . . 'cause I had never wanted to do that. I really didn't share a needle that day; later I did. We would use water, rinse [the needles] out, and then I would share [the needle] with someone, like, mostly my friend Antoine. But I was scared. I was afraid of getting AIDS or hepatitis or anything. You know you can get anything from that, anything from blood to blood. But the high? You know I was scared, but then again, I didn't care. The high is, like, I mean I don't want to say it because it's so inappropriate, but it makes you feel all warm and stuff and then it feels good. I mean, I know it's inappropriate, but the high makes you feel like you wanna come. That's the best way I can describe it.

The stories of Christina, Samantha, and Lindsay illustrate how parent–adolescent conflict can push some young women to run away so they can be free to do what they want without interference from parents (Bloom et al., 2003). These young women generally viewed running away as an opportunity to live a carefree life characterized by drug use, partying, and fun. Some young women, like Christina and Lindsay, grew up seeing their parents using drugs, partying, and having fun and were attracted to this lifestyle from an early age. As adultified children, they had been exposed to adult situations and drug use contexts since childhood, so using drugs "was no big deal." For the most part, these young women were not apprehensive about using drugs for the first time, because many of them had grown up with parents and other family members who used drugs. From a young age, they had been exposed to adult role models who used drugs for a variety of reasons ranging from having a good time to dealing with intense emotions.

Like many teens who run away from home, these young women were not just running away from something, but also toward something (Kempf-Leonard & Johansson, 2007; Schaffner, 2014). As Laurie Schaffner (2014) pointed out in her study of runaway teens, both push and pull factors influence young people's decisions to go "on the run." Furthermore, while girls' drug use often escalated while they were on the run, most were already using drugs before running away from home. While many found out that life was not always "one big party" on the streets, they still continued to use drugs. Although they were likely physically addicted to methamphetamine, they framed their continued use as a personal choice. Unlike the young women whose stories are presented in the next section, young women who described their drug use escapades as adventurous and fun did not state that they wanted to stop using drugs.

LOOKING FOR A WAY OUT

In this section, I present the stories of three young women whose lives were plagued by neglect, abuse, and trauma as a result of their parents' drug use. Consistent with the gendered pathway model, all three sought to escape their troubled home lives by running away (Chesney-Lind & Shelden, 2013; Kempf-Leonard & Johansson, 2007; Salisbury & Van Voorhis, 2009). One of these young women was White, one was Mexican American, and one was biracial (Mexican American/African American). At the time of the interviews, two were under the care of child protective services and living in group homes while the other was incarcerated at the Arroyo Verde correctional facility.

Paige's Story

It was a brutally hot summer day when I showed up at the Green River group home, a four-bedroom stucco house located in the middle of the suburbs. No doubt due to Homeowners Association (HOA) requirements, the one-story house was indistinguishable from every other house on the block, and I passed by it several times before I found it. Once at the house, I knocked on the door, and a petite woman of Ethiopian descent invited me in. She asked me to wait in the living room while she summoned Paige from her bedroom. As I sat waiting, I could hear the TV in the den along with girls joking with staff. Other girls, like Paige, were holed up in their rooms. Finally, Paige entered the room with the staff member who asked where we would like to meet. I asked if we could meet in the office, which was the only private room in the house. My request was granted and Paige and I headed to the office.

The first thing I noticed about 15-year-old Paige was that she had blonde hair, blue eyes, and was petite. Originally from California, Paige fit the image of the stereotypical California beach girl. I soon learned, in intimate detail, however, that Paige was no California beach girl. She had lived through horrors that most of us cannot even imagine. At the time of our interview she was under the care of child protective services and had lived in over 15 youth facilities, foster care homes, and in the homes of various family members and friends. She had been at the Green River group home for four months, and had been off of drugs for six. As we sat in that small office, Paige opened up about her relationship with her mother.

Paige was born in a mid-sized city in California to a 20-year-old mother who was addicted to methamphetamine and a father who had been imprisoned when Paige was an infant (see Chapter 3 for more on Paige's father). When Paige was about 6 or 7, she and her mother moved to Arizona for a "fresh start." Unfortunately, her mother's attempt to "get off meth" was unsuccessful and she relapsed soon after arriving in Arizona, often disappearing on drug binges and leaving Paige to take care of her younger brother and sister. When her mother was around, she often had various drug-using friends and boyfriends "getting high" and "staying over all night." Paige was sexually abused by several of her mothers' "friends" beginning in the sixth grade. To cope with the ongoing abuse, Paige began to cut herself. She said, "I used to cut for a really long time and stuff. Cutting was just my thing that helped me. I remember one night I cut really badly and like nothing was making the pain or anxiety go away because I was scared someone was going to come back in and I was just so tired of it." Eventually Paige ran away to escape being sexually victimized.[2]

Once on the street, Paige began using drugs. She said, "I just started using, like, a lot of pills and stuff and anything I could find, and then I did cocaine for a while, and then I started meth and heroin, and I've done a lot of things on occasion, but the main thing was cocaine and meth, and in the last year I got into bath salts, and I traded things for bath salts." When I asked if she used drugs to deal with what had happened to her, Paige said, "That's part of it. My therapist and I talk about that. But I'm more at peace with everything that happened to me now than what I used to be. I mean it still hurts and stuff . . . . I feel really sad that that happened, but now it's more, like, I don't think I would be the same person if that stuff hadn't happened. It sounds, like, really cliché and stuff, but I know I can help other people, and it's, like, just part of my background and it made me who I am and stuff."

Deanna's Story

Deanna was a petite 15-year-old Mexican American girl.[3] Of all the girls I interviewed for this study, she was the most expressive and our interview lasted about three hours as she reflected upon her life leading up to her current incarceration at Arroyo Verde. As we sat in a conference room at Arroyo Verde, Deanna talked at length about her early family life and struggles with addiction. It was hard to imagine that this diminutive girl had already been through so much in her young life. Speaking of her early life, Deanna disclosed that her father sold drugs and that both her parents and sisters were addicted to methamphetamine. She recalled being shuttled back and forth between relatives when she was younger and feeling like she was not wanted or loved by her parents who were often emotionally and physically unavailable due to their own drug use. For Deanna, drug use became a way of life on the streets. By the age of 14, Deanna had injected drugs, overdosed, lost more than 30 pounds due to methamphetamine use, stolen money to fuel her drug use, and ended up in various residential treatment centers and finally a youth correctional school. At the time of our interview, Deanna had been locked up for 11 months and was proud of her 11-month sobriety. Below is Deanna's story of how she first started using methamphetamine and how she eventually used methamphetamine with her father as a way of forging a connection with him, a connection that resulted in her getting raped by her father's friend.

> My dad had turned his back on me and wasn't talking to me even though I made several attempts to talk to him behind my mom's back, but he just wanted to be with his girlfriend. And it kind of broke my heart because I was

his little girl, daddy's little girl. I was always by him or with him when I was younger. And I just wasn't feeling right that day I started [using methamphetamine]. I had gotten $20 for my birthday. My mom gave it to me, and she was, like, 'What are you going to use it for?' And I said, 'I don't know . . . probably some food, maybe buy little things like some toys, bubbles or something, maybe cards.' But then I went to this girl Crystal's house to hang out. I knew she and her friends did [methamphetamine] and I asked her . . . I didn't know how to say it so I was, like, 'Can you get any dope?' and she was, like, 'What weed?' and I was, like, 'No, methamphetamine' and she was, like, 'Yeah, hold on for a minute.' And she got this other girl, and the third girl called up this guy, and he came and brought us meth for about $20, which is not that much, but I was curious, real curious about, like, how does it feel like to use? I didn't know nothing about what it felt like.

Like many of the other girls whose stories were presented in Chapter 3, Deanna remembered being "daddy's little girl" prior to his escalating drug use. Although she did not initially use drugs with her father, she eventually used methamphetamine with him. As Deanna talked, it became apparent that her father, who was addicted to methamphetamine, played a central role in her own decision to use drugs and was a major source of personal conflict in her life. "I always wanted to spend time with my dad even if it meant doing drugs. We got to the point where we used together all the time." Deanna then described how this desire to spend time and be close to her father resulted in her father's friend sexually assaulting her.

Me and my dad went over to a tweaker motel [a motel frequently used by methamphetamine users], the Regents Inn, and we were up there with my dad's friend Roger. We were getting high. I was smoking [methamphetamine]. They shot up together and then my dad's cell phone rings and [he] was, like, 'Deanna, I'm going to leave you here for, like, two hours. I'll be back in two hours. Don't go nowhere, I'll be back. I gotta go deal with this crazy girl Veronica.' And he went to deal with her. It was at night, it was getting dark, and he left me there with Roger. And I shot up with Roger and . . . I knew where I was at and everything but I just didn't . . . . It wasn't real to me, you know. I shot up with him, I got high, and I ended up getting raped by him. I tried calling my dad's phone after two hours, but my dad didn't answer. He probably unplugged it and then turned it off and he never called. And then the next morning,

I realized what happened. You know, I just left, and I went to my boyfriend's house, and since that day, I felt really bad. I was shooting up, like, all the time, smoking meth a lot. If they didn't get it for me, I'd get it. I was doing heroin, pills, anything. I was stealing things. I didn't feel 'cause when I was high I didn't feel nothing. I had no emotions. I wasn't scared of nothing. I wasn't happy. I wasn't stable. I wasn't nothing. I was just cold-hearted, like, I didn't care about nobody or nothing. I didn't care about myself. I didn't care where I was going to be in 24 hours. I didn't care about my mom. I didn't care about a guy I was going out with, anything. I treated people like crap. I just didn't care.

As a result of the rape, Deanna spiraled out of control. Although she never spoke to her father about the rape, she eventually concluded that he had abandoned her in a precarious situation. He was not there to protect her in the way that fathers "should" be there for their daughters. This, along with her father's attempts to sell drugs to her friends, made Deanna question the wisdom of continuing to have a relationship with him. Even though she still wanted a relationship with her father, she knew that a relationship with him was "not good for" her own "recovery."

Alana's Story

My interview with 16-year-old biracial Alana took place on a hot summer day. Alana was slightly overweight with light brown hair and a light complexion. She wore large hoop earrings, chewed gum, and seemed eager to talk as we sat in the living room of the Oak Canyon group home. Alana was in a good mood, because she had just received $25 from the group home "CEO" for making As in two classes. As we sat in the office, she seemed relaxed and ready to share her story.

According to Alana, her mother was "raped when she was 16 or 17" by Alana's biological father who was a member of the Bloods gang in Los Angeles. She said, "To my understanding, my father was in the Bloods and my mom was in the Crips. But once they found out [my mother] had got raped and got pregnant, my father got shot the day before I turned one, from what I understand, and he died." As a result, Alana said her mother's drug use escalated and she became "hard core into crack, meth, whatever she could lay her hands on." Alana never met her biological father who died soon after raping her mother. Due to neglect, Alana and her sisters were placed under the care of child protective services. "My mother had four kids and I was the oldest and from what I understand she just couldn't take care of us anymore. She was a prostitute herself and addicted to a lot of drugs so we all just got put into CPS." At the time of our interview, Alana had not seen her mother in several years. She said, "I haven't seen my mother in forever. To tell you the truth, I don't even know if she's alive. She was addicted to so many drugs."

Once in foster care, Alana began to run away on a frequent basis and became a prostitute when she was 12 after being "on the run" with an older teen girl, who introduced Alana to her boyfriend/pimp. "I was on the run and the girl that I ran with who used to be my closest friend, her boyfriend took us and he told us that the only way we could stay there was to be in prostitution, and I wasn't up for that, so he started with, 'Just smoke this. Oh, just hit this,' and I had never smoked cigarettes or used any type of drugs or alcohol. I had never done that, so I was just, 'Okay, whatever,' and I started smoking and I got addicted to [methamphetamine]." Alana eventually was able to escape from her pimp when she was arrested for drug use. When I asked her if she was worried about running into her pimp, she said, "No, because he's locked up for pimping and pampering as they call it . . . ." Eventually, though, she met another pimp who she referred to as her boyfriend. She was around 14 or 15 and her boyfriend/pimp was 18, but this relationship did not last long. She said:

I was on the run, and the boyfriend that I was dating was my pimp, and he was 18 while I was, like, 14, 15 and one night . . . because my foster mom, my foster parents, and my foster sister had always told me, 'Never let a man hit you, and if they do, you'd better hit back,' so I was taught how to not just fight girls, but also men. So one day he slapped me in the face because I didn't bring him back a certain amount of money, so when he slapped me, I just decked him in the face and we just started fighting, and my nephew had called, and I pushed the button and he heard everything where I was, and he came with my cousin, my older cousin, and my older cousin beat [my boyfriend] up and they took me home.

Unlike young women who are attracted to the allure of the street, Paige, Deanna, and Alana sought to run away to escape troubled home lives characterized by neglect and abuse. They often used hard drugs such as methamphetamine while on the street and were sometimes victimized. They did not laugh as they shared their stories and did not view their running away as an adventure, but rather as a way out of a troubled home life. In this sense, their narratives closely aligned with gendered pathways perspectives of girls' offending which suggest that young women who have been victimized and traumatized run away and use drugs to cope with their abuse, which in turn, leads to their involvement in the juvenile justice system (Chesney-Lind & Shelden, 2013; Kempf-Leonard & Johansson, 2007; Salisbury & Van Voorhis, 2009).

CONCLUSION

The vast majority of girls in the juvenile justice system have experienced trauma, abuse, and victimization (Acoca & Dedel, 1998; Cauffman, Feldman, Waterman, & Steiner, 1998; Chesney-Lind & Shelden, 2013; DeHart, 2009; Lederman, Dakof, Larrea, & Li, 2004; Lopez et al., 2011; Schaffner, 2006). Much of this trauma, abuse, and victimization is related to parental substance abuse (Kroll & Taylor, 2003; National Center on Addiction and Substance Abuse, 1999). Parents who use drugs are often not well-equipped to take care of their children, and as was the case with Paige and Alana, neglect is common (Barnard & McKeganey, 2004; Kroll & Talyor, 2003; National Center on Addiction and Substance Abuse, 1999). In other instances, as illustrated by Paige's and Deanna's narratives, parents are unable to protect their daughters from victimization. In both of these instances, parents' drug-using acquaintances sexually assaulted their daughters.

To escape home lives characterized by neglect and/or abuse, many girls run away (Chesney-Lind & Shelden, 2013). This is unfortunate because running away places young women at risk for further exploitation and victimization on the streets (Thrane, Yoder, & Chen, 2011; Tyler, Hoyt, Whitbeck, & Cauce, 2001). This was certainly true for Paige, Deanna, and Alana who grew up in urban crime-ridden neighborhoods. By virtue of being young, desperate, and female, Paige, Deanna, and Alana fell prey to adult men who sexually victimized and/or pimped them out on the streets. The fact that girls' perceived worth is rooted in their youth and gender is not surprising given that we live in a culture that sexualizes and objectifies children (Faulkner, 2010) and privileges the sexual desires of boys and men (Wesely, 2012).

Not all girls run away from home to escape neglect and abuse. Many young women are attracted to the freedom that "being on the run" provides where parental intrusions are minimal and socializing with peers is optimal (Bloom et al., 2003). As demonstrated in the narratives of Christina, Samantha, and Lindsay, arguments with parents (most often mothers) usually precipitate girls running away, but these arguments do not constitute neglect or abuse. Like many teens who run away from home, Christina, Samantha, and Lindsay were not only running away from something, but also toward something (Kempf-Leonard & Johansson, 2007; Schaffner, 2014).

Irrespective of why girls run away, many soon realize that life on the street is not always easy. While on the streets, girls live day by day. Housing is usually transitional as they flit back and forth between friends' homes, parents' homes, motel rooms, and shelters. Drug use is part of this lifestyle. Unfortunately this drug-fueled lifestyle is a risky one. Christina, Samantha, and Lindsay experienced bad trips and overdosed; Deanna was sexually assaulted; Alana engaged in prostitution; and Lindsay began to inject drugs even though she was scared of contracting HIV. Sadly, drug use often turns into an addiction. Even when girls want to quit, they often find that their addiction is much stronger than any fears they might have about themselves or their futures. They are willing to take the chance of contracting a disease or even dying from an overdose because they either maintain a fatalistic perspective or they do not feel very hopeful about their lives. For many, using drugs to numb the pain, escape abuse, and cope with life stressors is a way to self-medicate when treatment is not available (Carbone-Lopez & Miller, 2012). Faced with "out of control" daughters, parents often struggle to intervene on their behalf, and this is true even of those parents who use drugs, who have used drugs in the past, or who are married to drug users. The next chapter describes how girls' parents do the best they can to support and intervene on behalf of their daughters who use drugs.

6 · PARENTS' ATTEMPTS TO INTERVENE ON BEHALF OF DRUG-USING DAUGHTERS

In 2003, Liz Garbus released *Girlhood*, a powerful documentary that chronicles the life of 16-year-old Megan. At the beginning of the documentary, Megan is locked up in the Waxter Juvenile Detention Center in Baltimore for cutting up another girl with a box cutter. As the documentary ensues, we learn that Megan's mother is a heroin addict who has been in and out of prison for drug use and prostitution. As a result, Megan has lived in 11 foster homes and run away from 10 of them. At Waxter, she is playful and sometimes silly, and the staff members appear to be quite fond of her; however, once she is released from Waxter, Megan enters another foster care home. Eventually she runs away from that foster care home because she does not get along with her foster care mother and resents her rules. Megan then moves in with a friend. Soon after, Megan's mother is released from prison. Upon being released from prison, Megan's mother attempts to forge a relationship with her, but Megan struggles with accepting her mother who continues to battle a heroin addiction. During one intense emotional scene, Megan's mother asks for some Xanax, and Megan becomes clearly agitated and upset that her mother wants to use drugs. When Megan's mother asks why she is upset, Megan screams: "You wanna know why? 'Cause I gotta go through this shit every motherfucking day with my father, with you. He's a fucking drunk; you're a fucking dope fiend,' and I gotta go through that shit.

That shit hurts me. I can't take that fucking shit no more. I can't take that shit. And I'm tired of it. I'm tired. I'm about to say, 'Fuck all of y'all. For real. All of y'all. I don't want your money. I don't want shit from y'all. I can do this on my own.' I'm about to say, 'Fuck all of y'all' because I'm tired, and I can't handle it. I'm tired and I'm too young to be stressing like this."

Unable to deal with Megan's emotional outburst, Megan's mother leaves the car with Megan screaming after her to go ahead and leave and get high. Once she realizes that her mother is not coming back, Megan turns to her friend and begins to sob, "I cannot be strong no more. I can't hold it in. It's so much in my head. My mother . . . she's fucking killing me, yo. Look at my fucking hands, yo. I be having issues, yo. I be hearing voices, yo. I'm going crazy. I can't take this shit. I'm gonna have a nervous breakdown. I'm gonna have a heart attack." Like many girls in this book, Megan struggles with her relationship with her mother. While Megan knows her mother loves her, and she loves her mother in turn, Megan just "can't take it no more." Like her mother, Megan also uses drugs as a way to escape and cope with her feelings.

I share Megan's story because it illustrates how complicated the relationship between a drug-using parent and daughter can be. It is clear that Megan's mother wants a relationship with her daughter, but she is unable to consistently provide love and support because of her own struggles with addiction. Furthermore, even when Megan's mother attempts to parent Megan, Megan resists her efforts. As the documentary unfolds, it becomes clear that Megan is angry with her mother for failing to be a good mother, and resents her mother's attempts to parent her. Struggling with her own problems and desire for drugs, Megan's mother responds to this rejection by running away. While both mother and daughter love one another, their relationship is fractured, and they are at an impasse.

This chapter examines how parents like Megan's mother struggle to help their drug-using daughters and how their daughters who have often had to depend on themselves resent their mothers' intrusions during adolescence. Contrary to popular stereotypes about drug-using parents as selfish and uncaring, some girls shared stories about how their parents intervened on their behalf in an attempt to curtail their drug use or control their angry/violent behaviors. Unfortunately, these parents—almost always mothers— were largely ineffective because their daughters, like Megan, resented their mothers' intrusions. It is also quite possible that mothers struggled with their own emotional problems, which further compromised their ability to effectively parent their daughters (Belsky, 1984; Giordano, 2010).

Mothers' attempts to parent their daughters during adolescence were further hampered by the enormous challenges they faced as a result of living in impoverished neighborhoods characterized by drug use, violence, and crime (S. E. James, Johnson, & Raghavan, 2004; Maher, 2000; Sterk, 1999). Neighborhood characteristics that can undermine parenting include poverty, residential instability, inadequate public services, limited social networks, and danger (Pinderhughes, Nix, Foster, & Jones, 2001). Parents who use drugs, have used drugs, or are in relationships with drug-involved partners face additional stressors and challenges especially if they have been jailed or incarcerated. As discussed throughout this book, formerly incarcerated parents and their families face a number of state sanctions and collateral consequences that can also negatively impact their ability to parent their children (Arditti, 2012; Hagan & Coleman, 2001; Siegel, 2011). Parents often respond to such chronic stressors by employing harsh and inconsistent parenting strategies (Pinderhughes et al., 2001). Even within such contexts, distressed parents still care and advocate for their children (Arditti, Burton, & Neeves-Botelho, 2010).

STIGMATIZATION OF DRUG-USING PARENTS

Parents who use drugs are often stigmatized as "bad parents" and this is especially true for mothers (Baker & Carson, 1999; Banwell & Bammer, 2006; E. J. Brown, 2006). The stigmatization of drug-using parents, especially mothers, further compromises their ability to parent their children by making it less likely they will seek help for their drug problem out of fear of losing their children (Haight, Ostler, Black, Sheridan, & Kingery, 2007; McKeganey, Barnard, & McIntosch, 2002). Many drug-using mothers also have limited support networks and struggle to deal with their own issues while parenting their children (S. E. James, Johnson, & Raghavan, 2004; Maher, 2000; Sterk, 1999; Strauss & Falkin, 2001). Mothers who are undocumented or have felony convictions face additional layers of stigma (Romero, 2011). Thus, it is not surprising that parental drug use lies at the heart of many system-involved youths' families, and this was true for the girls in this study (Kroll & Taylor, 2003; Lee, 2016). As pointed out in the Introduction, 70% of the girls whose stories are shared in this book reported that at least one of their parents used drugs either currently or in the past. Many girls were exposed to drug use from an early age. As demonstrated in Chapter 1, growing up with drug-using parents was "normal" within their families and neighborhoods, and it was not until they were older that they began to recognize that their parents were different from other children's parents.

Despite parents' personal struggles with addiction, many of them love their children and seek to balance their addictions with parenting demands. While many are ashamed of their drug use, they do their best to keep their drug use hidden from their children and other relatives (Haight, Carter-Black, & Sheridan, 2009). For example, in one study of mothering, Cathy Banwell and Gabriele Bammer (2006) found that drug-using mothers struggled with isolation, often choosing to exclude themselves from other mothers and relatives out of fear of being stigmatized for their drug use, which further eroded their social support systems. Other qualitative studies poignantly highlight the shame, remorse, and guilt that many drug-using parents feel when it comes to their children (Rhodes, Bernays, & Houmoller, 2010). Like Megan's mother, they often feel ashamed, hopeless, and like failures when it comes to parenting their children.

In contrast, some drug-using parents actively resist being stereotyped as bad parents and believe they are "good enough" parents. They profess their love for their children and point out various strategies that demonstrate how much they care about their children. These strategies include hiding drug use and drug paraphernalia, ceasing drug use during pregnancy, telling children not to use drugs, and slowing down drug use (Baker & Carson, 1999; E. J. Brown, 2006; Rhodes et al., 2010). Tim Rhodes, Sarah Bernays, and Kathrin Houmoller (2010) discussed such strategies in terms of "damage limitation" which center on parents' attempts to create a "sense of normalcy of family life" for their children. While parents' motives for creating the appearance of normalcy may be for self-protection, they are also concerned with protecting their children. This study, along with other work in this area, indicates that drug-using parents are not uncaring individuals who are concerned only about themselves, but rather distressed individuals who are struggling with their own problems while also trying to parent their children under challenging conditions (E. J. Brown, 2006; Rhodes et al., 2010). Of course, this is not to minimize the harm that parental drug use can have on children's development, but rather to contextualize it while also acknowledging parents' strengths (Barnard & McKeganey, 2004).

This chapter presents alternative representations of drug-using parents as shared by system-involved girls. It should be noted that drug-using parents do not always use drugs, and often cycle through periods when they temporarily abstain from using drugs. In other instances, parents cease drug use altogether. Given the fluid nature of parental drug use, parents with a history of drug use, whether past or present, are considered "drug-using parents" for the purposes of this chapter. It should also be emphasized that not all parents used drugs. Some parents never used drugs, but were romantically involved with drug users at some point in their lives. In almost all instances, mothers were the ones who intervened on behalf of their daughters. The role of mothers as sources of social support for drug-using daughters is not uncommon (Boyd & Mieczkowski, 1990; Strauss & Falkin, 2001). Shiela Strauss and Gregory Falkin (2001), for example, interviewed 100 women offenders in drug treatment about their sources of social support. Two-thirds indicated that their mothers provided them with at least one type of social support, which included affirmational, emotional, practical, or informational support. Unfortunately, while their mothers were anxious to do whatever they could to help their daughters stop using drugs, they often inadvertently enabled their daughters by providing them with money, which their daughters then used to buy drugs. Furthermore, while many of the drug-using women appreciated the support they received from their mothers, they also struggled with trusting their mothers and sometimes received unwanted help from well-meaning mothers. Although data on the women's mothers were not available, it is possible that their mothers also struggled with their own issues. Nevertheless, like the mothers of the girls interviewed for this book, they still did their best to support their daughters and help them stop using drugs even if their efforts were sometimes counterproductive and lacked consistency.

PARENTS' STRATEGIES FOR TAKING CARE OF CHILDREN

Don't Be Like Me

Even when parents were actively using, many of them did not want their daughters to be like them, and verbally told them so. Crystal, a soft-spoken 15-year-old White girl at Arroyo Verde, grew up in a home with two drug-using parents. Her father died of a methamphetamine overdose when

Crystal was a child. Before his untimely death, her father regularly implored his young daughter to not be like him, to avoid using drugs. She said, "When I was young, my dad would always talk about me growing up to be a lawyer . . . tell me don't do what Daddy is doing, and I would go, 'I know, Dad.'" Eventually, Crystal did start using methamphetamine even though she had vowed never to do so. According to Crystal, she just sort of "fell into it."

Although Crystal may have been surprised that she just "fell into" drug use, research suggests that parental anti-drug messages alone are not enough to prevent youth from using drugs especially when others in their families and neighborhoods use drugs (Giordano, 2010). As Peggy Giordano (2010) noted in *Legacies of Crime: A Follow Up of the Children of Highly Delinquent Girls and Boys*, while most parents "do not set out to teach their children delinquent acts" and "express a strong interest in ensuring that their child avoids contacts with the police and other difficulties that they know firsthand are associated with negative consequences," they often inadvertently model and expose their children to delinquency, drug use, and other deviant acts (p. 127).

Despite parental implorations against drug use, many girls outright rejected their parents' anti-drug messages on the premise that if their parents used drugs, then why shouldn't they? For example, Erin, an 18-year-old Mexican American girl, said, "My dad would tell me to not do drugs, not to be like him. And I was, like, well, I was thinking in my head, like, 'Well, you did it, so why can't I? You use drugs, and my sister Janelle did it a couple times, and my sister Jennifer did it,' you know . . . they all did it, and then you tell me I can't do it? Why are you telling me that I can't do it when you all do it?" Annette, a 15-year-old White girl living at Green River, was even more direct. "You know my mom and all those older people she hangs out with, the ones I get high with? They all tell me, 'You don't know what you're doing. You better quit doing dope. You better stop doing this shit.' I'm, like, 'Dude, don't tell me what to do, you don't even know.' And they're, like, 'You'll learn, you'll learn the hard way.' But here they are doing drugs with me!" These narratives reveal that despite parental implorations to not use drugs, many of the young women were surrounded by drug use. Developmental factors may also have come into play as many of these young women outright defied their parents' wishes. While such conflicts with parents are generally higher during adolescence (Arnett, 1999), they were especially intense among the girls interviewed for this book given their complicated relationships with their mothers.

Other parents attempted to physically keep their daughters away from drug-using people. Fifteen-year-old Clarissa shared how her father, an active drug user, tried to protect her from her boyfriend who also used drugs. She said, "I guess my dad talked to my mom one day, and he was, like, 'Tell Clarissa to not go back to that guy 'cause he's no good. He does drugs. He's no good.'" Clarissa's father also tried to protect her from her brother, who used drugs. She said, "My dad tells me, 'You don't need to do that stuff [methamphetamine]. It's bad stuff.' He also knows my brother does meth. Like, I would do it with my brother sometimes, but not all the time 'cause I don't like the way he acts when he's on it. He's, like, a different person, and one time, my dad told him, 'You better not be giving that to my daughter. I'll mess you up if you give that to my daughter.'"

Like Clarissa, 17-year-old Nia also used methamphetamine and came from a family of drug users. Although in her case, her mother stopped using when Nia was 7. When asked why she started using drugs, Nia said:

> I was curious. Really curious. I mean when I was younger my mom and dad both used until I was seven. Then my mom stopped and got me and my brothers away from it, but my dad kept using. I had an idea about what drugs were back then, but I still wanted to know for myself. And no matter how much my mom always told me 'don't do it,' I did it anyway. I should have listened because when my mom and dad were together, they would fight, and my dad would abuse us kids. He tried killing my mom. And she said, 'That's how it will make you act. You won't care' and blah, blah, blah. She would always just tell me stuff to try and keep me from doing it. Maybe I should have listened, but I didn't. I mean I was really, really curious.

As the previous examples illustrate, many drug-using parents implored their children to "just say no." Despite parents' good intentions, their implorations did little to dissuade their daughters from using drugs in the absence of other protective factors. This is not surprising given that past research indicates that parental anti-substance use messages are rarely effective at preventing teen substance use (Ennett, Bauman, Foshee, Pemberton, & Hicks, 2001; Svensson, 2003). Furthermore, many of these young women had parents, siblings, and other family members who used drugs and lived in neighborhoods where drug use was normative. Against these odds, parental implorations had little effect on dissuading their daughters from using drugs. Still, these narratives reveal that many drug-using parents do attempt to dissuade their daughters from using drugs. Unfortunately, as was the case with Erin and Annette, parental anti-drug messages are often mixed and inconsistent.

Monitoring and Controlling Girls' Behaviors

Parents also tried to monitor and control their daughters' behaviors, but they often met with staunch resistance from their daughters who resented their parents' intrusion into their lives. Although some adolescents may resist parental attempts to control and monitor their behaviors (Arnett, 1999), the young women interviewed for this book may have been particularly bothered by such parental intrusions given their past histories of adultification. Furthermore, parents often relied on harsh discipline strategies to deal with their daughters' behaviors, which further exacerbated already tense situations. Fifteen-year-old Crystal, for example, began dating an older boy who introduced her to methamphetamine. Her mother, an ex-drug user who had been in recovery for many years, became suspicious of Crystal's boyfriend, as Crystal shared:

> My mom was suspicious of Jesse, my boyfriend, because I ran away for him. When I got caught, my mom started finding out that it was him [who introduced me to methamphetamine], and she didn't okay me being with him, so I would sneak off, and he would come pick me up, and I lived far from him, and I thought it was cool 'cause he would come pick me up. I thought that was so nice, and then one day, I actually got caught with [methamphetamine] 'cause he had gave me a bag, and he gave me stuff, and I was making up my own way on how to smoke it. And then my mom heard a lighter clicking in my room, and she busted in and saw it. She started screaming, 'What the hell is wrong with you? And, like, what's going through your mind? And, who did you get this from?' And I would lie even though she knew where [my boyfriend] was at, and she knew who he was at this point.

Sixteen-year-old Liza's mother, a former cocaine user, also tried to monitor and control Liza's behavior. At the time of my interview with Liza, her mother had been attending Narcotics Anonymous for two years. Liza, who did not live with her mother, described what happened on a recent visit. "She came to visit me, and she was, like, 'Look at your face . . . look at those pimples or whatever.' She's, like, 'It's from drugs.' And I just looked at her, and I was, like, 'Whoa.' When I walked in to see her, that's the first thing she said to me. What the .... 'Can't you say hi? How are you doing? You know I haven't seen you since March. Can't you say 'I miss you?' No, the first thing she does is ask me about my drugs." In response, Liza said she went "off" on her mother: "I'm, like, 'Oh, my gosh!' I went off! 'Why do you do that to me? Why do you disrespect me like that?'"

Both Crystal's and Liza's mothers were former drug users who reacted with anger when confronted with evidence of their daughters' drug use. They screamed at their daughters in an attempt to show their disapproval and to let their daughters know that they were aware of their drug use. These mothers were quite aware from their own personal experiences that drug use can lead to negative consequences, and they sought to prevent their daughters from making the same mistakes they had made. Unfortunately, their attempts to control their daughters were unsuccessful, as both Crystal and Liza reacted with anger and continued to use drugs on the sly.

Unlike Liza and Crystal, 14-year-old Lydia's mother did not use drugs, but had been married to men (including Lydia's father) who had used either drugs or alcohol and were physically abusive (see Chapter 2). Fueled by an intense desire to protect Lydia from negative influences and drugs, Lydia's mother often tried to monitor Lydia's whereabouts and prohibit her from interacting with drug users, which was challenging given that others in Lydia's family and community regularly used drugs. Her attempts to monitor and control Lydia's behaviors ranged from trusting her daughter to "do the right thing" to yelling and threatening Lydia when she did not. Lydia's responses to her mother's attempts to monitor and control her also varied. While Lydia recognized that her mother's attempts to control her were rooted in love, she still "took advantage" of her mother's leniency when her mother was too trusting, and resented her mother, when she was too harsh.

> We have a really good mother–daughter relationship. She's really understand-ing, and she knows what I'm thinking even when I don't even tell her, like, she knows what to say and stuff. I think she's too lenient on me, so I think that's why I take advantage of the situation sometimes. And, I think she should put her foot down some more. I mean I know she cares a lot 'cause she knows I was doing drugs and out in the streets. And every time I would try to leave somewhere, go out, she would tell me she had a bad feeling, or say 'don't

go, come back,' but I would leave. And, I think I just take advantage of her kindness sometimes 'cause she's like a good mother.

Lydia also said her mother sometimes used harsh language with her in an attempt to prevent Lydia from going out. As indicated by the following quote, Lydia's mother sometimes grew frustrated by her inability to control her daughter and prevent her from using drugs.

When she gets really mad, she's really harsh. She doesn't put her hands on me, but her words are very hurtful, very, very hurtful. She's really hurtful, like, she uses bad words in a very bad way . . . and it's, like, Spanish words and it's, like, very hurtful. It makes me feel, like, I should not be doing what I'm doing and, like, I should stop doing the stuff that I'm doing. And she tries to make me do what's right and tells me what's good and what's bad 'cause she knows, she's been through it, and she's lived, and she's my mother. It's hurtful, though. When I do something bad, like one time I came home high, it was hurtful. She said really hurtful words. 'This is gonna happen to you, and you're gonna end up like this, and stuff like that.' Really hurtful.

Although Lydia described her mother as kind and loving, it was clear that her mother sometimes resorted to hurtful language in an attempt to control Lydia's behavior. However, toward the end of our discussion, it also became clear that Lydia's mother sometimes became physically volatile. Lydia said, "I don't know. She just wants me to be happy, and she just lets me do a lot of things that I want. One time I was with one of my boyfriends, and my mom was at the house, like, he came over, and my mom just knew that it wasn't a good idea for your 14-year-old daughter to have a man in her house. Then she got really violent. She threw the beans on the wall. It was crazy! It was hot beans and she tried to throw 'em at me. It was terrible. It was crazy." Lydia's narrative reveals that while her mother was usually kind and loving, she did become frustrated when her attempts to control and monitor Lydia's behaviors proved unsuccessful.

Although parental monitoring and control behaviors are often thought of as protective factors, this is not often the case for parental drug users who lack legitimacy in their children's eyes. Also, many of these parents—perhaps due to their own troubled upbringing—lack the parenting skills needed to effectively monitor and control their daughters' behaviors

(Belsky, 1984). Faced with their daughters' opposition, many parents eventually give up, tune out, or resort to name calling and physical attacks, all of which serve to exacerbate an already tense situation. Ultimately, these efforts to control and monitor their daughters' behaviors often fail with the end result being that parents unintentionally push their daughters toward drug use and life on the streets.

Relying on Family Support

Drug-using parents often gave up full or partial custody of their children to relatives. Sometimes, if parents were incarcerated, they had no choice. Parents sometimes went on drug binges and left their children with relatives for short periods of time. In almost all cases, parents were attempting, at least in part, to protect their children. Well-meaning relatives, who were usually grandmothers and aunts, often stepped in to help with parenting. Selena, for example, had lived most of her life with her maternal grandmother because her mother was frequently on drugs and in and out of jail or prison. Although Selena loved her grandmother, and even viewed her grandmother as a mother, she often resented her grandmother's intrusion in her life.

> My grandma is like my mother. We have a good and bad relationship, mostly bad though. We argue a lot. I say that she don't understand me, and she says that I don't understand her. I don't know. We just don't get along. I'm always yelling at her, and I'm always irritated by her. And people see it as, like, 'Oh, that's your grandma.' No, that's my mom, and just like you and your mom argue, that's how me and my grandma argue. Just 'cause she's older or whatever don't mean nothing. She's like my mother. So, we always argue, I'm always yelling at her, telling her to leave me alone. She always wants to be in my business and know what's happening and stuff. I'm, like, 'No, I don't want you to know anything. I can do this by myself. I don't need your help.' She always says that she needs to help me, and I'm, like, 'No.'

When I asked why her grandmother felt like she needed to help her all the time, Selena sighed and explained that her grandmother still treated her like a little girl and did not want her to grow up. Selena, who had assumed the role of adultified child early on, resented her grandmother's attempts to control her and bristled at the thought of having to abide by her grandmother's rules and expectations.

'Cause I'm her little girl. She raised me. She likes to be right there. I don't know. She don't want me to be like my mom. She don't want me to grow up. It's hard for her to see that I am [growing up], and like, I'm going to be 18. And she says even though you're 18, I'm still going to be there for you, you know, she says, 'You've got a place to stay.' She wants me to be living with her forever, but it can't be like that. She thinks she's helping, but she's not. She's making me more angry, making me want to keep more stuff from her, because every time I tell her something, she always has to throw it in my face and always has to say something . . . that's why I don't tell her stuff.

Unlike other girls who physically moved into their relatives' homes, Desiree, a 14-year-old Mexican American girl, lived with her aunt, her mother, and her younger siblings and cousins. Desiree's aunt's financial contributions were essential to the household. Her aunt also assumed a coparenting role, but Desiree often resented her aunt's parenting attempts. In the following narrative, Desiree describes what happened when her aunt went looking for her after she failed to go home one night.

I was on the run, and I was staying at a friend's house. I wasn't just doing meth. I was drinking and doing some other stuff . . . coke. It was, like, 3, 4 o'clock in the morning, and we were out partying that night. And I looked bad, messed up, you could tell. I was around the corner, and I was, like, 'That's my aunt right there!' And she came around the corner, and she was shocked. She was, like, 'Get your ass over here right now!' and she started screaming at me. She was yelling at me and she was, like, 'Get in the car!' and I was, like, 'No!' and she was, like, 'If you don't get in the car, I'm going to go over there and yank you by your hair!' And I was, like, 'Oh, my gosh. Okay!'

As these narratives reveal, mothers in part, relied on relatives to help them with parenting. Unfortunately, grandparents and other relatives often lack the financial and emotional resources needed to raise other family members' children (Hayslip & Kaminski, 2005). Furthermore, as was the case with Selena, role confusion can be a problem in some families when relatives such as grandmothers act as both mothers and grandmothers. Finally, in families characterized by the intergenerational transmission of delinquency and drug use, grandparents and other relatives may also struggle with their own emotional and substance abuse issues, which further compromises their ability to parent other family members' children (Giordano, 2010).

SOLICITING ASSISTANCE FROM OUTSIDE SOURCES

Desperate to help their drug-using daughters, parents sometimes resorted to soliciting help outside the family. They sought emergency care for their daughters when they overdosed, staged interventions, or called probation officers and law enforcement. It should be noted that only parents who were "in recovery" or had never used drugs sought outside assistance for their daughters, and then only when the situation was extreme (e.g., overdose, extreme drug use, violent behavior). More often they sought to deal with their daughters' behaviors via informal mechanisms such as verbally reprimanding them, restricting access to negative influences, and closely monitoring their behaviors. Unfortunately, because I did not ask about parents' documentation status, I cannot say for certain that undocumented parents were less likely than other parents to solicit outside support; however, previous research along with the anti-immigrant sentiment in Arizona at the time of this study, strongly suggests that these parents might have been less likely to call upon outside sources such as law enforcement and more likely to rely on their own personal networks to deal with their daughters' behaviors (Quiroga, Medina, & Glick, 2014).

Seeking Emergency Care

Seventeen-year-old Lindsay, who was addicted to methamphetamine, acknowledged that her mother had often tried to dissuade her from using drugs, but that she resisted her mother's implorations. "She knew, but she couldn't do nothing about it 'cause I would tell her to 'Shut the fuck up and who was she to be in my life?'" Like other young women, Lindsay did not put much stock in her mother's implorations because "Why should I care what she says when she's never been there for me? When she's the one who went to jail for using drugs?" Although Lindsay's mother had struggled with her own addictions, she clearly did not want to see her daughter go down the same path. Lindsay's mother's willingness to help her daughter is evident in the narrative below.

I overdosed once. I came home one morning at, like, 3 in the morning, and I couldn't go to the bathroom, to go pee . . . . I couldn't pee or nothing. I'd been up for, like, a week, and then, like, I was crying and stuff in the bathroom, and my mom came, and she was, like, 'What's wrong with you?' and I was, like, 'I can't go to the bathroom. I can't pee.' And she was like, 'What are you doing?' She's, like, freaking out, and she made me go the hospital, and I was trying to get out of the car and stuff, and like, I was mad, you know, 'cause I didn't want to go and get tested. She tricked me into going. Said we were going somewhere else. Then when we got there, she like, gave them the right to put me in restraints and stuff 'cause I was kicking the doctors and nurses and stuff, and I'm surprised I didn't get an assault charge for that. I was freaking out and then they had to put a catheter in me 'cause I wouldn't go to the bathroom. I couldn't and it hurt really bad. And, then they're, like, 'What have you been doing? A lot of ecstasy? 'Cause I know ecstasy. I've seen it.' And my mom was, like, 'You're so fucking stupid and da-di-da' and they're, like, 'You need to drink water, and we're going to put this in you and make you drink.' And I was, like, 'no,' and I was just refusing and they really couldn't do nothing to me 'cause I was freaking out so much, and then they gave me pills and stuff, and I got released. Then I ran the next day. And my mom was, like, 'You a dumb bitch!' When I got home, I slept for, like, a day and a half, and then I ran.

Although Lindsay's mother's verbal attacks ("You're so fucking stupid" and "You a dumb bitch") were counterproductive, she was attempting to help her daughter. Understandably, Lindsay reacted with anger, which further escalated the situation. Looking back, Lindsay said, "I used to be, like, 'I'm gonna do what I want. I don't give a fuck. You can't tell me what to do. That's who I am. If you don't like it, don't talk to me.' Like, that was my attitude for a long time. Then I realized that other people have feelings and what I do affects them and stuff."

Staging an Intervention

A few mothers attempted to stage "an intervention" for their drug-using daughters. Fifteen-year-old Deanna's (whose story was presented in Chapter 5) mother, a former methamphetamine user, was desperate to help Deanna overcome her drug addiction. Realizing that Deanna would not go willingly to a drug treatment facility, her mother enlisted the help of family members to "trick" Deanna into going into rehab. Deanna reacted with anger.

I was at this girl's house and [my brother-in-law] came to pick me up. I was, like, 'Take me back to the east side.' And he had set me up with my mom, like, we were driving by the hospital, and I was, like, thinking, 'What if he turns in here?' And he did, and I was, like, 'RJ, what are you doing, for real, like, what the hell?' He's, like, 'Oh, I'm just turning around.' And I got all suspicious, and he turned around, and I see two security guards come out with my mom and my sister, and my sister was very pregnant. [My sister] tried yanking me out of the car, and I put my foot up on the dash. And I was, like, 'Bitch, you're not going to tell me what to do! You're not my mom so you better back up.' I kicked her in the stomach 'cause she was pregnant. I kicked her to get her away from me. We started fighting right there in the parking lot and the security was, like, 'We can do it two ways, the hard way or the easy way.' And when I got there, I was like, 'Screw you.' I was talking to the security guards like that and my mom, too. She was trying to put me in the hospital. I was just tripping. I was just telling them, like, crazy stuff, I was cursing at the nurses. The people that wanted to help me the most I hated. I felt hate towards my mom. I was telling my mom the same thing, 'You're a bitch. I hate you. You're ruining my life. Just stay away from me.' I got her to take me home again and I left the same hour 'cause of the crisis team, the guidance center, the psychs and everything. They didn't get there, and I stayed for, like, a couple of hours in the waiting room just bitching at my mom and telling her all these hateful things and everything, and my mom is sitting there crying, and I'm crying. And I just felt anger, like, I was mad. I always felt inside me that I just, like, wanted to be so mean to somebody. My mom took me home again. You know I just used her again and again. I didn't even care.

Like Lindsay, Deanna had spent time in the recovery unit at Arroyo Verde. While at Arroyo Verde, she had had time to reflect on the past. Looking back, she said:

Nothing was wrong with my mom and the people trying to help me. Instead of me asking, 'What is wrong with you?' I should have been asking, 'What was wrong with me?' I was in there and I was telling my mom all this kind of stuff like, 'I hate you. If you don't take me home, I hate you. You're such a bitch. I can't believe you would try to ruin my life like this and try to lock me up. You don't even want nothing from me. You just want to lock me up. You

just want to be mean to me, and you never want me to have no fun.' I was saying all this mean, hateful stuff towards my mom, the person I loved more than
anything or anyone in the world, and I was telling her, just like, 'You are just
trying to ruin my life. You're stupid. I hate you.' I didn't even care. I didn't feel
nothing. I was really high. I was like, 'Ooohhh, you dumb, you dumb lady, like,
go away . . . just let me alone . . . . Why do you have to care about me? Why do
you care about what I do or who I'm with? It's not your life so stay out of it.
Just fucking don't bother me. Stay away from me.'

Erin also shared a story about how her mother tried to stage an intervention and get help for her. Like Deanna, Erin was also addicted to methamphetamine and deeply resented her mother's attempts to help her. She
described what happened after her mother caught her using methamphetamine in her room: "My mom called a crisis team one time. They didn't
show up for, like, hours. I was outside smoking like a whole pack of cigarettes, and I was telling my mom, 'If you let me stay home, I promise I won't
go nowhere. I'm sorry.' I was, like, 'Poor me. Feel sorry for me.' And she
believed me. That was the first time my mom tried to set me up. I manipulated her. I stayed at my house the whole rest of the day and two hours of
the night and then I took off again. And I was back to the same stuff I used."

Thinking back about that time in her life, Erin said, "When you mess
up like that, you use people and use them and use them and use them until
there is nothing that you can use them for or you take and take and take
until there's nothing more. And I was just, like, 'Screw you, you can't tell
me what to do, fuck you. What is wrong with you people? Why can't you
just leave me alone? What's wrong with you?'" Like Deanna, Erin expressed
regret at the way she treated her mother in the past. Looking back, she recognized that her mother was trying to help her. Sobriety, counseling, and
maturation may have contributed to both girls being able to reflect upon
and understand why their mothers intervened on their behalf even when it
meant facing their daughters' wrath.

Calling Law Enforcement/Probation Officers

Some mothers called law enforcement and probation officers to help deal
with "out of control" daughters, but never for drug use. The most common
reason mothers called law enforcement or probation officers was when girls

were exhibiting angry or violent behaviors. For example, Deanna's mother called the police when Deanna became confrontational. Deanna said:

> My mom called the cops because I was yelling at her, and I had took off to my friend's house. My mom followed me to my friend's house 'cause my friend set me up, and when my mom showed up, I was yelling at her. When the cop came, I was, like, 'Screw you!' The cop had to follow us home, and the cop was, like, 'I'm going to follow you and if I see you yelling at your mom or raising your hands at your mom, then I'm going to pull you guys over, and you're going to sit in the back of the car, and you're going to ride with me.' And I was telling this cop, 'Fuck you! You're not my dad! Don't tell me what to do! You're nothing to me! You're just a fucking pig, that's all you are.'

Similarly, 17-year-old Kathy's mother called the police after she arrived home unexpectedly and caught Kathy getting high in the backyard. The situation escalated quickly and Kathy's mother called the police. Kathy described this incident as follows:

> I was a day to day huffer since I was about 11 or 12. And one time, when I was about 13, my mom had gone away for the weekend to Mexico and I was at home. And I was sitting at home, huffing, just laying low, and my mom came home unexpectedly, and she tried to call the police. That's when I got very violent and spit at her and everything to the point where I was going to hurt her really bad. And the police showed up and that's when I assaulted that police officer, and I was taken to jail, and I was there in jail for about a couple of months. Pretty much like a slap on the hand . . . . 'Be good, don't do it again.' That was my first time in jail I believe, when I was 13.

Although Kathy was using drugs, this was not the reason her mother called police. Her mother called the police because she needed help handling Kathy's violent reaction. Brianna's mother also called upon outside forces to control her daughter's behavior. In this instance, Brianna's mother called Brianna's probation officer after Brianna repeatedly violated the terms of her probation. According to Brianna, she was in Arroyo Verde for "violation of probation and not listening to my mom." She explained: "My mom was saying, 'You're not going out,' and I'd be, like, 'Why not? It's the weekend, and I just got off of work, and I want to go out with my friends,' and so I would just leave because I felt that I had the right to leave, and so my mom would write down every time I left. She let me get away with it four or five times, but after that she got fed up with me and called my [probation officer] and told her, and so my PO violated me, which sent me to court, and then once you go to court, you either get detained, consequences, house arrest, whatever. I got sent here."

CONCLUSION

Young women growing up with drug-using parents often face a number of other issues such as exposure to parental violence, child maltreatment, constant residential mobility, and poverty (Kroll & Taylor, 2003). As pointed out in Chapter 2, many young women struggle to support their mothers and families. As children they are adultified in the sense that they give their mothers relationship advice, help care for siblings, attempt to protect their mothers from abusive partners, and hide evidence of maternal drug use from other family members and authorities. For the most part, these young women grow up very quickly. As demonstrated in Chapter 5, they often run away from home and begin using drugs as a way to achieve freedom and/or escape from their problems. At this point, many parents either initiate or intensify attempts to protect their daughters from drugs and other negative influences. This is true even of drug-using parents who are often stereotyped as being selfish, uncaring, irresponsible, distracted, neglectful, intolerant, aggressive, and as putting drugs before their children (Klee, 1998). As demonstrated in this chapter, parents often attempt to intervene on behalf of their daughters by imploring them to not use drugs, monitoring and controlling their behaviors, relying on support from relatives, staging interventions, and calling upon assistance from law enforcement and probation officers.

Unfortunately, parents' attempts to monitor and control their daughters are often inconsistent. A father high on methamphetamine, for example, might use drugs with his daughter. While sober, this same father might implore his daughter to refrain from using drugs. Even when parents do attempt to do something positive for their daughters, such as staging an intervention, the way they go about it might further isolate their daughters rather than draw them closer. This was certainly the case with

Lindsay's mother who called her daughter "a dumb bitch" while trying to help her. Faced with extreme resistance from daughters, parents might also resort to calling upon law enforcement and probation officers for support (C. P. Davis, 2007). One unintended consequence of parents calling upon law enforcement is that police officers might arrest their daughters under domestic violence arrest policies and charge them with simple assault (Strom, Warner, Tichavsky, & Zahn, 2010). For some girls, an arrest might be their entry into the juvenile justice system, whereas for others, an arrest might further mire them in the system. The next chapter discusses what happens when girls become "property of the state."

7 · PROPERTY OF THE STATE

Locked Up, Locked Out, and in Need of Treatment

The road to the deep end of the juvenile justice system is not unknown, but it is a treacherous one. Girls growing up in families characterized by victimization, abuse, and trauma are at increased risk for depression and anxiety (Chesney-Lind & Shelden, 2013; DeHart, Lynch, Belknap, Dass-Brailsford, & Green, 2014). To cope with these feelings, many young women run away, use drugs, and engage in other survival acts that are delinquent in nature (Chesney-Lind & Shelden, 2013; DeHart et al., 2014; Kempf-Leonard & Johansson, 2007; Salisbury & Van Voorhis, 2009). As illustrated in Chapter 5, while some young women do not experience abuse, they are exposed to harsh and inconsistent discipline, parental drug use, family violence, poverty, and they often "go on the run" to escape these conditions. These adverse childhood events also increase the likelihood that young women will become involved in the juvenile justice and criminal justice systems (DeHart et al., 2014).

Once girls officially come into contact with the juvenile justice system, their cases are dismissed, referred to diversion, or formally petitioned. If their cases are formally petitioned, then they can either plead guilty to the charge and their case moves toward disposition (sentencing), or they can plead not guilty and receive an adjudicatory hearing where a judge hears their case. If they go the latter route, then the judge can decide to dismiss their case, place them on probation, detain them, or commit them to a long-term out-of-home facility such as a youth correctional facility (Pasko, 2010). While this initial contact with the juvenile justice system may be enough to prevent some young women from further offending, for other young women, it is just their first step toward the deep end of the juvenile justice system. Once in the deep end of the juvenile justice system, they will either be criminalized or medicalized with the underlying assumption being that there is something wrong with them as individuals: They are either "bad" or "sick."

SOCIOCULTURAL VIEWS OF YOUTH

Saving Wayward Youth

Conceptions of youth shape juvenile justice policy and practice. Furthermore, such conceptions change over time and are often classed, gendered, and raced. For example, beginning in the 19th century, U.S. conceptions of what it means to be a child shifted. Children were no longer considered little adults, but rather blossoming youths who were in need of care and support. During this time, a group of child advocates, who were primarily middle-class White women, began to advocate on behalf of "wayward" and "delinquent" youth. These so-called "child savers" viewed children as vulnerable, fragile, innocent, and dependent on parents for nurturance and care (Feld, 1999). They believed it was the state's responsibility to care for children by "acting as a kindly parent (parens patriae) when parents were judged as unwilling or incapable of doing so" (Moon, Sundt, Cullen, & Wright, 2000). This cultural shift toward viewing wayward and delinquent children as dependent, innocent, and in need of saving coincided with the development of the juvenile justice system. Indeed, "the stated intent of early juvenile justice institutions was to save at-risk youths by removing them from criminogenic environments and families and then socializing them to middle-class values" (Pickett & Chiricos, 2012, p. 674). The underlying assumption was that lower- and working-class parents, many of whom were recent immigrants, were to blame for their children's delinquency. Thus, during this era "houses of refuge, reform schools, and juvenile courts served primarily to control and warehouse the children of impoverished and immigrant parents" (Pickett & Chiricos, 2012, p. 674).

Controlling the Female Sexual Delinquent

For girls, this control translated into policing sexuality, which was tightly linked to girls' morality as a result of bad parenting (Odem, 1995). As Mary Odem discussed in her book *Delinquent Daughters: Protecting and Policing Adolescent Female Sexuality in the United States, 1885–1920*, middle-class White reformers sought to protect working-class girls' sexuality during the late 1800s/early 1900s. During this era "female reformers challenged the widespread perception of the 'fallen woman' as depraved and dangerous by portraying her instead as a victim of male lust and exploitation" (p. 4). The focus was on punishing male seducers and it was during this time that many age-of-consent laws came into place; however, by the early 20th century, reformers had replaced this "model of female victimization with one of female delinquency that acknowledged the sexual agency of young women" (p. 4). These reformers now looked to "social and family environments to explain the immorality of working-class female youth" and "focused on controlling young women and their environments instead of their male partners" (p. 4). To accomplish these goals, they relied on special police officers, juvenile courts, detention centers, and reformatories to police and correct girls' sexual morality. The underlying assumption was that the state needed to intervene on behalf of sexually delinquent young women when parents were unable to do so. During this era, the primary cure for girls' moral offenses was "rescue from and of the family" (Pasko, 2010, p. 1101).

Punishing Dangerous Youth

Flash forward to the 1960s. During this decade, conservative critics began to critique the child saver orientation of the juvenile court. They argued that the "juvenile justice system was flawed" and that child saving had "led to the lenient treatment of dangerous youths and to the victimization of the public" (Moon et al., 2000, p. 39). This view intensified during the 1980s and 1990s and was directed primarily at African American and Latino boys. This emphasis on blaming young men of color was fueled in no small part by rampant media coverage of marauding gangs of African American and Latino youth causing mayhem against unsuspecting members of the public (Haberman, 2014). Academics such as John DiIulio, a professor of political science and public affairs at Princeton, further contributed to this view of youth of color as violent and dangerous. In 1995, DiIulio coined the term "super predator" to denote a "new breed" of stone-cold juvenile predators who lacked remorse for their violent actions. Despite no research to back up the super predator thesis, media newscasters and politicians on both sides of the political spectrum ran with the story of juvenile super predators (Haberman, 2014). Although the media did not overtly connect youths' race and ethnicity with the super predator thesis, the images that typically accompanied such reports depicted young African American and Latino men.

Latina and African American girls did not escape being painted as menacing and dangerous during this era. As with boys, the media attributed girls' rising arrest rates for violent offenses to an upswing in girls' involvement in gangs, drugs, and violence (Chesney-Lind & Irwin, 2013) as opposed to changes in policies and practices that unfairly targeted young people of color (Feld, 2009). Seeking to better understand why girls' arrest rates for violence increased from 1980–2005, Barry Feld (2009) analyzed juvenile arrest and confinement data for girls charged with violent offenses. He concluded that the rise in girls' arrest rates for violence was due to changes in law enforcement policies that emphasized punishing youth. He also noted that the relabeling of status offenses as simple and aggravated assaults—a process known as bootstrapping—further explained the increase in girls' arrests for violent offenses. Policies of mandatory arrests when responding to domestic violence calls also account for the increase in girls' arrests for other and simple assaults (Buzawa & Hirschel, 2010; C. P. Davis, 2007).[1] Girls are more likely than boys to be arrested for altercations with family members—incidents that were previously handled informally or documented as status offenses (e.g., incorrigibility; Chesney-Lind, 2010). This is unfortunate because girls who are repeat offenders or reach later stages of the juvenile justice system as a result of being labeled a violent offender are more likely to be incarcerated and for longer periods of time than boys (Javdani, Sadeh, & Verona, 2011b). Girls of color are even more vulnerable because they are more likely than White girls to be detained and incarcerated for violent offenses (Chesney-Lind & Eliason, 2006).

Treating Traumatized Girls

While the 1980s through early 2000s emphasized punishing dangerous juvenile offenders, the pendulum currently appears to be swinging back toward rehabilitation in the form of renewed interest in assessment, diagnosis, and treatment (Dohrn, 2004; Pasko, 2010). Juvenile detention and correctional facilities are now charged with providing mental health and substance abuse treatment—usually in the form of individual counseling, group therapy, and medication—to youth who have been formally assessed and diagnosed with a mental health or substance use/abuse problem. This movement toward treatment has had a tremendous impact on how the juvenile justice system responds to girls, many of whom have been victimized, traumatized, and exposed to adverse childhood events (see DeHart et al., 2014).

While the majority of juvenile offenders meet the criteria for mental health disorders (Golzari, Hunt, & Anoshiravani, 2006; Teplin, Abram, McClelland, Dulcan, & Mericle, 2002), girls exhibit higher rates than boys. Gail Wasserman, Larkin McReynolds, Susan Ko, Laura Katz, and Jennifer Carpenter (2005), for example, found that over 80% of girls met criteria for at least one disorder at probation intake compared to 67% of boys. These findings are consistent with other research, which has found that girls have much higher rates of internalizing disorders, such as anxiety and mood disorders, than boys (Abram, Teplin, McClelland, & Dulcan, 2003; Golzari et al., 2006; Teplin et al., 2002).[2]

Recognizing the high rates of mental health and substance use diagnoses among youth in the juvenile justice system, the National Commission on Correctional Health Care (NCCHC) developed guidelines for ensuring that system-involved youth receive appropriate treatment services while confined in juvenile detention settings. Specifically, the NCCHC advocated that:

1. Every detainee should be screened quickly for potential psychiatric problems and current medication;
2. Treatment plans should be developed by qualified mental health staff and appropriately documented, reviewed regularly, and communicated to detention staff;
3. Current medication regimens should not be interrupted, if possible;
4. Acute psychiatric symptoms should be treated appropriately, either within the facility under the supervision of a qualified clinician or in an alternate clinical setting such as a hospital;

5. Psychotropic medication should be used in accordance with scientific evidence and professional standards to treat psychiatric symptoms, not merely to control behavior;

6. The facility should have appropriate suicide prevention measures in place; and

7. Efforts should be made to provide links and referrals to mental health care in the community, as appropriate. (Desai et al., 2006, p. 207)

Despite these recommendations, many youth in the juvenile justice system do not receive treatment. According to a relatively recent study, only 64% of youth with a diagnosed mental disorder and only 35% of youth with a diagnosed substance use disorder received treatment in the juvenile justice system (see Skowyra & Cocozza, 2007). Research further indicates that youth of color are even less likely to receive mental health and substance use treatment than White youth (Herz, 2001; Teplin, Abram, McClelland, Washburn, & Pikus, 2005). African American and Latino youth with mental health problems also receive harsher sentences compared to White youth with similar mental health problems (Dorhn, 2004; White, 2015). While White youth with mental health problems are more likely to be placed under community supervision, Latino and African American youth are more likely to be confined (White, 2015).

Even when treatment is offered in juvenile justice facilities, it is often inadequate, fails to include family members, and does not take contextual factors or structural barriers into account (Goodkind, 2005; Lewis, 2006; Sedlak & McPherson, 2010). Furthermore, several reports indicate that line staff with little or no training in mental health and substance abuse treatment often provide "counseling" and "group therapy" in juvenile detention and correctional facilities (Decker, Taylor, & Katz, 2013; Lewis, 2006; Sedlak & McPherson, 2010; Tosouni, 2010, 2014). As a result, many youth who have been diagnosed with mental health and substance use problems receive inadequate treatment. Despite the lack of adequate treatment, juvenile justice professionals (judges, lawyers, probation officers) continue to routinely recommend that youth with mental health and substance abuse treatment needs be sent to youth correctional facilities where they can at least get some treatment as opposed to no treatment (Moore, 2009).

SHIFTING VIEWS OF YOUTH, POLICIES, AND PRACTICE

Sociocultural views of youth are not static, but rather constantly shifting. They are also classed, gendered, and racialized. The early child saving movement conceptualized wayward children as needing to be saved, but focused only on poor, working-class, and immigrant children who were White (Feld, 1999; Moon et al., 2000; Pickett & Chiricos, 2012). Similarly, the women reformers who spearheaded efforts to control young women's sexuality during the late 1800s/early 1900s were primarily concerned with working-class White girls as opposed to girls of color (Odem, 1995). Race also came into play during the Get Tough era of the 1980s and 1990s when youth of color irrespective of gender were vilified (Rios, 2008). Reacting to public concern over violent juvenile crime, state legislatures enacted a number of punitive laws to crack down on youth violence (Rios, 2008). These new laws coupled with more punitive law enforcement practices contributed to the disproportionate confinement of youth of color (Durán, 2008; Rios, 2008). While the juvenile justice system is currently focused in large part on assessing, diagnosing, and treating youth with mental health and substance use problems, it should be emphasized that other views of youth continue to inform juvenile justice policies and practices. For girls, this means that the juvenile justice systems and its actors are often charged with simultaneously saving, controlling, punishing, and treating them; however, which charge gets emphasized may differ in accordance with girls' race, ethnicity, and class.

Although views of youth and juvenile justice policies and practices have shifted over the years, the idea of parens patriae continues to prevail. The juvenile justice system can step in and assume custody of children judged to be in need of saving, controlling, punishment, or treatment. For some youth, such as the young women interviewed for this book, this means being remanded to an out-of-home facility where they are separated from their families and communities. Such separations are especially common for youth in state juvenile correctional facilities whose opportunities to see parents are limited to strict visiting hours schedules. All too often, these visiting hours/times are not conducive to parents' schedules if they work on the weekends or lack transportation to the facility (Lewis, 2006). Furthermore, as is the case with adult prisons, juvenile correctional facilities are usually located far away from youths' families, which results in many youth feeling isolated and disconnected from their parents, partners, and communities. The underlying assumption, and one that continues to prevail, is that the juvenile justice system, in the form of state actors and institutions, must take over when the parent has failed. In today's world, this means that the juvenile justice system must now be responsible for making sure that system-involved youth receive the assistance they need in the form of mental health and substance abuse treatment while also controlling and punishing them for their transgressions.

The next section provides an overview of my experiences working as an unpaid clinical intern at Arroyo Verde and addresses how budgetary constraints, competing messages about rehabilitation and punishment, conflicting job roles, and a lack of training and resources impact incarcerated girls. The focus is primarily on how these various factors severely undermined the juvenile correctional facility's ability to provide adequate mental health and substance abuse treatment for the incarcerated girls in its care.

BECOMING "PROPERTY OF THE STATE"

Tension between Rehabilitation and Punitive Orientations

As a clinical intern at Arroyo Verde, I observed firsthand the challenges that state juvenile correctional facilities face when attempting to provide mental health and substance abuse treatment services to girls within a correctional facility. Arroyo Verde, which is part of the Arizona Department of Juvenile Corrections, reflects the tension that exists within institutions whose mission is to simultaneously punish, control, and rehabilitate youth. This tension is evident in the various types of staff (security-control versus clinical-rehabilitative) as well as the physical makeup of the facility itself. Like individuals and families, juvenile justice institutions are influenced by larger social forces such as political climates, policies, and economic constraints. When I started my clinical internship in Arroyo Verde in 2009, the state of Arizona was dealing with a significant economic crisis as a result of the recession. The state legislature was threatening to slash state budgets and the Arizona Department of Juvenile Corrections was rumored to be on the chopping block (Taylor, Decker, & Katz, 2015). While the state ultimately decided not to close the Arizona Department of Juvenile Corrections, staff was cut, facilities were closed, and the number of youth remanded to youth correctional facilities declined (ADJC, 2010; Taylor et al., 2015). None of these decisions centered on the best interests of youth and families, but rather on sustaining the already poorly funded Arizona Department of Juvenile Corrections.

These cost-saving measures came to a head a couple of weeks after I started working at Arroyo Verde. A young girl slashed her arms with a piece of broken light bulb while in the bathroom. The story spread across the campus like wildfire and eventually a local alternative newspaper reporter picked up the story and wrote a scathing indictment of the Arizona Department of Juvenile Corrections. The title of her story was "Suicidal Tendencies: The Arizona Department of Juvenile Corrections is a Bloody Mess" and was accompanied by photos of the bloodied girl in handcuffs and lurid descriptions of the incident (Silverman, 2009).[3] The reporter concluded her article by calling into question the Arizona Department of Juvenile Corrections' ability to take care of youth diagnosed with mental illness. She wrote: "The Arizona Department of Juvenile Corrections is supposed to educate and rehabilitate juvenile delinquents. Instead, the agency has become the state's adolescent mental hospital, a job it's clearly not equipped to handle." Although this sensationalized account made it sound like the state-operated juvenile correctional facility was a dumping ground for severely mentally ill youth who are routinely ignored, punished, and victimized, this was not the case. While the state agency has certainly been found guilty of such atrocities in the past, I did not see any evidence of such blatant disregard for youths' well-being and safety while I was at Arroyo Verde.[4] While some line staff tried to be friends with the girls, others attempted to police them, but none of their behaviors, at least that I observed, constituted blatant neglect or abuse.[5] This is not to say that the agency provided adequate services for system-involved youth. It did not, but to be fair to the agency and its many dedicated employees, it was forced to operate under the constraints of a severely limited budget, which meant that at least while I was an intern, Arroyo Verde was operating with a skeleton crew as a result of having to lay off both clinical and security staff.

College Campus or Youth Prison?

Located on the outskirts of a large southwestern city, Arroyo Verde is bordered by a freeway on one side, the boys' correctional facility on another, and the desert on the other two sides. To enter Arroyo Verde, you must empty your pockets. The security staff then inspects your bags to make sure you do not bring in any contraband. Once you receive the green light, you sign in, and walk through a metal detector. After you clear the metal detector, a guard buzzes you into the facility. Occasionally a drug-sniffing dog will be there to greet you before you are allowed access into the bowels of the institution.

Not all of Arroyo Verde resembles a prison. The interior yards and buildings resemble a small college campus in many ways. Green grass, a rare commodity in the middle of the desert, and picnic tables dot the yard. Scattered throughout the campus are four residential units, a cafeteria, a chapel, classrooms, and the two administrative buildings that house the visiting room, staff offices, and the security center where guards monitor a bank of cameras 24/7. The campus also houses a pavilion with basketball courts, a gym, and a baseball diamond surrounded by a track. Unfortunately, the college campus-like environment is limited to the nicely landscaped yards and neatly maintained buildings. Youth, staff, and visitors are reminded that they are in a youth prison, once they enter the housing units, which consist of cell-like rooms with metal beds, thin mattresses, and concrete walls along with a common area with tables and couches.

Neglected and Abused Youth? Or Dangerous and Manipulative Youth?

One thing that became apparent during my internship was that the staff members could be categorized as having either a security-control or rehabilitation-clinical orientation. Prior to beginning my clinical rounds, I had to complete several full days of training, which consisted of *How to Be a Correctional Professional, Suicide Prevention, Mental Health Documentation Basics,* and the *New Freedom Program* (the state agency's official mental health and substance abuse treatment program). The trainer came from a military and law enforcement background and endorsed a strong security orientation. During training, he lectured us about the importance of setting clear physical and emotional boundaries with youth. My sense was that he viewed clinicians as too naïve and trusting to work with such dangerous, manipulative, and out of control youth. My suspicions were confirmed when he distributed a 7-page handout titled *Verbal Counters to Ways Youth Attempt to Groom & Manipulate*

```
           Verbal Counters To Ways Youth Attempt To
        Groom & Manipulate Staff Into Sexual Relationships

      Let's look at how Youth attempt to build deceptive-rapport with
  staff (their targets) & how to handle the approaches.  A few of the
  redirects below are not responding to sexual comments... but most are.

      These recommendations are Better Business Practices and are not
  supported by a lot of staff in this industry, but I don't care. My job
  is to give YOU the best info to keep you from:

  1.) Missing cues when grooming has begun

  2.) Creating a cloud around your name or bad reputation

  3.) Crossing the legal line
```

FIGURE 2. Training handout provided at an Arizona Department of Juvenile Corrections new employment training session. This was the individual trainer's handout and not an official agency handout.

Staff Into Sexual Relationships. The handout clearly presented youth as predators who might groom adult staff members into sexual relationships.[6] The message was clear: These are dangerous youth, not neglected and abused young people in need of mental health and substance abuse treatment.

This staff member knowingly undermined the state agency's overarching rehabilitation mission by sharing materials that he had personally designed to reflect his own views of incarcerated youth. I share his materials (see Fig. 2) to illustrate how individual juvenile justice staff members' views can influence other staff members, shape staff interactions with youth, and reinforce damaging stereotypes. In this instance, a staff member who was in charge of training new employees presented the youth as dangerous, scheming, and manipulative despite a plethora of research, which indicates that many incarcerated youth have been victimized and traumatized in their own homes as well as in secure juvenile detention and correctional facilities (Acoca & Dedel, 1998; Decker et al., 2013; Lewis, 2006). The trainer was not alone in his assessments of the youth, as other security staff members maintained similar views. In contrast, and as expected, the clinical staff appeared to be more rehabilitation-oriented. These various staff perceptions of youth were no doubt influenced by their positions (security versus clinical), training, and the overall tension that continues to exist within juvenile correctional facilities that are charged with both punishing and treating incarcerated youth.

MENTAL HEALTH AND SUBSTANCE ABUSE
TREATMENT AT ARROYO VERDE

Reception, Assessment, and Classification

Upon entering Arroyo Verde, all youth are assigned to the Reception, Assessment, and Classification (RAC) unit for approximately 23 days. During this time, they complete tasks and are assessed to determine their treatment and educational needs. All youth complete the Criminogenic and Protective Factor Assessment, which covers "education, behavior, medical, substance abuse, aggression, and [the] child's attitude toward delinquent behavior" (ADJC, 2014a, p. 8). Once their treatment and educational needs are assessed, they are assigned to one of several units that specialize in anger management, substance abuse, and mental health needs.

Substance Abuse and Mental Health Treatment

At the time of my internship, Arroyo Verde offered the New Freedom program, which is described on the program website as a "comprehensive substance abuse and behavioral health program" that is used in "more than 2,500 correctional programs and facilities nationwide" (A New Freedom, 2016). According to their website, the New Freedom programs are based on "evidence-based strategies that are absolutely top-tier and have been proven effective in countless studies featuring rigorous experimental designs" (A New Freedom, 2016). The program website further states that all program curricula incorporate elements of cognitive-behavioral therapy (CBT), motivational interviewing (MI), and the stages of change model. According to the stages of change model, individuals in treatment should move from "being unaware or unwilling to do anything about the problem (pre-contemplation) to considering the possibility of change (contemplation), to becoming determined and prepared to make the change (preparation), and finally taking action (action) and sustaining or maintaining that change over time" (New Freedom PowerPoint). As the model suggests, the emphasis is on individuals becoming ready to change and eventually changing their behaviors.

The New Freedom program is workbook based. Youth must complete assignments on specific topics (e.g., substance use, gangs, PTSD, grief/loss) during treatment groups and then process what they wrote in process groups which meet 4 to 6 times a week and are facilitated by Arroyo Verde staff.[7] Expected outcomes for New Freedom include decreased incidence of recidivism, decreased incidence of post-release substance abuse, increased compliance with drug testing, decreased post-release probation violations, and active participation in post-release treatment, counseling, and support group activities.

Other Mental Health and Substance Abuse Services

In addition to New Freedom, some youth also participated in individual counseling. Counselors were usually doctoral students in training under the supervision of a licensed doctoral-level psychologist. During my time at Arroyo Verde, state budget cuts resulted in the termination of mental health positions, and only one doctoral-level licensed psychologist was left to supervise 5 or 6 part-time student interns. A full-time licensed clinical social worker was also on staff, and a psychiatrist was on contract. These mental health professionals were expected to meet the mental health and substance abuse treatment needs of the approximately 72 girls who were at the facility during the time of my internship (ADJC, 2012). This lack of qualified, credentialed mental health professionals meant that not all youth received adequate mental health and substance abuse treatment. Furthermore, since the facility relied primarily on an ever-changing pool of clinical interns, turnover was high.

GIRLS' VIEWS OF COUNSELING

As a clinical intern at Arroyo Verde, I was often frustrated when one of the girls I was working with was released back into the community with limited aftercare support. Unfortunately, many of these young women relapsed and ended up in the system again. For me, seeing these girls return to Arroyo Verde was heartbreaking, but not unusual. Despite the revolving nature of the system, I would like to believe that the girls did glean something from their individual and group counseling sessions. As I read back through the transcripts of the interviews I conducted at Arroyo Verde between 2006–2007, I was heartened by the number of times girls reported that treatment was beneficial as well as the number of times that "therapy talk" seeped through in their language; however, I am not convinced that counseling had any long-term effects since the services were piecemeal and generally focused only on individual change as opposed to taking other contextual factors (e.g., family, relationships, patriarchy) into account.[8] Still, many of the young women found counseling helpful if they felt like they could trust their counselor. Talitia, a 16-year-old biracial girl with a shy smile, for example, had only positive things to say about counseling and her counselor. Like many of the girls I interviewed, Talitia struggled with an addiction to methamphetamine. She believed that being at Arroyo Verde had helped her open up about her problems.

> I used to be really, really shy when I was in here. A lot of it came from major depression and from when my dad went to prison the first time. The only person I'd talk to was my mom. I wouldn't talk to pastors or psychs, or nothing. And then I just barely started talking to my doctor . . . . I just recently started talking to my doctor psychologist person. I'm close with her, and a lot of really expensive doctors and psychs and stuff had tried getting through to me, and tried talking to me, and I wouldn't talk to none of them, but I'm close to Dr. _____. Before I would shut down when I went in there [to see the therapist]. I wouldn't shake my head. I wouldn't say 'yes' or 'no.' I wouldn't say 'hi,' nothing for them. But with Dr. _____ I talked a lot more, like, I'm more of an outgoing person now. I know now what's right and what's wrong. [Using methamphetamine is] not a game.

It is clear from her narrative that Talitia trusted, respected, and believed her counselor cared about her, which allowed her to feel safe enough to share her experiences in counseling. Other young women tended to have a negative view of counseling if they believed their counselors were uncaring, judgmental, and incapable of understanding their diverse experiences and backgrounds. Seventeen-year-old Selena, for example, was one of the few girls that I interviewed who was critical of counseling. She resented the intrusion of counselors whom she described as not really caring about the girls in their care. She said, "I think they're fake. And I think that they're always about their books, read their books, and that's where they get their information from . . . . And I hate it when they sit down and they're, like, 'How does that make you feel?' and I'm, like, 'You know what? Shut up. Don't ask me how I'm feeling. It irritates me.'" Selena was annoyed with the counselors at Arroyo Verde who she viewed as not really caring for her or even understanding what had led to her incarceration. For Selena, it was important that the counselors understand her, which is why she had a much more favorable view of group counseling that included her peers. She said, "I think groups are better because everybody knows what you're going through. You feel more comfortable .... I don't know. Everybody is on the same page, and you know what they've been through, their behaviors, and where they are coming from. It's easier to talk to people my age who have been through stuff that I've been through, and I can tell them something, and they won't look at me, like, what the hell? And they won't judge me or look at me all different. I can sit there and tell them something, and they're, like, 'Oh yeah. I understand.' They can't judge me otherwise. Why you gonna judge me if you do the same thing?" Like Selena, young women who feel stigmatized and judged resent having to share their feelings and insights with people they believe do not understand or care about them (Belknap & Cady, 2008). Focus groups indicate that feeling respected and cared for by staff members more generally is very important to incarcerated girls (Belknap & Cady, 2008; Belknap, Holsinger, & Dunn, 1997).

Counseling Helps You Stand Up for Yourself

Most girls were more positive when they spoke about counseling. These results are consistent with a recent national survey of youth in custody, which found that the majority of youth in custody find counseling helpful (Sedlak & McPherson, 2010). In general, girls appreciated being able to talk about their relationship problems with caring counselors in a confidential space. Sixteen-year-old Yesenia, for example, said that counseling had helped her with "unhealthy relationships." More specifically, she said, "Not only does [counseling] help you with substance abuse, but it also helps you recover from unhealthy relationships, you know, like, basically anything you can think of, you know .... [Counseling] really helped me a lot." When I asked her to explain what she meant, Yesenia said: "I feel, like, if you want to change for the better, counseling can help you. Like my relationship with my boyfriend ... I've been through a lot of tough times with him and sometimes I sit there, and I cry when I talk to him, because, like ... I want things to be good and perfect, but they're not going to be like that with us using drugs, you know. But it's hard to break up with him, you know? He's my baby's daddy. I talk to my counselor here, and I tell her how I feel. We're really, really close, and I tell her I don't want to be with him." From our conversation, it was clear that Yesenia felt very close to her counselor, which is an important ingredient in the therapeutic relationship (Lambert & Barley, 2001), but one that is often hard to develop in institutional settings where girls sometimes feel like they cannot trust counselors and other staff members (Lewis, 2006; Tosouni, 2010). Still, in this instance, Yesenia, with the support of her counselor, was able to talk with her boyfriend on the phone and express her desire to break up with him. An important part of this talk, as indicated in the following quote, was being able to express her feelings to her boyfriend and clearly explain what she wanted from him in return: "I talked to him on the phone, and I tell him I don't want to be in a relationship with him. I don't want to be with him. I tell him to get over me, because I want to get over him. I tell him to leave me alone. He's never going to change and until he proves to me that he's going to change, then maybe things will be different. Until then I don't think he's going to change. I tell my counselor that I have to tell him this over and over and over. And she told me 'That's okay since he knows how you feel and you've gathered all the information that you want gathered and you have made a decision.'"

Yesenia's counselor assisted her with gathering information and then making a rational decision based on this information. The counselor then had Yesenia practice what she was going to say to her boyfriend when she saw him in person and asked her to identify what "coping skills" she planned to employ: "She helps me with what I'm going to say when I see him in person. I am determined to not go back to him. She tells me what I need to start working on . . . 'cause I leave on Thursday. She asks: 'What are you going to do when you see him?' She said, 'cause he'll be looking all cut up [looking good] and I got to think about that when I see him. What can I tell myself, you know? What am I going to do, what coping skills am I going to use when I see him?"

As we spoke, it became clear that Yesenia was still struggling with how to deal with her boyfriend and what coping skills she was going to use when she saw him. Although she acknowledged that she "learned so much" at Arroyo Verde about how to "stand up for [myself]," she understood that standing up to or breaking up with her boyfriend was not going to be easy. While talking with her counselor had certainly helped her develop awareness that the relationship was unhealthy, it failed to provide her with any sources of support and resources "on the outside." Her primary strategy was to just tell her boyfriend that she wanted to break up with him, as she described:

And the way I see it, I'm going to talk to him. I really do care about him, but I feel that my love that I had for him faded away. If I'm being honest, it faded away and I want to sit down and talk to him like I'm talking to you, but I want him to be sober. I really need to tell him that if wants me back, if he really wants me back, he has to follow my expectations if he wants me back. I don't deserve to be with somebody like that, I really don't. I learned so much here [at Arroyo Verde]. I learned to stand up for myself, to be straight up, you know. 'You don't like it, then bye!' There's other people out there. I don't deserve that kind of lifestyle anymore. I need to really change for my daughter. It ain't about me no more. It's about my daughter.

While individual agency grounded in positive coping skills is important, young women like Yesenia also need support and resources to deal with such complicated issues as domestic violence, substance abuse, and teen parenting. In addition, Yesenia, like many other girls in the juvenile justice system could benefit from participation in teen dating violence prevention programs that are evidence-based (Hickman, Jaycox, & Aronoff, 2004; O'Keefe, 2005). Unfortunately, such programs are practically nonexistent in juvenile corrections despite the fact that many system-involved girls have a history of being involved in abusive relationships (Kelly, Cheng, Peralez-Dieckmann, & Martinez, 2008).

Working through Addictions

Girls also believed that counseling helped them work through their addictions, but again, as was the case with relationships, the focus of counseling was solely on individual cognitive and behavioral change. While such a focus is important, counseling will be limited if other contextual and structural issues are not considered (Dohrn, 2004; Goodkind, 2005; Javdani & Allen, 2016). Fifteen-year-old Deanna talked at length about how counseling had helped with her addiction to methamphetamine. Like Yesenia, "therapy talk" seeped through her narrative as she mentioned terms like "criminal thinking," " compulsive thinking," and "the disease of addiction." She said:

Yeah, [counseling at Arroyo Verde] helped. Last time I [was released from Arroyo Verde], I was sober for a while and then I got high again. It wasn't fun. It wasn't fun anymore. It wasn't, like, the old times. I picked up right where I left off. It felt nasty, like, it was fun to a certain extent, and then it just got old quick, and it was nasty. The feeling it gave me ... the places it got you. I realized things more than before [counseling]. I realized that ... one day I just realized, 'What the hell am I doing in a dope house with this girl?' And, she's sitting there cleaning her pipes out with a Q-tip and she broke the pipe, and thought that was the end of the world for her. She was, like, 'Oh, fuck! Oh my God, my pipe! I don't know what I'm going to do!' She was bitching about all her stuff, and she didn't know what to do. Even though I was getting high, it was nothing to me. I was, like, 'Here you can have [my pipe].' It was the end of the world for her, and that's how it was, how it used to be for me. If you don't have a pipe or your needle, or anything to get high with, it was the end of the world.

Ultimately, Deanna ended up back at Arroyo Verde. However, as she reveals in the following narrative, this time around, she was grateful for her time at the facility because being locked up physically prevented her from "getting high, getting in trouble, and getting hurt." In this sense, she viewed being forced to abstain and removed from her community as a positive step toward her 'recovery.'

I came back because of stupid shit I was doing, doing things like gang stuff. I didn't care. I would step up to the biggest, baddest chick. You know a lot of times those people had guns and I had guns pulled out on me before ... drug deals and, like, just people tripping out on meth, you know. I would have either got killed that way or I would have killed myself by not eating and staying dehydrated and walking long distances without food or water or sleep and just so much meth in my system that, like, something would have failed in my body, my heart. I probably would have had a heart attack or something and just died, you know. I would be walking by myself somewhere and nobody would have found me for days because, you know, that's how I was like back then . . . . I would disappear from my family. They didn't know where I was at for weeks or days and sometimes even months. I probably would have died. I was so glad when I got arrested, but I was so mad, but inside, like deep, deep down in my heart, I was relieved. I was, like, no more of this shit. But the disease is addiction. I know that now. It takes over your body, takes over your actions, your thinking. You know, your life becomes all about the disease of addiction. You're addicted to crystal meth. It isn't easy still. I still have cravings sometimes, but you know I'm here. I'm glad I'm here [at Arroyo Verde], but I was mad. I still have cravings, like, every once in a while, but it isn't every day, like, constantly on my mind. I'm not constantly getting in trouble for criminal behavior. I stop and I think before I act now. Now I realize all this stuff, like, all of a sudden, it was, like, a big hit in the forehead to me, but I know that I cannot live a happy life with crystal meth in my life. I'd rather feel like shit, feel real sad and depressed than not be able to feel at all. I'd rather get fat than get really, really skinny and not healthy. I'd rather be able to take showers, wear clean clothes, eat food, drink water, you know, brush my teeth, get medical help than not be able to do any of that at all. It changed my life, smoking crystal meth and shooting it up. It changed my life a lot. But being here makes me realize that it can be different.

Deanna, more than any other girl I interviewed, was grateful for being court ordered to serve time in Arroyo Verde because it meant she was finally able to get treatment for an addiction to methamphetamine. She had been at Arroyo Verde for 11 months. As a result of participating in individual and group sessions on the recovery unit, she had gained insight into herself. Like Yesenia, she used certain phrases that I refer to as "therapy talk." For example, she said, "I'd rather feel like shit, feel real sad and depressed than not be able to feel at all." This statement suggests that Deanna was beginning to develop an understanding of how she used methamphetamine as a means to cope with her problems, including the trauma of being raped. Although only 15, she was able to articulate her feelings well. While Deanna possessed insight into why she used methamphetamine and a desire to stop using, she continued to view her addiction as something she could overcome on her own as a result of this newfound insight. Furthermore, while she viewed incarceration as a positive because it forced her to stop using, the problem with such a mentality is that she will eventually return to her community where temptations to use will be present.

Although many girls expressed positive views about counseling, it was clear that the focus of counseling was on changing the individual as opposed to also addressing contextual issues and structural barriers that often impede "change" (Dohrn, 2004; Goodkind, 2005; Javdani & Allen, 2016). While individual change is important, it should be emphasized that individuals' capacity to change is rooted within and constrained by their raced, classed, and gendered positions within a larger set of interlocking contexts and structures.

CONCLUSION

This chapter began with a discussion of how girls' past trauma, victimization, and other adverse child events set the stage for their eventual entry into the juvenile justice system (Chesney-Lind & Shelden, 2013). It also addressed how sociocultural views of youth, gender, race, ethnicity, and class further contribute to the criminalization and medicalization of girls' survival strategies and deeper involvement in the juvenile justice system. While many girls receive mental health and substance abuse treatment in juvenile correctional facilities, this treatment is often inadequate. In many facilities, including Arroyo Verde, line staff and other unlicensed individuals (e.g., interns) carry out the bulk of the mental health and substance abuse treatment. Relying on line staff to run groups is problematic if they are not properly trained. While some line staff respected the young women in their care, others were more authoritarian in nature. Girls may interpret such an authoritarian style of communication as an indication that the staff do not genuinely care about or respect them (Belknap & Cady, 2008). Clinical staff should also be adequately trained. While I was a clinical intern at Arroyo Verde, one licensed psychologist supervised a cadre of clinical interns, the majority of whom were graduate students in clinical psychology. Unfortunately, most of the clinical interns, who comprised the majority of the clinical staff, lacked both clinical experience and experience working in juvenile corrections. They were also not at the facility on a full-time basis and were only at the facility for a semester or two at a time. Still, despite budgetary constraints, the agency did manage to creatively "make do" with very limited resources, and many of the clinical interns and line staff, despite their lack of experience, appeared to be committed to their charges. Still, given the nature of the girls' histories and problems, a more experienced staff of licensed clinical professionals would have been preferable.

Despite the issues I observed, many of the young women that I interviewed in 2006–2007 had a lot of positive things to say about counseling and cited trust and respect as important ingredients of the client–counselor relationship. They frequently spoke about how counseling helped them with their relationships, addictions, and past traumas. For the most part, they appreciated the opportunity to talk with their counselors and work through their problems in groups, and many peppered their narratives with words such as "coping skills," "criminal thinking," and "the disease of addiction." While girls appreciated counseling, more evidence-based treatment programs are needed to address dating violence, substance use, and past traumas. When possible, these efforts should include families, address contextual and structural factors, and be community-based (Dohrn, 2004; Goodkind, 2005; Javdani & Allen, 2016). As it stands, girls continue to view their ability to change as a personal prerogative, but lack the skills, support, and resources to do so. For example, while many girls wanted to stop using drugs, they often relapsed upon release from the facility. To me, the saddest part about being a clinical intern was seeing young women with serious addictions released too soon, only to have them return a few months later. Not surprisingly, as will be shown in the next chapter, many young women had mixed feelings about their ability to "make it on the outside," but even those who felt confident often relapsed. Thus, the next chapter also presents practice and policy recommendations that can help us better address the treatment needs of system-involved girls that go beyond just focusing on individual change.

8 · MOVING BEYOND THE INDIVIDUAL TOWARD PROGRAMMATIC, SYSTEMIC, AND POLICY SOLUTIONS

As I interviewed girls for this book, one thing became clear. Many of them were hopeful about their futures. They were optimistic despite having been in and out of various treatment centers, youth correctional facilities, and group homes. Yet, some of them were also anxious about their ability to abstain from drug use and stay away from "negative influences on the outside." The first part of this chapter presents some of these fears, hopes, and dreams. While most of the narratives presented in this chapter are from my interviews with girls, I also draw upon some written work from the *Portraits in Pen* project that I facilitated with incarcerated girls in 2003.[1] Although some of the girls were anxious about being released, many still maintained hope for a better future. Unfortunately, despite their best intentions, many of these young women will relapse or reoffend upon release and most will once again be court ordered to an out-of-home placement (ADJC, 2014b).[2] Consistent with dominant U.S. sociocultural views of individual responsibility, many of them will then blame themselves for their perceived failures, which is not surprising given that the juvenile justice system has tended to either criminalize or medicalize them (Bosk, 2013).

While individual agency and change is important, we also need to be cognizant of how larger social structures and forces shape system-involved girls' experiences across a variety of contexts and systems. Given the importance of parents in the lives of system-involved girls, we should also consider how we can better work with parents as opposed to blaming them for their wrongdoings while doing little to address the larger social forces and structures that contribute to family problems. Thus, the second half of this chapter presents recommendations for working with system-involved girls and their families that involve moving beyond placing the onus of change on individual girls toward developing programmatic, systemic, and policy solutions that can better support girls and their families. Consistent with an ecological framework, a strength-based, multilevel approach is proposed to address the various contexts and systems that girls and their parents are embedded in. Such approaches, whether they be practice or policy-oriented, should also consider how race, ethnicity, class, gender, and age intersect to shape girls' identities and experiences. Finally, evidence-based interventions that build upon girls' strengths are needed.

LOOKING AHEAD: FEARS, HOPES, AND DREAMS

Not surprisingly, like the women in Susan Starr Sered and Maureen Norton-Hawk's *Can't Catch a Break: Gender, Jail, Drugs, and the Limits of Personal Responsibility* (2014), all of the young women whom I interviewed for this book blamed themselves for their problems. They did not minimize responsibility for their problems and behaviors nor did they make the connection between their past victimization and their subsequent offending (see also Gaarder & Belknap, 2002). Despite the myriad challenges they faced, they were still cautiously optimistic about their future upon their release. Like many young people, they wanted to do well in school, get a good job, and have a family. They typically gravitated toward jobs in the helping professions such as social work, teaching, nursing, and veterinary care. They also displayed tremendous empathy and wanted to help others, especially children and animals. School was also important to them with most wanting to complete their General Equivalency Diploma (GED). The majority also wanted to abstain from using drugs and wanted to avoid being sent to an adult prison when they were older. As I listened to their narratives, I was struck by their optimism, hope, and dreams. They seemed rather "normal," but like those young women who expressed anxiety about being "able to make it on the outside," I also worried that, despite their best efforts, they would relapse.

Going to School and Getting a Good Job

Although most of the young people who participated in the *Portraits in Pen* project expressed themselves through poetry, a couple of them opted to use "I want . . ." writing prompts. One young woman wrote the following:

> I want to accomplish my goals of my life, so I can be happy.
> I want to study hard for my G.E.D., so I can learn a lot to help me in my career.
> I want to make my parents proud of my successes and accomplishments.
> I want to help support my family and the friends that are close to me.
> I want my family to see and know that I made it in life.
> I want them to know that I not only did it for me, but for them as well.
> I want to be a role model for my little brother, nieces, nephews, and cousins.
> I want all the youth in this country to find positive role models to look up to.

This young woman's wants are not outrageous. Like many young people, she is goal-oriented. She wants to earn a GED, make her parents proud, support her family, and be a positive role model. The young women I interviewed typically aspired to careers in helping professions. Motivated by their own experiences, many of them wanted a career that would allow them to help others. They wanted to be teachers' aides, nurses, and vet techs. Ashley, whose parents both used drugs, said: "I want to be a nurse because my baby sister died when she was real little, and she was premature because my mom did drugs and stuff when she was pregnant with her, and so I just want to help little babies." Lolo, who was at a group home at the time of our interview, wanted to be a teacher's aide and foster care parent. She was very specific about her future educational and career goals.

> I want to go to a community college, and from there to NAU [Northern Arizona University]. I want to be a teacher's aide to see what it's like, and when I get a permanent job, I want to work with younger kids from, like, 3rd grade and down. I love younger kids, and I'm in an early childhood professional development class right now, and I really like it. I also want to be a

foster care mom some day, because there's no point in making new people in the world when there are kids suffering in CPS or living on the streets. I would have been living in the streets if my foster parents hadn't taken me in. So I want to do the same thing that my parents did for me ... for other kids.

While many of the young women's aspirations are fairly conventional, they are difficult to achieve for many system-involved girls who typically have a history of victimization and trauma, significant gaps in their education, and a lack of social support. Yet, despite these challenges, many of these young women still maintain hope for a brighter future that involves achieving conventional goals such as going to school and obtaining a good job. In their study of detained and incarcerated girls, Joanne Belknap and Bonnie Cady (2008) also found that many of the young women wanted to achieve conventional goals, but lacked the confidence and skills to do so. Thus, these young women recommended that juvenile justice facilities incorporate more life skills training that would help them survive in the real world.

Many of the young women interviewed for this book also wanted to help others like themselves. Their narratives hinted at an understanding of how larger issues impact children. For example, Lolo wanted to help other children "suffering in CPS or living on the streets." In this sense, Lolo, like many of the other young women, was aware of how trauma, exposure to adverse life events, limited opportunities, and poverty impact other young people. Nevertheless, despite this implicit awareness, they still tended to frame their aspirations within an individualistic framework that emphasized individual agency as opposed to also considering how larger social structures and contextual factors work together to limit individuals' choices and opportunities.

Keeping Busy and Staying Away from Negative Influences

Many young women said they wanted to keep busy and stay away from negative influences such as drug-using peers, boyfriends, parents, and other relatives. Moving away and keeping busy represented two strategies for staying away from negative influences and the temptation to use drugs. Sixteen-year-old Sharon, for example, believed that moving in with her father would help her stay away from negative influences. Like many of the young women whose stories I share in this book, Sharon had repeatedly run away from home and was addicted to methamphetamine. While "on the run," she stayed in various motels with an older boyfriend or at various friends' houses. At the time of our interview, Sharon had been incarcerated for three months. Prior to her incarceration at Arroyo Verde, she had been in a drug treatment facility. Upon being released from the drug treatment facility, Sharon relapsed and eventually ended up in Arroyo Verde for the third time. As we spoke, it became clear that she was ready to give up her previous lifestyle and wanted to move in with her father who lived in a different city. She believed that doing so would allow her to stay away from drug-using peers and the temptations that come along with them.

> I'm going to my dad's house 'cause he lives in a different city, and things are going to be better 'cause I don't even know where none of those [drug-using] people are at, and I don't want to know. I want to get a job now. I want to make something of myself. I don't want to be involved in [that drug-using lifestyle] anymore. I hated it when I was involved in it anyway. I hated it because it was, like, the same crap every day. And [those drug-using people] would try to get me to do stuff that I didn't want to do, and I really didn't want to do the drugs, but I did them anyway. Now . . . I don't think I would use drugs. If I know that somebody is doing drugs, I don't even want to be around them at all. Drugs were literally poisoning my body. I'm more spiritual now. I'm into God now. I have a God. I have help now.

Although Sharon had been in treatment before her latest stay at Arroyo Verde, she believed that she could avoid relapse upon release if she moved in with her father. Like many of the other young women, she had actively worked out a plan for what to do upon release. Moving in with her father and staying away from "negative peers" played a major role in her plan to stay clean, sober, and out of trouble. Unfortunately, for Sharon and other young women, their ability to "move away" is constrained by their age and economic positions. As adolescents, they have relatively little control over where they can live. Furthermore, even when they can move in with relatives, their relatives often live in similar communities plagued by poverty, drug use, and violence.

Other young women also vowed to keep busy upon release by working or going to school. Seventeen-year-old Brianna said, "When I get out of [Arroyo Verde], I plan on working, going to school, and spending time with my boyfriend and eventually moving out once I hit 18. I don't want to come back here. 'Cause if I come back then that's a waste of my life. That's how

I feel right now. I don't want to come here. I don't want to be in the adult system either because I'm about to be 18. I don't want to be in the adult system like my brother and my dad. That's why I'm going to keep myself busy and out of trouble." For Brianna, the primary reason for going to school and working was not economically motivated, but rather to keep herself busy and "out of trouble." She viewed turning 18 as an important milestone that would allow her to exercise more agency over her own fate and life circumstances. Unfortunately, due to educational gaps and limited job opportunities, turning 18 might not confer as many choices as young women believe, as their choices will most likely be constrained by their limited education and life skills (Belknap & Cady, 2008).

Seventeen-year-old Catalina also talked about going to school and keeping busy as a way of staying out of trouble. Like Brianna, Catalina knew that once she turned 18, she would be charged as an adult if she got into legal trouble again. Like other young women who were approaching 18, she said structure was needed to keep her from relapsing and entering the adult system. She also seemed to recognize that the juvenile justice system at least attempted to rehabilitate youth, but knew that the same might not be true of the adult criminal justice system, which she viewed as more punitive in nature. She said, "I don't want to end up back in here, and I'm going to be 18, I don't want to go to adult [prison], that's another thing. That's something different. They don't play around. They don't care. They don't have programs like juveniles have, you know, stuff like that." In order to avoid ending up in the adult system, Catalina vowed to keep busy and stay away from negative influences. She said, "I'm going to keep myself busy so I don't have time for stuff like that. I just want to keep myself busy so that when someone does want to call or whatever . . . well I'm going to change my phone number 'cause we've had the same phone number since I was, like, 14, so I want to do that." Like many of the girls I interviewed, she also emphasized the importance of having a plan upon release. She said:

> I just want to see myself motivated 'cause when I did do that stuff, I would go to school high. When I didn't go to school, I was at home. I had nothing to do. I had nothing planned. But when I get released, I need to have a plan, you know, things that I need to do, that I need to accomplish. Even daily, even little things, it don't have to be big, you know, like read a book by this day, go to school, do something, keep busy. I want it to be structured. I can see myself

at home doing what I want to do, going to school every day. On the weekends, I'll clean the house, go to the library, go check out a book, keep myself busy. Before I came here, I didn't have nothing to do so when someone would call, 'Hey, let's go out, come on,' but now when I get released and someone does call or come by, I'm going to be, like, 'I can't. I have to go to school. I have to go to this appointment in the counselor's office.' You know, I'm going to be busy.

As Catalina's narrative illustrates, many young women believed they need structure and routine to avoid negative influences. Their narratives also hinted at how challenging it was going to be for them to abstain from drug use given that most of them were surrounded by peers, friends, and family members who used drugs. Deanna, for example, whose story I presented in Chapter 5, discussed at length how difficult it would be to sever ties with her father. Yet, she recognized that she might have to do so in order to maintain her sobriety. Still, she struggled with the emotional ramifications of such a decision because she loved her father and still wanted a relationship with him.

Issues with my dad is, like, my number 1 big issue, like, the one that is on the top of the list. It's not the drug use anymore, but it's related to the drug use. I used to be really close to him. I used to go to work with him every day when I was good or after school all the time. I used to ride motorcycles with him, three wheelers and stuff. I was always there. I wanted the same thing, everything he wanted. I looked up to him a lot, and always wanted to be with him. About a year ago, I didn't see no problem with him. I was, like, 'Oh, yeah. He's cool. He gets high. No big deal.' Like around this time last year, I was in juvie, and I didn't see a problem with him. I didn't see a problem with getting high. I didn't see none of that, but then he left me at that motel and said he was coming back and never did and his friend raped me. Then he sold me drugs after I had been locked up and away from my home for over a year. He sold me drugs when I got out and got my best friends high off the needle. Now it's, like, I see him for who he really is and right now I'm in between, like, 'I hate you, and I don't ever want to talk to you, and I want you out of my life' and 'Yeah, I accept you and everything' . . . and I know it's going to take a long time and a lot of help and a lot of counseling for me to be able to make up my mind. He's just done a lot of stupid things, and hurtful things, and emotional abuse. So it's going to take a long time, you know, but I think at least for now, I have to stay away from him.

While avoiding the temptation of drug use was the most common reason girls gave for avoiding negative influences, it was not the only one. A few
girls mentioned the importance of staying away from gang-affiliated people,
including family members. Victoria, a 16-year-old Mexican American girl at
Desert Star, for example, said it was going to be difficult to stay away from
negative influences because her parents, siblings, and other family members were all involved in gangs, used drugs, and engaged in violence to deal
with problems. Despite not wanting to grow up to be like her family members, Victoria found herself pulled into the gang lifestyle from a young age.

A lot of it does have to do with your surroundings. I have five brothers and
one sister. You just watch them. Like, all my brothers are older than me, and
they're all, like, gangsters. We're from _____ and there's a lot of gangsters there. They are all from the same gang. The oldest one is still in a gang
and is in prison even though he's 34. He still has to do 10 years or so. He'll
never change. Some of my brothers have changed. The youngest one just got,
like, five years. He's the most corrupted one. You can't even talk to him in a
civil way because he's so rude. He's like the young one, 23, and he's, like, 'gangster this, gangster that,' but it's just what you see as a child. What a child sees
has some kind of impact. I've always wanted to do good in school and not be
like that, and I tried, but I still ended up in here.

Victoria discussed how difficult it would be to refrain from using violence
when her family members and other people in her neighborhood endorse
violence as a means for handling conflict. While Victoria did not want to
use violence upon her release from Desert Star, she believed that she would
be compelled to do so by her brothers and other family members unless she
managed to stay away from them. Victoria's narrative illustrates how important context is when discussing why adolescents engage in behaviors such
as drug use, delinquency, and gang violence.

I don't want to be here. I want to go home. I want to go to school. I want to
go to college. I don't want this for myself. It's just hard because I have that bad
anger type thing and that's what always gets me in trouble, and I have to be
around my dad and my brothers when I leave [Desert Star] and my brothers will be, like, 'Don't let nobody disrespect you. If you let them disrespect
you, you're a punk.' I always have that in the back of my head. If someone

disrespects you, you have to do something. I usually hit them or do something. I don't want to think that way, but it's hard. It's hard when that's how you grow up. It's hard. It's crazy. I mean that's how it is, and if I don't want to live like that, I have to stay away, and it's going to be hard to stay away from everybody.

As Deanna's and Victoria's narratives reveal, "staying away from negative influences" is not always cut and dry especially when those negative influences are parents and other family members. Also, as pointed out by Victoria, larger street culture norms can dictate how young women should behave in neighborhoods characterized by drugs, gangs, and crimes (Valdez, 2007). Simply staying away from negative influences can be challenging, as young women often care about the people they "should" avoid. Furthermore, in many instances, young women lack the financial resources to move. As teens, many of them are dependent on adults (e.g., parents, partners) for survival.

Wanting to Do Better for My Child's Sake

One of the young women who participated in the *Portraits in Pen* project wrote a letter to her infant daughter. In her letter, she spoke about wanting to earn her GED and obtain a full-time job for her daughter's sake. The letter eloquently illustrates how motherhood can motivate some young women to make "better life choices" (Chumbler, Bute, Huff, & Cherry, 2015; SmithBattle, 2007):

To My Dearest Love,

Today is June 23, 2003, and as I sit here I cannot help but think about you. In my life, I have made some mistakes, but I work hard every day to prove myself as a mother to you. To prove to myself I made the hardest decision of my life to keep you at the foster home. I made this decision for your benefit. I made that choice for the best interest of both of us. In about sixty days, I will be starting a new beginning at [name of residential treatment center]. At [name of residential treatment center], I will continue taking classes that will help me reach my GED. By that time, I want to have a full-time job. That will be one step closer to me having you at home and back in my arms. I want to provide you with a better opportunity in life that I took for granted. I know you cannot read this letter yet, but by the time you can, I hope I have already fulfilled all my promises to you as a good mother. You have been my strength, and I want to love and protect you and give you the best life I can.

Love Always and Forever,
Your Mommy

All of the young mothers (or mothers to be) in this study wanted to do better (as defined by staying out of the system, completing high school/GED, getting a good job, abstaining from drug use) for their children's sake. Despite their young age, these young mothers cared deeply about their children and regretted not being able to see them while incarcerated. Talitia, an attractive 16-year-old biracial girl with a sparkling smile, had been pregnant while at Arroyo Verde. Because Talitia gave birth to her daughter while incarcerated, her daughter was immediately whisked away upon birth and given to Talitia's mother to care for while Talitia continued serving her time. Talitia spent a good portion of the interview talking about how much she missed her baby. As I listened to her, I found myself wishing that the facility had done a better job of facilitating and nurturing this young mother's relationship with her daughter. Unfortunately, as is the case with adult prisons, many youth correctional facilities are not family friendly and teen parents are not awarded special privileges that would allow them to spend quality time with their children (Acoca, 2004; Nurse, 2002). Thus, teen parents like Talitia feel the loss of their children deeply and often vow to "make better choices" upon their release. Talitia, for example, said, "Once I leave here in three months, I will take care of my daughter, and I'll get my GED so I can start college classes on the Internet, and so I can be home for my daughter and work on school, and after I graduate, I want to go work for a vet and get more experience with animals, like, go to a shelter and work there. I don't feel like I will come back here because the motivation that I have to just take care of my daughter is too strong."

A few young women also mentioned wanting to stay away from their babies' fathers once they were released. Bianca, for example, said she had stopped "partying, doing drugs, and getting into trouble" for the sake of her baby. Unfortunately, as she reveals in the narrative that follows, her boyfriend continued to drink heavily and hang out with friends. While Bianca believed that her boyfriend loved their child, she worried that his drinking would negatively impact his ability to be a good father. She said, "Our relationship was really, really good in the beginning, but now it's kinda harder 'cause we have a baby together, and we kinda get into arguments 'cause I don't like some things he does, and it's just that, that's the only problem. 'Cause before, you know, when I was into drinking and all that, we would hang out and drink together, party, whatever. Now that I have a baby, I don't drink, I don't do nothing and I've changed a lot, but he still wants to hang around with the same friends and drink with them, and I hate it." In contrast to girls who said they wanted to stay away from negative influences for their own personal recovery, Bianca wanted to stay away from her baby's father because she did not want her son to grow up around someone who drinks and parties all the time. Thus, while she believed that her boyfriend was a good person who respected her and loved their son, she struggled with his excessive drinking and partying and contemplated leaving him in order to protect her son. As illustrated by Talitia's and Bianca's narratives, being a mother can be a transformative experience for young women who are motivated to refocus their lives for their children (Chumbler et al., 2015; SmithBattle, 2007).

It's All Going to Be Up to Me

Girls expressed varying thoughts about their ability to remain trouble-free upon being released from the youth facility. Some girls were optimistic despite previous relapses and setbacks. Catalina, for example, had been in treatment prior to relapsing and being remanded to Arroyo Verde. Yet she remained optimistic about her future. When I asked what she thought would be different this time around, she said:

> I've been away from [drugs] for almost three months before I came here because I spent a month in juvie, so it's been three months that I've been away from it. And I'm not craving it. My body doesn't want it. My body is not calling for it, but it's just my mind that's going to be messing with me. It's just inside of my head 'cause my body is not craving it, but I don't think I'm going to mess up this time. It's all going to be up to me. I don't want to do it, and I'm not going to go back [to using drugs] because I'm better than that. I'm more hopeful this time. I believe in myself. I have faith and I'm a strong person. I can do whatever I want to do as long as I put my mind to it, you know, and I have to be patient 'cause nothing is going to happen all at once, take it step by step.

While some young women like Catalina were optimistic about being successful "on the outside," others expressed trepidation about being able to stay clean and sober upon being released from the youth facility. This was especially true for girls at Arroyo Verde and Desert Star who had more extensive histories of drug addiction and treatment than the girls in the group homes. For example, Nia, a 17-year-old White girl, described how difficult it would be to stay away from methamphetamine upon release from Arroyo Verde despite her personal conviction to do so. She said, "I don't know. I want to say that I am going to do my best when I get out, that I'm not going to get high, but I can say that when I'm in here, but when I'm out there, it's different. Once you're a tweaker, you're always a tweaker. You know. You can pick out who is on drugs, and who is not. I mean I know [relapse] can happen to me, but I still have the mentality that it can't happen to me. I don't want to get high no more, but there's still a big part of me that wants to get high. A big part of me. I can say that I won't use as much as I want while I'm in here, but when I get out, let's face it, it will be hard not to use. If I was to leave today, I would get high."

As mentioned in Chapter 7, it was not uncommon for the girls I was counseling to be released from Arroyo Verde only to return a few months later, dejected, crestfallen, and once again going through withdrawals. Many of these young women had professed ambivalence about leaving the facility. They knew they were not ready, and I knew they were not ready, but they were released anyway. Some went to drug treatment facilities, others to residential treatment and independent living centers, and still others to their parents', relatives', or foster care homes. While these young women were armed with post-release plans, which included strategies for staying away from negative influences and situations, many relapsed despite their initial attempts to stay drug-free. Not surprisingly, some of the young women interviewed for this book knew full well the challenges they would face upon release, and were anxious about being able to stay drug- and trouble-free on the outside. This was especially true for 17-year-old Kathy who had spent most of her teen years in a variety of youth facilities.

> I had a parole reinstatement meeting to see if I could go back into the community, and I was given five more months here [at Arroyo Verde]. They said that I'm not ready. I'm institutionalized, I guess. They say I have anti-social traits so they're trying to work with me to go through those things. Yes, I know I have anti-social traits. I know I'm institutionalized considering the fact that I've been here most of my teenage life. These people have seen me grow and mature. It's kind of hard to break away from this. I'll be 18 in December so they are going to

release me two months before I'm 18 and send me to some type of independent living program. It's pretty much all I know. Every time I think about leaving, I get this tight feeling, like, fear, but then I tell myself, 'You're going to have to do it eventually,' but I'm not strong enough to deal with that right now.

What is interesting about Kathy's narrative is that she had internalized the institution's message that she was "institutionalized" and had "anti-social traits." Like the women in Jill McCorkel's book *Breaking Women: Gender, Race, and the New Politics of Imprisonment* (2013), many of the young women interviewed for this study received messages from staff that there was something wrong with them as individuals. These traits were either framed within a medicalization (e.g., anti-social traits) or criminalization (e.g., manipulative) framework. As was the case with Kathy, these messages served to undermine some of the girls' beliefs about whether they could abstain from drug use and stay out of trouble upon release. Girls' anxiety over their ability to be "successful" on the "outside" is merited. Recidivism is a major problem for youth involved in the juvenile justice system. Barriers to successful reentry into the community include a lack of support, a high likelihood of reengaging with negative peer influences, substance abuse relapse in the absence of ongoing treatment, family conflict, lack of a place to stay, and poor employment options (Abrams, 2007; Altschuler & Brash, 2004; Fields & Abrams, 2010).

MOVING BEYOND THE INDIVIDUAL TOWARD PROGRAMMATIC, SYSTEMIC, AND POLICY SOLUTIONS

In the previous section, I shared girls' fears, hopes, and dreams. While some were optimistic about their futures, others were anxious about being able to make it on their own upon release from the youth facility. What was perhaps most striking to me is that almost all of the young women who shared post-release plans conceptualized their efforts to stay drug- and trouble-free in individual terms. Whether or not they could succeed on the outside was largely attributed to their individual strengths and efforts to stay strong and resist temptation. For the most part, girls' beliefs that their "success" was up to them was correct given that aftercare programming for juvenile offenders is scant and only moderately effective (C. James, Stams, Asscher,

De Roo, & van der Laan, 2013). Not surprisingly, many young women end up back in the system (ADJC, 2014b). More efforts are needed to support girls upon release from youth facilities as well as preventing girls from entering the juvenile justice system in the first place.

The remainder of this chapter contains recommendations for working with system-involved girls and their families by unknotting the tangled web of systems they often find themselves in. The focus is on developing, implementing, and evaluating: 1) alternatives to court involvement and confinement, 2) evidence-based interventions that address issues that matter most to girls such as substance use/abuse and dating violence, and 3) family-based aftercare strategies and programmatic efforts. The importance of making sure that these programmatic efforts are both gender-specific and culturally tailored to address the unique needs of girls from a variety of backgrounds is stressed. Taking into account the various contexts in which girls and their families are embedded should also be a salient feature of programmatic efforts. A system-wide critical caring approach should also be adopted when working with girls and their families (González & Ayala-Alcantar, 2008). A key feature of such an approach would be developing trust-based relationships with girls and their families by not stigmatizing, blaming, and ostracizing them. The chapter concludes with a discussion of why it is important to incorporate a "family perspective" when developing criminal justice and other policies (Arditti, 2012, p. 7).

Alternatives to Court Involvement and Confinement

Girls are disproportionately arrested for status offenses (Acoca & Dedel, 1998; Chesney-Lind & Shelden, 2013). Despite the Juvenile Justice and Delinquency Prevention Act (JJDPA) and its emphasis on diverting status offenders from the juvenile justice system, girls are still entering the system for status offenses through bootstrapping and relabeling (Javdani, Sadeh, & Verona, 2011b). In the spirit of the JJDPA, a growing number of juvenile court judges have refused to use locked confinement as a sanction where the valid court order (VCO) exception is permissible. Instead, they have banded together with practitioners, providers, parents, families, and others to build community-based and family-centered programs to address the needs of youth status offenders (Coalition for Juvenile Justice Project/SOS Project, 2012). In Connecticut, for example, first-time status offenders are automatically diverted to community-based programs, or if identified as high risk, they are diverted into the state's new system of Family Support Centers (FSC) where they and their families can receive 24-hour crisis intervention, family mediation, educational advocacy, group or one-on-one therapy sessions, and if necessary, respite care for two weeks. Ohio also has implemented an alternative program called the Unruly Diversion Program, which was designed to "intercept complaints from parents about their child's behavior before they become formal charges of ungovernability/ incorrigibility" (Coalition for Juvenile Justice/SOS Project, 2012, p. 10). If parents need assistance handling their child, they can contact the court and request an intervention. Kentucky's Truancy Diversion Project is yet another example of an alternative program that diverts status offenders from the juvenile justice system. This program involves school personnel identifying truant youth and then working with them and their families to develop and meet small, achievable attendance goals. Families participating in the program also receive other mental health, counseling, drug treatment, and health services as needed. These three programs along with the other programs presented in the *Positive Power: Exercising Judicial Leadership to Prevent Court Involvement and Incarceration of Non-Delinquent Youth* represent family-centered alternatives to remanding youth status offenders to secure detention and correctional facilities. Such programs would be particularly beneficial for girls who continue to be arrested for status offenses and who are disproportionately impacted by bootstrapping and the relabeling of status offenses as violent offenses (Acoca & Dedel, 1998; Chesney-Lind & Shelden, 2013; Strom, Warner, Tichavsky, & Zahn, 2010).

Alternatives to Out-of-Home Placement

As discussed throughout this book, many girls involved in the juvenile justice system have histories of neglect and abuse, have been exposed to domestic violence and parental substance use, and have moved often in their young lives (Ryder, 2014; Schaffner, 2006). Not surprisingly, these young women often develop significant mental health and substance use/ abuse problems, which are not often addressed until they enter the juvenile justice system (Cauffman, Feldman, Waterman, & Steiner, 1998; Giaconia et al., 1995). Unfortunately, treatment and intervention options in juvenile correctional and other out-of-home facilities are often inadequate for a variety of reasons, not the least of which is funding constraints. All too often, counselors and therapists are not licensed, and in some facilities, line care staff are responsible for "counseling" youth (Tosouni, 2014). Many treatment approaches and programs currently being offered in secure juvenile correctional facilities as well as other out-of-home placements are not evidence-based nor have they been systematically evaluated (Chesney-Lind, Morash, & Stevens, 2008; Foley, 2008). Furthermore, due to significant barriers, families are rarely included in treatment efforts. Thus, I support the growing trend toward developing, implementing, and evaluating family- and community-based alternatives to out-of-home placements that go beyond individual-focused treatment.

Two family- and community-based programs, in particular, have demonstrated effectiveness in the field. The first is Multisystemic Therapy (MST), which is a family- and community-based intervention that focuses on youth with serious problems such as substance abuse who are at high risk for out-of-home placement (Henggeler, Schoenwald, Borduin, Rowland, & Cunningham, 2009). MST typically uses a home-based model of delivery, which means that youth are not separated from their parents, families, and communities. They receive intensive services with the support of a dedicated therapist who is available 24/7 to address the young person's and family's concerns. Therapists have small caseloads of four to six families, work as a team, and provide services at times convenient to the family. One of the many strengths of MST is that therapists do not stigmatize, shut out, or blame parents. In contrast, MST therapists "concentrate on empowering parents and improving their effectiveness by identifying strengths and developing natural support systems (e.g., extended family, neighbors, friends, church members) and removing barriers (e.g., parental substance abuse, high stress, poor relationships between partners)" (Office of Justice Programs, 2015).

A second program, Multidimensional Treatment Foster Care (MTFC; Chamberlain, 2003), is a family- and community-based program that addresses the needs of youth who are dually adjudicated or crossover youth. MTFC involves connecting foster care parents with a program supervisor who checks in with the family on a daily basis, individual therapy and skills/training for youth, support and parenting skills groups for foster care parents, a behavioral modification plan for youth, and monitoring of youths' academic progress. The original MTFC program was recently adapted to address the needs of girls. This newly adapted program—which includes a focus on avoiding social/relational aggression, building peer relationship skills, improving emotion regulation, avoiding risky sexual encounters, and decreasing substance use—has been found to reduce delinquency among girls in a randomized clinical trial (Leve, Chamberlain, Smith, & Harold, 2012).

Enhanced Programming in Out-of-Home Placements

While family- and community-based alternatives to out-of-home placements are preferable, this is not always possible. Many youth continue to be remanded to out-of-home placement facilities where they are isolated from their families and communities. Given this reality, evidence-based programs are urgently needed in such facilities. These programs should be gender-specific and address issues that are important to girls such as substance use, relationships, and trauma.

Gender-specific programming is a "multidimensional strength-based approach based on theoretical perspectives that consider females' pathways into the system and provide interventions that specifically address social, cultural, and psychological factors" (Wolf, Graziano, & Hartney, 2009, p. 296). Barbara Guthrie and Laurie Flinchbaugh (2001) identified the following criteria for developing and identifying gender-specific programs for girls:

1. Include girls' voices and input during program development.
2. Present girls with a safe place to express themselves without the "attention of boys."
3. Utilize peers and women facilitators to guide girls in ways that are emotionally safe and nurturing.
4. Provide girls with the opportunities to develop relationships with other girls and women.
5. Tap into girls' cultural strengths.
6. Focus on girls' emotional and physical health and relational contexts.
7. Include reference to gender, gender socialization, self-in-relation, self-efficacy, and the societal influences of racism, sexism, and classism.
8. Provide girls with opportunities to effect change at individual, relational, and community levels.

While the call for gender-specific programs in juvenile justice facilities and other out-of-home placements is not new, it has gone largely unheeded in the juvenile justice system (Chesney-Lind et al., 2008). As Allison Foley (2008, p. 263) pointed out, many existing programs for system-involved girls "do not incorporate meaningful discussions, especially deconstructions, of gender, gender roles and what it means to be a female in this (U.S.) society." Furthermore, very few of the programs that do exist have been formally evaluated (Chesney-Lind et al., 2008; Foley, 2008). A recent review of gender-specific programs for "at-risk" and delinquent girls yielded only eight programs that had been formally evaluated and presented in the published literature (Chesney-Lind et al., 2008). Of these eight programs, only two specifically served girls in the system.

While few gender-specific programs exist for girls in the juvenile justice system, even fewer address the specific needs of girls of color. Juvenile justice professionals often rely on stereotypical explanations that blame girls of color for their problems rather than considering how abuse, victimization, and trauma might have contributed to their problem behaviors (Lopez & Chesney-Lind, 2014; Pasko & Lopez, 2015). One way to better meet the needs of girls of color is to culturally tailor existing interventions. Two important reasons exist for developing or culturally adapting interventions for racial/ethnic minority groups. First, culturally tailored interventions are more likely to engage and retain ethnic minority individuals (Kumpfer, Alvarado, Smith, & Bellamy, 2002; Prado, Pantin, Schwartz, Lupei, & Szapocznik, 2006). Second, different sets of risk and protective factors are associated with risk behaviors (e.g., drug use, unprotected sexual activity) for different ethnic groups (Barrera, Castro, & Biglan, 1999). Consequently, culturally tailoring interventions to meet the needs of specific racial/ethnic groups might result in higher levels of engagement, retention, and success (Kumpfer, Alvarado, Smith, & Bellamy, 2002; Prado, Pantin, Schwartz, Lupei, & Szapocznik, 2006). Ideally, culturally tailored interventions should be based on the cultural values of the particular subgroups under study and take into account the attitudes, norms, and expectancies of this group with respect to particular behaviors. Incorporating culturally tailored and gender-specific programs within the juvenile justice system will move beyond superficial efforts and go a long way toward addressing the needs of girls of color.

Aftercare Services

Girls sometimes express anxiety about being released from out-of-home placement settings, and this was especially true for girls at Arroyo Verde who were used to a very structured routine. While some of the girls were confident about their ability to stay drug-free and not reenter the juvenile justice system, others worried about their ability to survive on the outside.

Their concerns are merited because the individual focus of most juvenile justice treatment and programming places the onus of change on the individual girl to stay away from drugs, crime, and negative peer influences. Such expectations set up many young women for failure because all too often their families need support and assistance as well.

Research indicates that aftercare programming can be moderately effective. A recent meta-analysis of 22 aftercare programs designed to reduced recidivism among juvenile and young adult offenders found that the programs had a small and positive effect on recidivism for program participants relative to juveniles and young adults who had received no aftercare or received care as usual upon reentry into the community (C. James et al., 2013). The programs with a larger proportion of minority youth had even larger effects, which suggests that aftercare programs might be particularly effective for youth of color. Unfortunately, the moderating role of gender was not examined. Of the 22 programs, none were gender-specific nor did any include girl-only participants. As mentioned earlier, girls have specific needs that should be addressed. Continued treatment for mental health and substance abuse issues should be a necessary part of aftercare programming for girls. Culturally tailored interventions that are gender-specific are also needed for girls once they reenter society. Ideally these interventions should be family-focused and evidence-based. An emphasis also should be placed on making sure that girls' services are coordinated across various contexts and systems.

ADOPTING A SYSTEM-WIDE SOCIAL JUSTICE CRITICAL CARING APPROACH

Avoiding Stigma, Developing Trust

Juvenile justice and other youth professionals often blame parents for youths' problems. They rely on stereotypes about gender, race, and class to form their impressions of youth and their parents (Gaarder, Rodriguez, & Zatz, 2004; Lopez & Chesney-Lind, 2014; Pasko & Lopez, 2015). Mothers often bear the brunt of the blame. My focus groups with clinicians at the Desert Star residential treatment center indicated that clinicians often blamed mothers for their daughters' problems. One clinician, for example, said, "I find that a lot of the (girls') moms are single themselves. They had many boyfriends, and they're looking for a man to take care of them. They have their 13-, 12-year-old daughter dating a 20-something-year-old-man, and they're fine with that. Those are the moms that I usually meet when I go to court. The ones who don't care." Another added that Latinas are "more likely than any other group to need a man to take care of them." It was clear that they attributed Latina girls' problems to cultural and gender stereotypes that present Latinas as subservient to the men in their lives, a finding that is consistent with other research on Latinas (Pasko & Lopez, 2015).

Parents can sense when juvenile justice professionals blame them for their children's problems. Several recent surveys indicate that parents often feel shamed, blamed, and stigmatized by juvenile justice professionals (Aldridge, Shute, Ralphs, & Medina, 2011; Justice for Families, 2012; Walker, Bishop, Pullmann, & Bauer, 2015). Judith Aldridge, Jon Shute, Robert Ralphs, and Juanjo Medina (2011), for example, found that parents of gang-involved youth often felt like juvenile justice professionals blamed and belittled them for not being able to control their children. Parents believed that juvenile justice professionals had no idea what it was like to parent a child who repeatedly got into trouble. Parents also touched upon how difficult it is to parent while poor and lamented that most juvenile justice professionals could not relate to their backgrounds. One parent in the Aldridge et al. study said:

> I've been to court more times with [my son] than I care to remember, yeah? You go in there and there's all these bloody solicitors and all these— magistrate or judge or whatever. And all these people are snobs. They've been to private schools [. . .]. They have no real idea of our life, they have no real idea about being poor. Whether you're poor and white, whether you're poor and Asian, whether you're poor and black, they have no idea. They've no idea what it's like to wake up fucking hungry and cold. They've no idea about having no clothes or shoes on your feet. They've no idea whatsoever. So all they see is a criminal. (p. 376)

As this example illustrates, parents often feel as if juvenile justice professionals look down upon them and blame them for their children's problems. Parents of color may feel especially stigmatized and distrustful of juvenile justice professionals due to historical and systematic racism in the justice system (Holley & VanVleet, 2006).

Research also indicates that drug-using parents whose children are under the purview of the child protective services system feel ostracized and stigmatized (Cleaver, Nicholson, Tarr, & Cleaver, 2007; Kroll & Taylor, 2003). Hedy Cleaver, Don Nicholson, Sukey Tarr, and Deborah Cleaver (2007, p. 96) asked parents to share how they felt about their treatment in the child protective services system. Parents with substance-use problems were dissatisfied with their treatment because they felt like child protective services workers did not care about their needs and feelings as parents (e.g., "I was never asked what was important to me and what help would benefit me"; "No one talked to me about my feelings. I could not tell anyone how I felt. I did not feel able to talk openly about myself.") Parents in the study by Cleaver and colleagues (2007) as well as drug-using parents in other studies fear disclosing their own drug use out of fear of losing their children (e.g., "I felt a bit worried about if I was doing anything wrong and they might take my child away"; Haight, Ostler, Black, Sheridan, & Kingery, 2007; McKeganey, Barnard, & McIntosh, 2002). As discussed in Chapter 6, drug-using parents' fears are not unfounded. Society stigmatizes drug users and this is especially true for parents who use drugs (Haight et al., 2007; McKeganey, Barnard, & McIntosh, 2002).

Many parents care about their children irrespective of their own drug use and criminal backgrounds. In many instances, mothers assume primary responsibility for their children. While some mothers had used drugs in the past, many had stopped using drugs and were attempting to prevent their daughters from following in their footsteps. In other instances, mothers did not use drugs, but had been or were currently involved with men who did use drugs and/or were violent. While mothers relied on support from relatives, they still often struggled to support their children. Although some fathers were involved in their daughters' lives, most did not live with their daughters on a consistent basis nor were they generally the ones who were primarily responsible for their daughters' care. Still, like mothers, fathers attempted to intervene in their children's lives albeit to a more limited extent. Thus, juvenile justice, child protective, and other professionals should build upon parents' strengths whenever possible and operate under the assumption that parents do care about and want the best for their children as opposed to relying on cultural deficit thinking and stereotypes when making assessments about parents' commitment to their children, and this is especially true for parents of color (Aldridge et al., 2011).

Moving beyond Cultural Competency Training

One way to enhance juvenile justice staff members' interactions and engagement efforts with parents of color is by moving beyond cultural competency training to take into account how other factors such as gender, race, ethnicity, class, and substance use influence girls' (and parents') lived experiences. In order to effectively work with system-involved girls and their families, probation officers, clinicians, direct care staff, and other youth professionals must overcome their own biases against youth and their parents. Historically, clinicians and other youth professionals have received little training to address culture beyond a superficial understanding of "cultural values" and "cultural competency training" that are specific to one racial/ethnic group (Betancourt & Green, 2010; Knox, Burkard, Johnson, Suzuki, & Ponterotto, 2003). Unfortunately, learning about a set of cultural values and behaviors that are attributed to a specific group "can lead to stereotyping and oversimplification of a culture, rather than respect for its complexity" (Betancourt & Green, 2010, p. 583). Cultural competency training should be expanded upon to help juvenile justice professionals understand how larger structural disadvantages such as social inequalities, institutional racism, patriarchy, and violence against women can shape girls' and parents' experiences. The use of pedagogical techniques that challenge juvenile justice and other youth professionals to critically reflect upon their own assumptions about race/ethnicity, gender, class, and drug use are needed. An anticipated outcome of such training would be that clinicians and other juvenile justice professionals working directly with girls from "troubled" families would stop relying on cultural deficit explanations for girls' problems in favor of a more empathetic and critical approach to care (González & Ayala-Alcantar, 2008).

Fostering Multi-Agency Collaborations

A significant portion of the girls interviewed for this study were involved in the child protective services and the behavioral health systems. Unfortunately representatives from various youth systems rarely work together on behalf of the youth in their care. Part of the reason for this lack of collaboration is that youth professionals across youth agencies and systems are often overworked and overwhelmed with large numbers of clients and caseloads (Cleaver et al., 2007). Consequently, critical aspects of young people's histories can get lost in the cracks despite the good intentions of well-meaning professionals. Turf battles, funding disputes, and different perspectives on how to address young people's needs also hinder multi-agency collaborations (Cleaver et al., 2007; L. Jones, Packard, & Nahrstedt, 2002).

Overcoming barriers to multi-agency collaboration is no easy feat; however, it is well worth the effort as enhanced collaboration and communication across systems and agencies results in better outcomes for system-involved youth and their families (Cleaver et al., 2007). One promising strategy for enhancing such collaborations is the Interdisciplinary Training Model for Collaborative Practice (IT Model) developed by an interdisciplinary group (I. Davis, Litrownick, & Weinstein, 1997) and implemented and evaluated by L. Jones, Packard, and Nahrstedt (2002). The objectives of the IT Model program are to help trainees: "1) gain interdisciplinary knowledge in the topical area of child protection and maltreatment, 2) gain knowledge of the relationship between child maltreatment, domestic violence, substance abuse, and mental health, and 3) develop attitudes and communications skills conducive to effective collaboration" (L. Jones et al., 2002, p. 24). These goals and objectives can very easily be extended to include the juvenile justice system as well as a focus on understanding how structures and systems such as economic inequities, institutional racism, and unequal gender and power relations also shape girls and their families' experiences. Attention to such factors can greatly enhance multi-agency collaboration among key players across various youth and adult systems, and such collaborations can in turn benefit system-involved girls and their families.

POLICY IMPLICATIONS AND RECOMMENDATIONS

Consistent with Joyce Arditti (2012), I am in favor of policy makers incorporating a "family perspective" when developing criminal justice and social welfare policies. Policy makers should also consider how such policies might differentially impact families of color and the communities they live in. Drug policies are a case in point. Parental drug use played a critical role in the lives of many of the young women interviewed for this book and many reported that either one or both of their parents had been jailed or incarcerated for drug use, which had a tremendous impact on the quality of girls' relationships with their parents. Not surprisingly, the vast majority of the girls interviewed for this book also struggled with their own personal addictions. The intergenerational transmission of substance use/abuse must be severed if we want to help system-involved girls and their families. Doing so requires that we destigmatize parental drug use. Destigmatizing parental drug use might make drug-using parents more likely to disclose their drug use and seek help from social services earlier rather than later (Kroll & Taylor, 2003). Policies such as the one in Tennessee that criminalizes mothers whose babies are born with drugs in their system should be abolished (ABC News, 2014). More strength-based, family-focused policies should be developed to support drug-using parents in their efforts to stay sober and clean for the sake of their children. As demonstrated throughout this book, most system-involved girls love their parents and are deeply attached to them. Their parents also seem to care about them in turn. Yet, despite parents' love for their children, their drug use and associated behaviors often place their children in harm's way (DeWit, 1998; Kroll & Taylor, 2003; National Center on Addiction and Substance Abuse, 1999; Rhodes, Bernays, & Houmoller, 2010). If parents seek assistance earlier, then perhaps the intergenerational transmission of drug use can be severed.

CONCLUSION

The stories of 65 system-involved girls who used drugs were shared in this book. The main focus was to better understand how girls' relationships with parents—many of whom were current or former drug users—shaped their early lives and set the stage for their eventual involvement in the juvenile justice system. In attempting to present these girls' narratives, I had to walk a tightrope between acknowledging the role that parents played in girls' lives while avoiding the tendency to stigmatize and blame them for their daughters' problems. This was a tough balance to maintain, and I am not sure I always succeeded. After all, system-involved girls are often neglected, abused, and traumatized at the hands of their parents (Acoca, 1998; Chesney-Lind & Shelden, 2013; Lederman, Dakof, Larrea, & Li, 2004). Thus, while I advocate for a family-focused approach, I also recognize the importance of privileging girls' emotional well-being and physical safety over that of their parents', especially in extreme cases of neglect and abuse. In other instances, which make up the majority of cases, I advocate in favor of supporting parents in their efforts to more effectively parent their daughters.

This book also situated girls' experiences within and across various contexts. Consistent with ecological systems theory, system-involved girls' experiences are situated within a larger set of interlocking contexts and systems. In turn, their relationships with parents, romantic partners, and clinicians are situated within these larger contexts and systems. A critical need exists to develop context-specific interventions that move beyond placing the onus of change on individual girls. Strategies for enhancing parental involvement in the juvenile justice system are also needed to improve system-involved girls' developmental outcomes. Juvenile correctional facilities should develop more family-friendly policies and practices and provide enhanced cultural competency training for all juvenile justice professionals. At the agency-level, stronger and more sustainable interagency partnerships and collaborations between and across youth and adult serving systems and agencies are needed. Finally, policy makers should incorporate a family perspective when creating policies (e.g., sentencing laws, immigration laws) with special attention focused on how these proposed policies might disproportionately impact families and communities of color (Arditti, 2012).

As I conclude this book, I remain hopeful that we, as a society, can do a much better job at addressing the needs of system-involved girls. That is why I devoted so much time and space in this final chapter to discussing how we can better meet the needs of this underserved population of youth. I hope this book will provide students, practitioners, researchers, policy makers, and others with a deeper appreciation of system-involved girls' lived experiences while also inspiring them to do the type of groundbreaking, social justice-oriented work that is critical if we are to more systematically and effectively address the diverse needs of these young women and their families.

APPENDIX A
DOING RESEARCH WITH
SYSTEM-INVOLVED GIRLS

Gaining access to system-involved girls was no easy feat as they are considered a vulnerable population due to their involvement in these various youth systems. Since the interviews took place between 2006 and 2013 in a variety of out-of-home placement facilities, I had to obtain permission from multiple agencies, stakeholders, and my university Institutional Review Board (IRB) for each series of interviews. To maintain confidentiality, I assigned pseudonyms to study participants, the people they referenced in their interviews, the out-of-home placement facilities they lived in, and the broader county and state youth systems they were embedded in. And, with the exception of self-identified racial/ethnic identities and ages, I also altered the physical descriptions for all girls in order to further safeguard their anonymity. All interviews were audiorecorded and transcribed verbatim.

PHASE 1

The first series of interviews took place between 2006 and 2007 at Arroyo Verde, the state correctional facility for girls. After a year and a half, I was finally granted access by the Arizona Department of Juvenile Corrections to interview girls at the facility. Despite my request for a parental consent waiver, the Arizona Department of Juvenile Corrections refused to let me conduct interviews unless the girls' parents or legal guardians consented. The agency also limited the number of interviews I could conduct to 25, and only allowed me to conduct 1 to 2 interviews per week on Saturday and Sunday mornings. The Arizona Department of Juvenile Corrections provided me with a master list of girls' parents' names and home addresses. Upon receiving this contact information, I mailed an information letter explaining the purpose of the study, a parental consent form, a document from the Arizona Department of Juvenile Corrections endorsing the study, and a stamped return envelope to girls' parents/guardians. Parents were told that the study was about girls' experiences leading up to their involvement in the juvenile justice system. I emphasized that information obtained from their daughters would contribute to a greater understanding of why girls end up in juvenile correctional settings, information that could potentially help other girls in the future. Unfortunately, due to agency restrictions, I was unable to provide compensation for girls who participated in the study. These interviews—along with the other interviews that I conducted for this book—usually lasted between 90 minutes and 2 hours, but some were longer.

The interview consisted of two parts. Part one consisted of collecting pertinent demographic data (i.e., race/ethnicity, age, family composition, parenting status) and legal background information on girls and their parents (i.e., personal as well as parental drug use, parental incarceration) via a standard form. The second part consisted of open-ended questions. I asked girls to describe their experiences leading up to their involvement in the juvenile justice system. The girls at Arroyo Verde spent a lot of time talking about drugs and their relationships with parents and partners. They also talked a lot about their experiences at Arroyo Verde. While a few girls were hesitant to share personal details about their lives, most talked quite openly about why and how they ended up in the juvenile justice system. During these interviews, I often found myself sitting and listening while girls jumped from one subject to another. They were eager to share and often viewed the interview as a means to alleviate the boredom of spending an otherwise dull Saturday or Sunday on their units. I was willing to let them share what was important to them without interference on my part. Given that their relationships with parents played such a critical role in their life stories, I decided to conduct additional interviews with other system-involved girls to learn more about how family relationships shaped their early childhood experiences, and how these experiences in turn influenced their future involvement in the juvenile justice system. I also sought to include additional questions about how they thought their relationships with parents impacted their relationships with others (e.g., partners, youth professionals).

PHASE 2

From 2010–2011, with funding from a National Institute of Mental Health (NIMH) subcontract, my graduate research assistants and I interviewed an additional 18 girls living at the Desert Star residential treatment center. Given that the NIMH subcontract stipulated that my research focus on an underserved minority population, I only included Latina girls at this site. Like the girls at Arroyo Verde, the girls at the Desert Star facility had histories of drug use and current or prior involvement in the juvenile justice system.

Gaining access to girls at Desert Star was much easier than gaining access at Arroyo Verde and I was fortunate to have staff support in part because of my service on the Arizona Girls Roundtable (AGR) steering committee, an organization whose mission was to bring together girl-serving agencies for collaboration and networking and to develop a collective vision for girls in Arizona. My affiliation with the AGR no doubt contributed to my success at garnering agency support and access to study participants. Thus, the clinical director and the intake staff members at Desert Star were motivated to partner with me on this project. Their assistance was instrumental in recruiting participants and collecting parental consent and teen assent forms, which made the recruitment and interviewing processes much easier than it had been at Arroyo Verde.

During this second round of interviews at Desert Star, I expanded upon my earlier interview protocol that I had used at Arroyo Verde, by including a number of open-ended questions about girls' relationships with parents and romantic partners in addition to specific demographic and legal history questions. As with the first series of interviews at Arroyo Verde, girls were eager to share their insights into how their relationships with parents and partners influenced their lives, including their eventual decisions to use drugs and commit delinquent acts.

I also conducted focus groups with 19 drug-involved Latina girls who were attending a charter school for "high-risk" youth at Desert Star and 8 clinicians who worked with Latina girls. The charter school was located on the same campus as the residential treatment center. Girls who were interviewed for the study were not included in the focus groups. During these focus groups, I asked both adolescent and adult participants to discuss how gender and ethnicity shaped Latina girls' experiences leading up to their involvement in the juvenile justice system as well as how they are treated once they are in the system. (More information about the focus groups can be found in Lopez & Chesney-Lind, 2014.)

PHASE 3

From 2012–2013, with funding from an ASU seed grant, I conducted 22 qualitative interviews with drug-involved girls living in three group homes referred to in this book as Moonlight, Green River, and Oak Canyon. Gaining access to these young women was initially quite challenging, as I had to rely on community contacts to distribute recruitment flyers at their agencies. Fortunately, several months into the recruitment phase, one of my community contacts invited me to present my study to a bimonthly group he ran for system-involved youth. Armed with recruitment flyers, I attended the group and was surprised to find between 50 and 65 youth in attendance, about half of whom were young women. I presented my study, answered questions, and passed out recruitment flyers. After the meeting several young women approached me to schedule an interview. Soon after I began receiving texts from other young women interested in participating in the study. Through word of mouth and repeated visits to the bimonthly group, I was able to recruit and interview 22 young women. Unlike the other girls interviewed for this book, these girls were involved in the child protective services system. Given that the girls were under the care of the child protective services system, parental and legal guardian consent was waived. The interview protocol remained exactly the same as the one I used at Desert Star.

DIFFERENCES ACROSS OUT-OF-HOME PLACEMENT SITES

It is important to emphasize that while all girls interviewed for this book shared certain backgrounds—drug use, involvement with the juvenile justice system, court ordered to live in an out-of-home placement facility—they did vary in terms of how many systems they were involved in as well as the types of facilities they were living in at the time of the study.

In Arizona, both the juvenile justice system and the child protective services system can court order youth to live in an out-of-home placement facility (Northern Arizona Regional Behavioral Health Authority, 2014). These placements can be county or state-run placements such as detention and juvenile correctional facilities or they can be operated within the community by private nonprofit agencies that contract with the state to provide treatment and care for youth involved in the juvenile justice system, the child protective services system, or both.

States vary in terms of how they refer to various youth out-of-home placement facilities. Arizona refers to Level 1 facilities as residential treatment centers, Level 2 facilities as therapeutic group homes, and Level 3 facilities as behavioral health group homes. Other states refer to therapeutic group homes as residential treatment centers. In this study, I refer to Level 2 facilities as residential treatment centers and Level 3 facilities as group homes in order to avoid confusing the two types of "group home" sites. Interviews for this study took place across five different sites: the Moonlight, Green River, and Oak Canyon group homes, the Desert Star residential treatment center, and the Arroyo Verde correctional school for girls.

The Moonlight, Green River, and Oak Canyon group homes were houses located in the suburbs and from the outside looked like every other house on the street. Direct care staff (all women) staffed the group homes around the clock. Girls who lived in the group homes were able to attend school in the community and were often visited by caseworkers and probation officers who sometimes transported girls off-site to visit with parents and therapists. The Desert Star residential treatment center was more secure and was located in the middle of a large city. Girls lived on-site in cottages and were allowed to earn the privilege of visiting their families on the weekend. Unlike the girls in the group homes, the girls in residential treatment attended school on-site and had a full schedule of therapeutic activities. The Arroyo Verde correctional facility was a youth prison that was located on the outskirts of a large city far away from most of the girls' homes. Girls were not allowed to leave the facility and were cared for by a variety of staff including security, line, and clinical staff. Family members were allowed to visit during set times. All three settings had strict rules and schedules.

INTERVIEW THEMES

This study focused primarily on girls' relationships with parents because I wanted to determine how these relationships qualitatively influenced girls' other relationships and experiences over time and across contexts and systems. Major themes included: 1) Relationships with Mothers During Childhood and Adolescence, 2) Relationships with Fathers During Childhood and Adolescence; 3) Relationships with Romantic/Sexual Partners (On the Streets, Drug Use Contexts); 4) Relationships with Clinicians (Youth Facilities); 5) Drug Use Experiences; 6) Running Away Experiences; and 7) Future Aspirations Upon Release from Youth Facility. Each of these major themes had multiple subthemes, which are presented throughout the book. Throughout the analysis, I consciously attended to how girls' relationships manifested across various contexts and systems as well as how girls' relationships and experiences in general were racialized, gendered, classed, and aged.

APPENDIX B
STUDY PARTICIPANTS

Name	Setting	Age	Ethnicity
Elana	Arroyo Verde	16	Puerto Rican
Isabel	Moonlight	16	Mexican American
Savannah	Arroyo Verde	17	Mexican American
Richelle	Moonlight	14	Mexican American
Xochitl	Oak Canyon	14	Mexican American
Janee	Green River	16	Mexican American
Melanie	Oak Canyon	17	White
Connie	Desert Star	16	Mexican American
Christine	Green River	15	White
Annie	Desert Star	17	Mexican American
Paige	Green River	15	White
Lexus	Arroyo Verde	14	White
Dee	Oak Canyon	16	White
Bianca	Desert Star	17	Mexican American
Lydia	Desert Star	14	Mexican American
Dolores	Green River	15	White
Olivia	Desert Star	16	Mexican American
Claudia	Arroyo Verde	17	Mexican American
Ophelia	Moonlight	15	Mexican American
Delia	Arroyo Verde	15	Mexican American
Jordan	Desert Star	14	Mexican American
Shannon	Oak Canyon	17	White
Debbie	Arroyo Verde	16	Mexican American
Dulce	Green River	14	Mexican American
Jessica	Desert Star	15	Mexican American
Renee	Arroyo Verde	17	Mexican American
Sandra	Desert Star	15	Mexican American
Karina	Desert Star	16	Mexican American
Julia	Desert Star	16	Mexican American

(continued)

Name	Setting	Age	Ethnicity
Ashley	Desert Star	16	Mexican American
Clarissa	Arroyo Verde	15	White
Gina	Arroyo Verde	14	Mexican American
Brianna	Arroyo Verde	17	Biracial
Yesenia	Arroyo Verde	16	Mexican American
Anique	Oak Canyon	17	Biracial
Selena	Arroyo Verde	17	Mexican American
Christina	Arroyo Verde	14	White
Tara	Arroyo Verde	17	Mexican American
Deanna	Arroyo Verde	15	Mexican American
Liza	Oak Canyon	16	White
Eva	Desert Star	17	Mexican American
Alana	Oak Canyon	16	Biracial
Nina	Desert Star	14	Mexican American
Nora	Green River	17	Mexican American
Angelina	Desert Star	15	Mexican American
Simone	Desert Star	15	Mexican American
Annette	Green River	15	White
Magda	Moonlight	17	White
Courtney	Moonlight	16	Mexican American
Melissa	Desert Star	14	Mexican American
Samantha	Arroyo Verde	17	White
Lindsay	Arroyo Verde	17	White
Catalina	Arroyo Verde	17	Biracial
Crystal	Arroyo Verde	15	White
Victoria	Desert Star	16	Mexican American
Nia	Arroyo Verde	17	White
Erin	Desert Star	18	Mexican American
Desiree	Moonlight	14	Mexican American
Kathy	Arroyo Verde	17	Mexican American
Talitia	Arroyo Verde	16	Biracial
Cindy	Arroyo Verde	16	Mexican American
Sharon	Arroyo Verde	16	Biracial
Gloria	Green River	16	Mexican American
Lolo	Green River	15	Mexican American
Quinn	Arroyo Verde	17	White

ACKNOWLEDGMENTS

When I started graduate school in 1994, I chose to focus on "gangs and juvenile delinquency" because I wanted to better understand what had led my brother down this path. During those early years as a graduate student, I read everything I could on delinquency and ended up writing a dissertation on adolescent boys' delinquent events under the guidance of my mentor Dr. Edmund Emmer who inadvertently placed me on an interdisciplinary track when he recommended that I read widely across a number of disciplines beginning with the classics.

Several years later, I began this study of girls. As a school psychologist, I never envisioned writing a book, but after many talks with my mentor and close friend, Dr. Cecilia Menjivar, I set out to do just that. Thanks to Cecilia, I wrote a very rough draft of this manuscript over the course of several months, polished it off, and sent it to various presses. I was very happy when Rutgers University Press via my wonderful editor, Peter Mickulas, offered me a book contract. As I continued revising the manuscript, Cecilia encouraged me every step of the way and believed in this project even when I did not, and for that, I am forever grateful.

In addition to Drs. Emmer and Menjivar, I would like to acknowledge several mentors and scholars who shaped my early career. I would like to thank my high school teachers at Jesse H. Jones in Houston, Texas. As a first-generation college student, I was fortunate to be accepted into the Houston Independent School District's Vanguard Program. Although I loved all my teachers, the following teachers had a profound impact on my development, and I remain in contact with most of them: Ms. Jan Brisack, Dr. Richard Doina, Mr. Jon Mallam, and the late Mr. Wayne Martin.

I also had a number of fabulous professors at the University of Texas at Austin where I earned all of my degrees. The late Dr. Dev Singh, a professor of psychology, inspired me to become a psychologist. Dr. Manuel Ramirez, who I affectionately refer to as my "academic father," deserves much gratitude for being my mentor and friend over the past 24 years. Dr. Mark Roosa also deserves a big thank you for being my mentor while I was a post-doc at Arizona State University.

I also would like to thank several feminist scholars who greatly impacted this work. A big thank you to Dr. Joanne Belknap for all her guidance, encouragement, and support. Joanne read multiple versions of this manuscript and was always gracious with her time and feedback. I am also grateful to Drs. Meda Chesney-Lind and Lisa Pasko who share a passion for studying girls' issues. Thank you also to my other criminologist friends for their support and friendship: Drs. Robert Duran, Wilson Palacios, Hillary Potter, Anthony Peguero, and Marjorie Zatz.

Through the years, I have been involved as a research affiliate or fellow in several research groups/centers. These affiliations informed, and in some cases, funded the research conducted for this book. I want to give my HIV Intervention Science Training Program (HISTP) colleagues a special shout out for their support, but I would like to personally acknowledge Dr. Rosalie Corona for being an amazing friend, colleague, and scholar. Thank you also to Drs. Nabila El Bassel and Elwin Wu at Columbia University who awarded me an NIMH subcontract to interview and conduct focus groups with Latina girls at the Desert Star Residential Treatment Center. I am also grateful for the support of Drs. Lalo Valdez, Charlie Kaplan, Alice Cepeda, and the National Hispanic Science Network Summer Training Institute. At ASU, I would like to thank Drs. Patricia Dustman, Wendy Wolfersteig, Flavio Marsiglia, and Kate Hamm from the Southwest Interdisciplinary Research Center. Thank you also to Dr. Victor Agadjanian, the former director of ASU's Center for Population Dynamics (CPD), whose center provided me with a seed grant to fund the costs associated with the group home interviews.

As a scholar, I am fortunate to work in a dynamic school with great colleagues. Many of my colleagues in ASU's School of Social Transformation have also become my friends and have shaped how I view the world. Thank you to every one of them, but especially my friends Alesha Durfee, Mary Margaret Fonow, Chris Holman, Sujey "Wonder Woman" Vega, Nancy Jurik, Gray Cavender, Lisa Anderson, Beth Swadener, Gabriel Escontrias, Heather Switzer, and H.L.T. Quan. Thank you also to my doctoral students and mentees Lidia Nuno, Sue Micetic, and Katherine Maldonado for our shared discussions on all things related to youth and justice.

In addition to my academic friends and colleagues, I would like to thank my running and triathlon buddies for their support, friendship, and laughter: Cindy Rash, Brian Smith, Lito Silla, Magda Johnson, Nora Carrillo,

Jim Hall, Tyson Koerper, Sharon Berger, and Damarys and Michael Nimeth. Thank you to Racelab coach Bettina Warnholtz who taught me how to be an endurance athlete; writing this book was definitely a test of endurance. A big thank you to my buddies at Runner's Den and the Easy Breezy Running Group, especially Ron French and Craig Davidson. Coach Dean Hebert also deserves a very special mention. Not only does Dean push me at track, but he has also helped me become a more mentally tough athlete, and by extension, scholar.

Of course, I am very grateful to the support of my husband, Maurice Valdez, who encouraged me to write this book. His unwavering love, support, and encouragement propelled me along this journey. Annie Buentello deserves special mention for keeping me entertained via her funny Facebook posts while I spent many lonely hours writing this book. I am forever grateful to and in awe of my mom, Olivia Murley, for being such a resilient powerful force in the face of many adversities. Thank you also to my two younger brothers, Joe and Steven Lopez. My furry buddies also deserve a shout out for keeping me company while I wrote this book.

I owe the biggest thank you of all to the young women who shared their stories with me. Sharing the most intimate details of your life is never easy, and I commend them for their courage. I learned so much from these strong, powerful, and resilient young women, and I sincerely hope that I have done their stories justice. I am also incredibly grateful for the support of the agencies and staff members who supported and contributed to this research.

Finally, I would like to point out that the research for this book took place in three different stages across five different youth facilities. Chapter 3 draws largely upon a previously published article in the *Journal of Family Issues* (2012), while Chapter 4 builds upon an article that was published in *Violence Against Women* (2012). Portions of Deanna's story previously appeared in a 2009 *Family Relations* article. Full citations for all three articles are in the reference list. I thank the reviewers and editors whose feedback informed these articles and ultimately this book.

NOTES

INTRODUCTION

1. I recognize that the DSM–V no longer uses the terms Substance Abuse and Substance Dependence (see http://www.samhsa.gov/disorders/substance-use) and now classifies substance use in terms of severity (mild, moderate, or severe). In this study, both the girls and their parents used a number of "hard" drugs in addition to alcohol and marijuana. The most frequently reported drug of choice for girls as well as parents (based on girls' reports) was methamphetamine and this was true irrespective of race/ethnicity. Cocaine was the second most frequently reported drug. Given that both girls and parents used "hard" drugs, I suspect they would have been classified as at least substance abusers based on the older DSM criteria. Still, I cannot say that definitively since I did not formally assess girls or their parents. Thus, in this book, I use the terms *drug use* and *substance use* to describe both girls' and their parents' use of drugs. When discussing other research, I use the terms that the researchers used in their manuscripts.

CHAPTER 1 GROWING UP IN A "DYSFUNCTIONAL" FAMILY

1. Not all girls were able to recall positive memories of their parents. As will be demonstrated in the next two chapters, a few girls were very angry with their parents. This was especially true for girls who reported being physically abused by their fathers.
2. Gross (1987) found that even children who considered stepparents family made qualifying statements about how their stepparents were not full parents. In a more recent study, only about one-fifth of adult children perceived current stepparents to be full parents whereas one third saw them as at least partial parents, and about one half did not see them as parents at all (Schmeeckle, Giarrusso, Feng, & Bengston, 2006). While these adult children were willing to concede that stepparents were family, they were less likely to view them as parents.
3. Some of the young women viewed their involvement in the child protective services system as a parental decision. Unfortunately because I was unable to triangulate their data with case files, I cannot judge the veracity of these statements. Nevertheless, I am fairly certain that these young women believed what they told me, and it is their perceptions that matter most.

CHAPTER 3 DADDY'S LITTLE GIRL: FEELING REJECTED, ABANDONED, AND UNLOVED

1. The structure of girls' families changed constantly and men other than biological fathers assumed partial parenting duties at various times throughout girls' lives. These

men included mothers' boyfriends, husbands, and male family members. In this book, I refer to biological fathers (or adoptive fathers) as fathers primarily because these were the men that girls spent most of the time talking about in the interviews. Girls' attachments to biological fathers were based in large part on their beliefs about the role that fathers should play in their daughters' lives.

2. According to the ARC report, the "287(g) program establishes agreements between ICE and a local police department that gives that department the authority to essentially act as ICE agents—questioning people about their immigration status and detaining them until ICE can take custody. Effectively, the program empowers local police officers to turn an alleged traffic violation or an arrest of any kind into an immigration enforcement operation" (Wessler, 2011, p. 11; see this report for more information about how ICE works with local law enforcement agencies to apprehend and detain noncitizens).

3. These data were previous previously presented in Lopez & Corona (2012) in the *Journal of Family Issues*. The full citation can be found in the references.

CHAPTER 4   LOOKING FOR LOVE IN ALL THE WRONG PLACES

1. Teen dating violence is a type of interpersonal partner violence that occurs between two people in a close relationship, and it can be physical, emotional, or sexual. Physical violence consists of pinching, shoving, hitting, slapping, or kicking. Emotional violence can include "threatening a partner or harming his or her sense of self-worth" (CDC, 2014, p. 1). Examples of emotional violence include bullying/shaming, embarrassing on purpose, and keeping someone away from friends and family. Sexual violence is defined as forcing a partner to engage in a sex act without their consent (CDC, 2014). Stalking is also a form of teen dating violence.

2. Not all girls interviewed for this book identified as heterosexual. Several also identified as bisexual or lesbians. Some of the girls were involved in same-sex relationships while living in out-of-home placements, but had never been involved with a same-sex partner "on the outside." None of the girls shared any stories about a controlling or abusive same-sex partner; however, it may be that they were not comfortable sharing this aspect of their lives. I also did not specifically ask girls to disclose information about same-sex partners, which is an unfortunate limitation of this study.

3. Portions of these data and analyses were previously published in *Violence Against Women*. See Lopez, Chesney-Lind, & Foley (2012).

4. All girls at the residential treatment center and group homes were asked about who typically maintained the most power in their relationships. I did not ask this question of the girls at Arroyo Verde.

5. Girls typically used passive language when talking about their virginity. They referred to "losing their virginity" or their boyfriends "taking their virginity." This language suggests that girls may not believe that engaging in sexual intercourse for the first time is entirely up to them or they may be hesitant to admit they wanted to engage in sex

due to the stigma associated with girls' wanting to have sex for pleasure (see Tolman, 2009).

6. The term Marianismo refers to an idealized version of Latinas. Characteristics of the idealized Latina include being "submissive to the demands of men, [willing to] withstand extreme sacrifices and suffering for the sake of the family, and [acting] like the Virgin Mary who is viewed as virginally pure and non-sexual" (Castillo, Perez, Castillo, & Ghosheh, 2010, p. 164).

7. These young women were first-generation Mexican Americans meaning that their parents were born in Mexico.

8. Simone's boyfriend also regularly cheated on her, which further eroded Simone's self-esteem and compromised her physical health when she contracted a sexually transmitted infection. She said, "I knew he was talking to other girls besides me. He always liked to have sex without a condom, and I knew that it was gonna cause me a problem, which it did, when I went to the clinic, they determined I had a STD, and I had Chlamydia . . . . I'm clean now, so that's good, but then he got with one of my friends, and he got her pregnant, so that was it. I broke up with him. I was like, 'I can't deal with it' so I just broke up with him."

CHAPTER 5 DOING DRUGS: THE GOOD, THE BAD, AND THE UGLY

1. With the exception of Lindsay, girls who reported conflict with parents were usually referring to conflicts with mothers most likely because most of them did not live with their biological fathers. It should be noted that some girls also reported conflicts with their mother's partners, though.

2. Like many sexual abuse victims, Paige did not initially disclose the abuse. It was not until Paige was in therapy that she told her mother. She said, "When I first told her it was about a year ago, and it was with my therapist and her, and at first she didn't believe me, but we came back [to therapy], and I mentioned it again. She told me how she just didn't believe it at first because she didn't want to admit it and she felt like a really bad mom." At the time of our interview, Paige was in therapy and working through past traumas and only had sporadic phone contact with her mother.

3. Portions of Deanna's story were previously published in a 2009 *Family Relations* article. See Lopez, Katsulis, & Robillard (2009) for full citation.

CHAPTER 7 PROPERTY OF THE STATE:
LOCKED UP, LOCKED OUT, AND IN NEED OF TREATMENT

1. One area of particular relevance for girls concerns status offenses, which constitute behaviors that are illegal for youth, but not adults (Chesney-Lind & Shelden, 2013). Examples of status offenses include running away from home or foster care, habitual truancy, and incorrigibility or behavior found to be beyond the control of parents/guardians. Recognizing that status offenses are often "manifestations of underlying

personal, familial, community, and systemic issues," Congress passed the Juvenile Justice and Delinquency Prevention Act (JJDPA) in 1974 (Peck, Leiber, & Brubaker, 2013). The JJDPA placed greater restrictions on the arrest and incarceration of status offenders. While the JJDPA initially had positive results for girls, these effects were short-lived. In 1980, Congress amended the JJDPA with the valid court order (VCO) protection exception. The VCO gave "judges and others the option of placing adjudicated status offenders in locked detention if they violated a VCO, or direct order from the court, such as 'stop running away' or 'attend school regularly'" (Coalition for Juvenile Justice Project/SOS Project, 2012, p. 3). This process of rearresting or incarcerating status offenders for violating a court order has negatively impacted girls whose status offenses often lead to formal juvenile court processing (Dohrn, 2004; Javdani, Sadeh, & Verona, 2011b).

2. Internalizing disorders include affective and mood disorders such as generalized anxiety disorder and major depressive disorder. Externalizing disorders include conduct disorder, attention deficit hyperactivity disorder, and oppositional defiant disorder. The Diagnostic and Statistic Manual of Mental Disorders (Versions I–V) contains descriptions and criteria associated with these various "disorders."

3. Description from news report: "The girl has a history of pulling out chunks of her own hair and drawing on the walls with her feces and blood, then wiping herself with pages she's ripped from a Bible. And she's a cutter. The scars from her self-abuse are visible on her arms and legs. She clearly requires constant supervision, but on September 21, staff at the [Arizona Department of Juvenile Corrections] facility in Phoenix left the girl alone in a bathroom for at least eight minutes. When a guard finally asked what was taking so long, the girl replied that she was constipated. She emerged from the stall covered in blood and deep cuts she'd made on both arms with a piece of a broken light bulb, then ran through the grounds with blood squirting everywhere."

4. The state agency that operates Arroyo Verde is no stranger to bad press, controversy, and lawsuits. In the past several decades, the state agency was the target of two federal investigations looking into possible civil rights violations (Decker et al., 2013). In April of 2002, July of 2002, and March of 2003, three boys committed suicide at Mesa Roja, the boys' correctional school next door to Arroyo Verde. In 2002, as a result of allegations of improper care and the high suicide rate, the Department of Justice (DOJ) began an investigation of all juvenile correctional schools operated by the agency. Alleged violations included "abuse, poor living conditions, inadequate education, poor mental health treatment, insufficient supervision, and failure to prevent suicide of youth in custody" (Decker et al., 2013, p. 6). Upon the conclusion of its investigation, the DOJ found that youth confined at the state schools "suffer harm or the risk of harm from constitutional deficiencies in the facilities' suicide prevention measures, correctional practices, and medical and mental health care services" (Acosta, 2004, p. 2).

Following the DOJ investigation, the U.S. Attorney General's office filed a lawsuit against the state agency in 2004 (Decker et al., 2013). At that time, the state agency entered into a consent decree with the DOJ. As part of the consent decree, the Arizona Department of Juvenile Corrections agreed to make significant reforms to address the needs of youth in its care. A subsequent investigation completed by the Auditor General in 2009 revealed that the Arizona Department of Juvenile Corrections was compliant in initiating and sustaining several reforms over time, including increased training of staff and monitoring of suicidal juveniles, an improved grievance process for reporting abuses committed by staff, and a zero tolerance policy for abuse (Decker et al., 2013).

5. While it is possible that staff might have altered their behaviors around me, it is unlikely because I was not there as a researcher. I was just another clinical intern who was there to meet with the girls on her caseload. The frontline and security staff were used to seeing clinical interns given the stage agency's partnership with a local clinical psychology training program that regularly assigned graduate students to work at Arroyo Verde as part of their practicum requirements.

6. Craven, Brown, & Gilchrist (2006) provide this definition in their article on the sexual grooming of children: "The process by which a child is befriended by a would-be abuser in an attempt to gain the child's confidence and trust, enabling them to get the child to acquiesce to abusive activity. It is frequently a pre-requisite for an abuser to gain access to a child" (p. 288). Note that the trainer at Arroyo Verde used this term to refer to adolescents grooming adults.

7. Program staff include youth program officers (staff who work as case managers), youth corrections officers (staff responsible for monitoring safety), psychology associates (staff who assists with treatment and assessment).

8. I created a code called "therapy talk" that consisted of terms like "criminal thinking," "compulsive thinking," and "the disease of addiction." I often found that these types of terms seeped through the girls' narratives.

CHAPTER 8 MOVING BEYOND THE INDIVIDUAL TOWARD PROGRAMMATIC, SYSTEMIC, AND POLICY SOLUTIONS

1. In 2003, I taught a summer course on youth and justice with a special emphasis on juvenile delinquency and the juvenile justice system. My undergraduate class had spent the first part of that scorching summer reading journal articles on juvenile delinquency. Toward the end of the course, my students were well-acquainted with theories of delinquency and crime. They had read national reports on youth offending, critiqued juvenile justice policies, and reviewed theories of crime causation. Yet, I did not feel as if they had truly connected with the lives of young people caught up in the system. For them, youth and justice was just another class, one more upper-division requirement to fulfill. That is why I decided to arrange a field trip to two state juvenile correctional facilities. My goal was to inspire my students to connect with incarcerated youth in a real world setting as opposed to just reading statistics about them in journal articles and national reports.

After talking with staff at two local state juvenile correctional facilities, I arranged for the male undergraduates to visit Mesa Roja (boys-only facility) and for the female undergraduates to visit Arroyo Verde. In collaboration with teachers at both facilities, I divided the undergraduate and incarcerated students into pairs. Each pair had to create a written piece on whatever topic they wanted to write about. I include some of these pieces in this chapter.

2. Data on recidivism rates for girls is scarce. According to the 2014 ADJC Recidivism Fact Sheet, approximately 46% of youth recidivated within three years of release. For 2012, the recidivism rate for girls was 25%, down from 37% in 2011. The recidivism rate was "measured by the occurrence of a new, subsequent offense or commitment leading to the second adjudication or commitment."

REFERENCES

ABC News. (2014, July 13). First woman charged on controversial law that criminalizes drug use during pregnancy. Retrieved from http://abcnews.go.com/US/woman-charged-controversial-law-criminalizes-drug-pregnancy/story?id=24542754.

Abram, K. M., Teplin, L. A., Charles, D. R., Longworth, S. L., McClelland, G. M., & Dulcan, M. K. (2004). Posttraumatic stress disorder and trauma in youth in juvenile detention. *Archives of General Psychiatry, 61*, 403–410.

Abram, K. M., Teplin, L. A., McClelland, G. M., & Dulcan, M. K. (2003). Comorbid psychiatric disorders in youth in juvenile detention. *Archives of General Psychiatry, 60*, 1097–1108.

Abrams, L. S. (2007). From corrections to community: Youth offenders' perceptions of the challenges of transition. *Journal of Offender Rehabilitation, 44*, 31–53.

Acoca, L. (1998). Outside/inside: The violation of American girls at home, on the streets and in the juvenile justice system. *Crime & Delinquency, 44*, 561–589.

Acoca, L. (2004). Are those cookies for me or my baby? Understanding detained and incarcerated teen mothers and their children. *Juvenile and Family Court Journal, 55*, 65–80.

Acoca, L., & Dedel, K. (1998). *No place to hide: Understanding and meeting the needs of girls in the California juvenile justice system.* San Francisco, CA: National Council on Crime and Delinquency.

Acosta, A. (2004). *CRIPA investigation of Adobe Mountain School and Black Canyon School in Phoenix, Arizona, and Catalina Mountain in Tucson, Arizona.* U.S. Department of Justice. Retrieved from http://www.justice.gov/crt/about/spl/documents/ariz_findings.pdf.

Aldridge, J., Shute, J., Ralphs, R., & Medina, J. (2011). Blame the parents? Challenges for parent-focused programmes for families of gang-involved young people. *Children & Society, 25*, 371–381.

Allard, P. (2002). *Life sentences: Denying welfare benefits to women convicted of drug offenses.* Washington, DC: Sentencing Project.

Altschuler, D. M., & Brash, R. (2004). Adolescent and teenage offenders confronting the challenges and opportunities of reentry. *Youth Violence and Juvenile Justice, 2*, 72–87.

Amaro, H., & Raj, A. (2000). On the margin: Power and women's HIV risk reduction strategies. *Sex Roles, 42*, 723–749.

Arditti, J. A. (2012). *Parental incarceration and the family: Psychological and social effects of imprisonment on children, parents, and caregivers.* New York: New York University Press.

Arditti, J., Burton, L., & Neeves-Botelho, S. (2010). Maternal distress and parenting in the context of cumulative disadvantage. *Family Process, 49*, 142–164.

Arditti, J. A., Smock, S. A., & Parkman, T. S. (2005). "It's been hard to be a father": A qualitative exploration of incarcerated fatherhood. *Fathering, 3*, 267–283.

Arizona Department of Juvenile Corrections. (2010). *Arizona Department of Juvenile Corrections Annual Report: FY 2010*. Retrieved from http://www.azdjc.gov/FactsNews/ADJCPublications/Annual%20Report%202010.pdf.

Arizona Department of Juvenile Corrections. (2012). *Arizona Department of Juvenile Corrections Five Year Strategic Plan: FY 2013–FY 2017*. Retrieved from http://www.azdjc.gov/FactsNews/ADJCPublications/SP%202013-2017.pdf.

Arizona Department of Juvenile Corrections. (2014a). *Family Handbook*. Retrieved from http://www.azdjc.gov/FamilyServices/HandbookFamily.pdf.

Arizona Department of Juvenile Corrections. (2014b). *2014 ADJC recidivism fact sheet*. Retrieved from http://www.azdjc.gov/OfficesPrograms/Research/RecidivismRates2014.pdf.

Arnett, J. J. (1999). Adolescent storm and stress, reconsidered. *American Psychologist, 54*, 317–326.

Backett-Milburn, K., Wilson, S., Bancroft, A., & Cunningham-Burley, S. (2008). Challenging childhoods: Young people's accounts of 'getting by' in families with substance abuse problems. *Childhood, 15*, 461–479.

Baker, P. L., & Carson, A. (1999). I take care of my kids: Mothering practices of substance abusing women. *Gender and Society, 13*, 347–363.

Banwell, C., & Bammer, G. (2006). Maternal habits: Narratives of mothering, social position and drug use. *International Journal of Drug Policy, 17*, 504–513.

Barnard, M., & Barlow, J. (2003). Discovering parental drug dependence: Silence and disclosure. *Children & Society, 17*, 45–56.

Barnard, M., & McKeganey, N. (2004). The impact of parental problem drug use on children: What is the problem and what can be done to help? *Addiction, 99*, 552–559.

Barrera, M., Jr., Castro, F. G., & Biglan, A. (1999). Ethnicity, substance use, and development: Exemplars for exploring group differences and similarities. *Developmental Psychopathology, 11*, 805–822.

Bauer, H. M., Rodriguez, M. A., Quiroga, S. S., & Flores-Ortiz, Y. G. (2000). Barriers to health care for abused Latina and Asian immigrant women. *Journal of Health Care for the Poor and Underserved, 11*, 33–44.

Becoña, E., Martínez, Ú., Calafat, A., Juan, M., Fernández-Hermida, J. R., & Secades-Villa, R. (2012). Parental styles and drug use: A review. *Drugs: Education, Prevention, and Policy, 19*, 1–10.

Belknap, J., & Cady, B. (2008). Pre-adjudicated and adjudicated girls' reports on their lives before and during detention and incarceration. In Ruth T. Zapan (Ed.), *Female offenders: Critical perspectives and effective interventions* (pp. 251–281). Washington, DC: Jones and Bartlett.

Belknap, J., Holsinger, K., & Dunn, M. (1997). Understanding incarcerated girls: The results of a focus group study. *The Prison Journal, 77*, 381–404.

Belknap, J., Winter, E., & Cady, B. (2003). Professionals' assessments of the needs of delinquent girls: The results of a focus group study. In Barbara E. Bloom (Ed.), *Gendered justice: Addressing female offenders* (pp. 209–240). Durham, NC: Carolina Academic Press.

Belsky, J. (1980). Child maltreatment: An ecological integration. *American Psychologist, 35*, 320–335.

Belsky, J. (1984). The determinants of parenting: A process model. *Child Development, 55*, 83–96.

Betancourt, J. R., & Green, A. R. (2010). Commentary: Linking cultural competence training to improved health outcomes: Perspectives from the field. *Academic Medicine, 85*, 583–585.

Black, K. A., & Schutte, E. D. (2006). Recollections of being loved implications of childhood experiences with parents for young adults' romantic relationships. *Journal of Family Issues, 27*, 1459–1480.

Blakeley, K. (2014). Mom arrested for bringing 7-year-old on drug deal. Cafémom blog. Retrieved from http://thestir.cafemom.com/in_the_news/177706/mom_brings_daughter_drug_deal?use_mobile=0.

Bloch, K., & Taylor, T. (2014). Welfare queens and anchor babies: A comparative study of stigmatized mothers in the United States. In M. Vandenbeld Giles (Ed.), *Mothering in the age of neoliberalism* (pp. 199–210). Bradford, ONT: Demeter Press.

Bloom, B., Owen, B., Rosenbaum, J., & Deschenes, E. P. (2003). Focusing on girls and young women. *Women & Criminal Justice, 14*, 117–136.

Bortner, M. A. (1982). *Inside a juvenile court: The tarnished ideal of individualized justice.* New York: New York University Press.

Bosk, E. A. (2013). Between badness and sickness: Reconsidering medicalization for high-risk children and youth. *Children and Youth Services Review, 35*, 1212–1218.

Bottcher, J. (2001). Social practices of gender: How gender relates to delinquency in the everyday lives of high-risk youths. *Criminology, 39*, 893–932.

Boyd, C. J., & Mieczkowski, T. (1990). Drug use, health, family and social support in "crack" cocaine users. *Addictive Behaviors, 15*, 481–485.

Brabeck, K. M., Lykes, M. B., & Hershberg, R. (2011). Framing immigration to and deportation from the United States: Guatemalan and Salvadoran families make meaning of their experiences. *Community, Work & Family, 14*, 275–296.

Brabeck, K., & Xu, Q. (2010). The impact of detention and deportation on Latino immigrant children and families: A quantitative exploration. *Hispanic Journal of Behavioral Sciences, 32*, 341–361.

Bronfenbrenner, U. (1986). Ecology of the family as a context for human development: Research perspectives. *Developmental Psychology, 22*, 723–742.

Brown, E. J. (2006). Good mother, bad mother: Perception of mothering by rural African-American women who use cocaine. *Journal of Addictions Nursing, 17*, 21–31.

Brown, L., Callahan, M., Strega, S., Walmsley, C., & Dominelli, L. (2009). Manufacturing ghost fathers: The paradox of father presence and absence in child welfare. *Child & Family Social Work, 14*, 25–34.

Burgess-Proctor, A. (2006). Intersections of race, class, gender, and crime future directions for feminist criminology. *Feminist Criminology, 1*, 27–47.

Burton, L. (2007). Childhood adultification in economically disadvantaged families: A conceptual model. *Family Relations, 56*, 329–345.

Buzawa, E. S., & Hirschel, D. (2010). Criminalizing assault: Do age and gender really matter? In M. Chesney-Lind & N. Jones (Eds.), *Fighting for girls: New perspectives on gender and violence* (pp. 33–55). Albany, NY: State University of New York Press.

Carbone-Lopez, K., & Miller, J. (2012). Precocious role entry as a mediating factor in women's methamphetamine use: Implications for life-course and pathways research. *Criminology, 50,* 187–220.

Carpenter, L. M. (2002). Gender and the meaning and experience of virginity loss in the contemporary United States. *Gender & Society, 16,* 345–365.

Castillo, L. G., Perez, F. V., Castillo, R., & Ghosheh, M. R. (2010). Construction and initial validation of the Marianismo Beliefs Scale. *Counseling Psychology Quarterly, 23,* 163–175.

Cauffman, E., Feldman, S., Waterman, J., & Steiner, H. (1998). Posttraumatic stress disorder among female juvenile offenders. *Journal of the American Academy of Child & Adolescent Psychiatry, 37,* 1209–1216.

CDC. (2014). *Understanding teen dating violence: A fact sheet.* Retrieved from http://www .cdc.gov/violenceprevention/pdf/teen-dating-violence-factsheet-a.pdf.

Chamberlain, P. (2003). *Treating chronic juvenile offenders: Advances made through the Oregon multidimensional treatment foster care model.* Washington, DC: American Psychological Association.

Chambers, D. (2001). *Representing the family.* Thousand Oaks, CA: Sage.

Chesney-Lind, M. (2010). Jailing "bad" girls. In M. Chesney-Lind & N. Jones (Eds.), *Fighting for girls: New perspectives on gender and violence* (pp. 57–59). Albany, NY: State University of New York Press.

Chesney-Lind, M., & Eliason, M. (2006). From invisible to incorrigible: The demonization of marginalized women and girls. *Crime, Media, Culture, 2,* 29–47.

Chesney-Lind, M., & Irwin, K. (2013). *Beyond bad girls: Gender, violence and hype.* New York: Routledge.

Chesney-Lind, M., Morash, M., & Stevens, T. (2008). Girls troubles, girls' delinquency, and gender responsive programming: A review. *Australian & New Zealand Journal of Criminology, 41,* 162–189.

Chesney-Lind, M., & Shelden, R. G. (2013). *Girls, delinquency, and juvenile justice.* West Sussex, UK: John Wiley & Sons.

Children's Action Alliance. (2008). *Racial disproportionality in the juvenile justice system in Maricopa County.* Retrieved from http://www.azchildren.org/MyFiles/PDF/Racial_Disproportionality_JJ.pdf.

Chin, G. J. (2002). Race, the war on drugs, and the collateral consequences of criminal conviction. *Journal of Gender, Race & Justice, 6,* 253–275.

Chumbler, N., Bute, J., Huff, A., & Cherry, C.O.B. (2015). Building a "better life": The transformative effects of adolescent pregnancy and parenting. *SAGE Open, 5,* 1–9.

Cleaver, D., Nicholson, D., Tarr, S., & Cleaver, D. (2007). *Child protection, domestic violence and parental substance misuse: Family experiences and effective practice.* London: Jessica Kingsley.

Coalition for Juvenile Justice/SOS Project. (2012). *Positive power: Exercising judicial leadership to prevent court involvement and incarceration of non-delinquent youth.* Retrieved from http://www.modelsforchange.net/publications/337.

Collins, W. A., Welsh, D. P., & Furman, W. (2009). Adolescent romantic relationships. *Annual Review of Psychology, 60,* 631–652.

Craven, S., Brown, S., & Gilchrist, E. (2006). Sexual grooming of children: Review of literature and theoretical considerations. *Journal of Sexual Aggression, 12*, 287–299.

Daguerre, A. (2008). The second phase of US welfare reform, 2000–2006: Blaming the poor again? *Social Policy & Administration, 42*, 362–378.

Davis, C. P. (2007). At-risk girls and delinquency career pathways. *Crime & Delinquency, 53*, 408–435.

Davis, I., Litrownick, A., & Weinstein, J. (1997). *Interdisciplinary collaboration and education in child welfare practice.* U.S. Department of Health and Human Services, Office of Development Services.

Decker, S. H., Taylor, M., & Katz, C. M. (2013). *A case study of the response of the Arizona Department of Juvenile Corrections to the Civil Rights of Institutionalized Persons Act consent decree.* U.S. Department of Justice. Retrieved from https://www.ncjrs.gov/pdffiles1/nij/grants/244085.pdf.

DeHart, D. D. (2009). *Poly-victimization among girls in the juvenile justice system.* Washington, DC: National Institute of Justice, Office of Justice Programs, U.S. Department of Justice.

DeHart, D., Lynch, S., Belknap, J., Dass-Brailsford, P., & Green, B. (2014). Life history models of female offending the roles of serious mental illness and trauma in women's pathways to jail. *Psychology of Women Quarterly, 38*, 138–151.

Delva, J., Horner, P., Martinez, R., Sanders, L., Lopez, W. D., & Doering-White, J. (2013). Mental health problems of children of undocumented parents in the United States: A hidden crisis. *Journal of Community Positive Practices, 13*, 25–35.

Desai, R. A., Goulet, J. L., Robbins, J., Chapman, J. F., Migdole, S. J., & Hoge, M. A. (2006). Mental health care in juvenile detention facilities: A review. *Journal of the American Academy of Psychiatry and the Law Online, 34*, 204–214.

DeWit, D. J. (1998). Frequent childhood geographic relocation: Its impact on drug use initiation and the development of alcohol and other drug-related problems among adolescents and young adults. *Addictive Behaviors, 23*, 623–634.

Díaz-Cotto, J. (2006). *Chicana lives and criminal justice: Voices from El Barrio.* Austin, TX: University of Texas Press.

DiIulio, J. (1995, December 15). Moral poverty: The coming of the super-predators should scare us into wanting to get to the root causes of crime a lot faster. *Chicago Tribune.* Retrieved from http://articles.chicagotribune.com/1995-12-15/news/9512150046_1_crime-talking-bomb/4.

Dohrn, B. (2004). All Ellas: Girls locked up. *Feminist Studies, 30*, 302–324.

Dreby, J. (2012). The burden of deportation on children in Mexican immigrant families. *Journal of Marriage and Family, 74*, 829–845.

Durán, R. J. (2008). Legitimated oppression: Inner-city Mexican American experiences with police gang enforcement. *Journal of Contemporary Ethnography, 38*, 143–168.

Ennett, S. T., Bauman, K. E., Foshee, V. A., Pemberton, M., & Hicks, K. A. (2001). Parent–child communication about adolescent tobacco and alcohol use: What do parents say and does it affect youth behavior? *Journal of Marriage and Family, 63*, 48–62.

Faulkner, J. (2010). The innocence fetish: The commodification and sexualisation of children in the media and popular culture. *Media International Australia, 135,* 106–117.

Feld, B. C. (1999). Transformation of the juvenile court—part II: Race and the crack down on youth crime. *Minnesota Law Review, 84,* 327–395.

Fields, D., & Abrams, L. S. (2010, August). Gender differences in the perceived needs and barriers of youth offenders preparing for community reentry. *Child & Youth Care Forum, 39,* 253–269.

Fine, M., & Weis, L. (1998). *The unknown city: Lives of poor and working class young adults.* Boston, MA: Beacon Press.

Fineman, M. L. (1995). Masking dependency: The political role of family rhetoric. *Virginia Law Review, 81,* 2181–2215.

Foley, A. (2008). The current state of gender-specific delinquency programming. *Journal of Criminal Justice, 36,* 262–269.

Foshee, V. A. (1996). Gender differences in adolescent dating abuse prevalence, types, and injuries. *Health Education Research, 11,* 275–286.

Foshee, V. A., Bauman, K. E., & Linder, G. F. (1999). Family violence and the perpetration of adolescent dating violence: Examining social learning and social control processes. *Journal of Marriage and the Family, 61,* 331–342.

Gaarder, E., & Belknap, J. (2002). Tenuous borders: Girls transferred to adult court. *Criminology, 40,* 481–517.

Gaarder, E., Rodriguez, N., & Zatz, M. S. (2004). Criers, liars, and manipulators: Probation officers' views of girls. *Justice Quarterly, 21,* 547–578.

Garbus, L. (Director, Producer). (2003). *Girlhood* [Documentary]. New York: Fox Lorber.

Garcia, L. (2009). Love at first sex: Latina girls' meanings of virginity loss and relationships. *Identities: Global Studies in Culture and Power, 16,* 601–621.

Gasper, J., DeLuca, S., & Estacion, A. (2010). Coming and going: Explaining the effects of residential and school mobility on adolescent delinquency. *Social Science Research, 39,* 459–476.

Giaconia, R. M., Reinherz, H. Z., Silverman, A. B., Pakiz, B., Frost, A. K., & Cohen, E. (1995). Traumas and posttraumatic stress disorder in a community population of older adolescents. *Journal of the American Academy of Child & Adolescent Psychiatry, 34,* 1369–1380.

Gilliard-Matthews, S., Stevens, R., Nilsen, M., & Dunaev, J. (2015). "You see it everywhere. It's just natural": Contextualizing the role of peers, family, and neighborhood in initial substance use. *Deviant Behavior, 36,* 492–509.

Giordano, P. C. (2010). *Legacies of crime: A follow-up of the children of highly delinquent girls and boys.* New York: Cambridge University Press.

Goldberg, W. A., Tan, E. T., & Thorsen, K. L. (2009). Trends in academic attention to fathers, 1930–2006. *Fathering: A Journal of Theory, Research, and Practice about Men as Fathers, 7,* 159–179.

Golzari, M., Hunt, S. J., & Anoshiravani, A. (2006). The health status of youth in juvenile detention facilities. *Journal of Adolescent Health, 38,* 776–782.

Gonzalez, R., & Ayala-Alcantar, C. U. (2008). Critical caring: Dispelling Latino stereotypes among preservice teachers. *Journal of Latinos and Education, 7,* 129–143.

Goodkind, S. (2005). Gender-specific services in the juvenile justice system: A critical examination. *Affilia, 20*, 52–70.

Gross, P. (1987). Defining post-divorce remarriage families: A typology based on the subjective perceptions of children. *Journal of Divorce, 10*, 205–217.

Guthrie, B. J., & Flinchbaugh, L. J. (2001). Gender-specific substance prevention programming: Going beyond just focusing on girls. *Journal of Early Adolescence, 21*, 354–372.

Gutiérrez, L., Oh, H. J., & Gillmore, M. R. (2000). Toward an understanding of (em) power (ment) for HIV/AIDS prevention with adolescent women. *Sex Roles, 42*, 581–611.

Guttmacher Institute. (2015, February 1). State policies in brief: Substance abuse during pregnancy. Retrieved from http://www.guttmacher.org/statecenter/spibs/spib_SADP .pdf.

Haberman, C. (2014, April 6). When youth violence spurred 'superpredator' fear. *New York Times*. Retrieved from http://www.nytimes.com/2014/04/07/us/politics/killing-on-bus-recalls-superpredator-threat-of-90s.html?_r=0.

Hagan, J., & Coleman, J. P. (2001). Returning captives of the American war on drugs: Issues of community and family reentry. *Crime & Delinquency, 47*, 352–367.

Haight, W., Carter-Black, J. D., & Sheridan, K. (2009). Mothers' experience of methamphetamine addiction: A case-based analysis of rural, Midwestern women. *Children and Youth Services Review, 31*, 71–77.

Haight, W., Ostler, T., Black, J., Sheridan, K., & Kingery, L. (2007). A child's-eye view of parent methamphetamine abuse: Implications for helping foster families succeed. *Children and Youth Services Review, 29*, 1–15.

Hamer, J. (2001). *What it means to be daddy: Fatherhood for black men living away from their children*. New York: Columbia University Press.

Hardwicke, C. (Director). (2003). *Thirteen* [Film]. California, USA: Fox Searchlight Pictures.

Harris, L. J. (2006). An empirical study of parental responsibility laws: Sending messages, but what kind and to whom? *Utah Law Review, 1*, 5–34.

Hayslip, B., & Kaminski, P. L. (2005). Grandparents raising their grandchildren: A review of the literature and suggestions for practice. *The Gerontologist, 45*, 262–269.

Henggeler, S. W., Schoenwald, S. K., Borduin, C. M., Rowland, M. D., & Cunningham, P. B. (2009). *Multisystemic therapy for antisocial behavior in children and adolescents*. New York: Guilford Press.

Hennessey, M., Ford, J. D., Mahoney, K., Ko, S., & Siegfried, C. (2004). *Trauma among girls in the juvenile justice system*. Los Angeles, CA: National Child Traumatic Stress Network.

Herz, D. C. (2001). Understanding the use of mental health placements by the juvenile justice system. *Journal of Emotional and Behavioral Disorders, 9*, 172–181.

Herz, D. C., & Ryan, J. P. (2008). *Bridging two worlds: Youth involved in the child welfare and juvenile justice systems, A policy guide for improving outcomes*. Washington, DC: Georgetown University Public Policy Institute, Center for Juvenile Justice Reform.

Hickman, L. J., Jaycox, L. H., & Aronoff, J. (2004). Dating violence among adolescents prevalence, gender distribution, and prevention program effectiveness. *Trauma, Violence, & Abuse, 5*, 123–142.

Hidalgo, R. (2013). Crossroads: The intersection of immigrant enforcement and the child welfare system. *Juvenile and Family Court Journal, 64,* 35–44.

Hirsch, A. E. (2001). "The world was never a safe place for them": Abuse, welfare reform, and women with drug convictions. *Violence Against Women, 7,* 159–175.

Holley, L. C., & VanVleet, R. K. (2006). Racism and classism in the youth justice system: Perspectives of youth and staff. *Journal of Poverty, 10,* 45–67.

Holt, S., Buckley, H., & Whelan, S. (2008). The impact of exposure to domestic violence on children and young people: A review of the literature. *Child Abuse & Neglect, 32,* 797–810.

Humphries, D. (1999). *Crack mothers: Pregnancy, drugs, and the media.* Columbus, OH: Ohio State University Press.

Hutchinson, T. C., Parada, G., & Smandych, R. (2009). "Show me a bad kid and I'll show you a lousy parent": Making parents responsible for youth crime in Australian and Canadian contexts. *Australasian Canadian Studies, 26,* 49–86.

James, C., Stams, G.J.J., Asscher, J. J., De Roo, A. K., & van der Laan, P. H. (2013). Aftercare programs for reducing recidivism among juvenile and young adult offenders: A meta-analytic review. *Clinical Psychology Review, 33,* 263–274.

James, S. E., Johnson, J., & Raghavan, C. (2004). "I couldn't go anywhere": Contextualizing violence and drug abuse: a social network study. *Violence Against Women, 10,* 991–1014.

Jankowski, M. K., Leitenberg, H., Henning, K., & Coffey, P. (1999). Intergenerational transmission of dating aggression as a function of witnessing only same-sex parents vs. opposite-sex parents vs. both parents as perpetrators of domestic violence. *Journal of Family Violence, 14,* 267–279.

Javdani, S., & Allen, N. E. (2016). An ecological model for intervention for juvenile system-involved girls development and preliminary prospective evaluation. *Feminist Criminology, 11,* 135–162.

Javdani, S., Sadeh, N., & Verona, E. (2011a). Expanding our lens: Female pathways to anti-social behavior in adolescence and adulthood. *Clinical Psychology Review, 31,* 1324–1348.

Javdani, S., Sadeh, N., & Verona, E. (2011b). Gendered social forces: A review of the impact of institutionalized factors on women and girls' criminal justice trajectories. *Psychology, Public Policy, and Law, 17,* 161–211.

Johnson, H. (2004). *Drugs and crime: A study of incarcerated female offenders* (Vol. 63). Canberra: Australian Institute of Criminology.

Jones, L., Packard, T., & Nahrstedt, K. (2002). Evaluation of a training curriculum for inter-agency collaboration. *Journal of Community Practice, 10,* 23–40.

Jones, N. (2009). *Between good and ghetto: African American girls and inner-city violence.* New Brunswick, NJ: Rutgers University Press.

Jouriles, E. N., Mueller, V., Rosenfield, D., McDonald, R., & Dodson, M. C. (2012). Teens' experiences of harsh parenting and exposure to severe intimate partner violence: Adding insult to injury in predicting teen dating violence. *Psychology of Violence, 2,* 125–138.

Jurkovic, G. J. (1997). *Lost childhoods: The plight of the parentified child.* Philadelphia, PA: Brunner/Mazel.

Justice for Families. (2012). Families unlocking futures: Solutions to the crisis in juvenile justice. Report retrieved from http://www.justice4families.org/file/famsunlockingfutures.html.

Kantor, G. K., & Little, L. (2003). Defining the boundaries of child neglect: When does domestic violence equate with parental failure to protect? *Journal of Interpersonal Violence, 18*, 338–355.

Kelly, P. J., Cheng, A. L., Peralez-Dieckmann, E., & Martinez, E. (2008). Dating violence and girls in the juvenile justice system. *Journal of Interpersonal Violence, 24*, 1536–1551.

Kempf-Leonard, K., & Johansson, P. (2007). Gender and runaways risk factors, delinquency, and juvenile justice experiences. *Youth Violence and Juvenile Justice, 5*, 308–327.

Kim, J.Y.S., & Fendrich, M. (2002). Gender differences in juvenile arrestees' drug use, self-reported dependence, and perceived need for treatment. *Psychiatric Services, 53*, 70–75.

Klee, H. (1998). Drug-using parents: Analyzing the stereotypes. *International Journal of Drug Policy, 9*, 437–448.

Knox, S., Burkard, A. W., Johnson, A. J., Suzuki, L. A., & Ponterotto, J. G. (2003). African American and European American therapists' experiences of addressing race in cross-racial psychotherapy dyads. *Journal of Counseling Psychology, 50*, 466–481.

Kotchick, B. A., & Forehand, R. (2002). Putting parenting in perspective: A discussion of the contextual factors that shape parenting practices. *Journal of Child and Family Studies, 11*, 255–269.

Kroll, B. (2004). Living with an elephant: Growing up with parental substance misuse. *Child and Family Social Work, 9*, 129–140.

Kroll, B., & Taylor, A. (2003). *Parental substance misuse and child welfare.* London: Jessica Kingsley.

Kumpfer, K. L., Alvarado, R., Smith, P., & Bellamy, N. (2002). Cultural sensitivity and adaptation in family-based prevention interventions. *Prevention Science, 5*, 41–45.

Lambert, M. J., & Barley, D. E. (2001). Research summary on the therapeutic relationship and psychotherapy outcome. *Psychotherapy: Theory, Research, Practice, Training, 38*, 357–361.

Lapidus, L., Luthra, N., Verma, A., Small, D., Allard, P., & Levingston, K. (2005). *Caught in the net: The impact of drug policies on women and families.* New York: American Civil Liberties Union.

Lederman, C. S., Dakof, G. A., Larrea, M. A., & Li, H. (2004). Characteristics of adolescent females in juvenile detention. *International Journal of Law and Psychiatry, 27*, 321–337.

Lee, T. (2016). *Catching a case: Inequality and fear in New York City's child welfare system.* New Brunswick, NJ: Rutgers University Press.

Leve, L. D., Chamberlain, P., Smith, D. K., & Harold, G. T. (2012). Multidimensional treatment foster care as an intervention for juvenile justice girls in out-of-home care. In S. Miller & L. D. Leve (Eds.), *Delinquent girls: Contexts, relationships, and adaptation* (pp. 147–160). New York: Springer.

Lewis, M. (2006). *Custody and control: Conditions of confinement in New York's juvenile prisons for girls* (Vol. 18, No. 4). Human Rights Watch.

Lonegan, B. (2007). American diaspora: The deportation of lawful residents from the United States and the destruction of their families. *NYU Review of Law and Social Change, 32*, 55–81.

Lopez, V., & Chesney-Lind, M. (2014). Latina girls speak out: Stereotypes, gender, and relationship dynamics. *Latino Studies, 12*, 1–23.

Lopez, V., Chesney-Lind, M., & Foley, J. (2012). Relationship power, control, and dating violence among Latina girls. *Violence Against Women, 18*, 681–690.

Lopez, V., & Corona, R. (2012). Troubled relationships: High-risk Latina adolescents and nonresident fathers. *Journal of Family Issues, 33*, 715–744.

Lopez, V., Katsulis, Y., & Robillard, A. (2009). Drug use with parents as a relational strategy for incarcerated female adolescents. *Family Relations, 58*, 135–147.

Lopez, V., Kopak, A., Robillard, A., Gillmore, M. R., Holliday, R. C., & Braithwaite, R. L. (2011). Pathways to sexual risk taking among female adolescent detainees. *Journal of Youth and Adolescence, 40*, 945–957.

Maher, L. (2000). *Sexed work: Gender, race, and resistance in a Brooklyn drug market.* New York: Oxford University Press.

Margolin, G., & Gordis, E. B. (2000). The effects of family and community violence on children. *Annual Review of Psychology, 51*, 445–479.

Marín, B. V., Coyle, K. K., Gómez, C. A., Carvajal, S. C., & Kirby, D. B. (2000). Older boyfriends and girlfriends increase risk of sexual initiation in young adolescents. *Journal of Adolescent Health, 27*, 409–418.

Marsiglio, W., Day, R. D., & Lamb, M. E. (2000). Exploring fatherhood diversity: Implications for conceptualizing father involvement. *Marriage & Family Review, 29*, 269–293.

McClelland, G. M., Teplin, L. A., & Abram, K. M. (2004). *Detection and prevalence of substance use among juvenile detainees.* Washington, DC: U.S. Department of Justice, Office of Justice Programs, Office of Juvenile Justice and Delinquency Prevention.

McCorkel, J. A. (2013). *Breaking women: Gender, race, and the new politics of imprisonment.* New York: New York University Press.

McKeganey, N., Barnard, M., & McIntosch, J. (2002). Paying the price for their parents' addiction: Meeting the needs of children of drug-using parents. *Drugs: Education, Prevention, & Policy, 3*, 233–246.

McKinney, S. (2014). *Runaway youth: A research brief.* Status Offense Reform Center. Retrieved from http://www.statusoffensereform.org/wp-content/uploads/2014/05/Running-Away_Final.pdf.

Miller, J., & White, N. A. (2003). Gender and adolescent relationship violence: A contextual examination. *Criminology, 41*, 1207–1248.

Miller, S., Malone, P. S., & Dodge, K. A. (2010). Developmental trajectories of boys' and girls' delinquency: Sex differences and links to later adolescent outcomes. *Journal of Abnormal Child Psychology, 38*, 1021–1032.

Mincy, R. B., & Sorensen, E. J. (1998). Deadbeats and turnips in child support reform. *Journal of Policy Analysis and Management, 17*, 44–51.

Moffitt, T. E. (1993). Adolescence-limited and life-course-persistent antisocial behavior: A developmental taxonomy. *Psychological Review, 100*, 674–701.

Moffitt, T. E., & Caspi, A. (2001). Childhood predictors differentiate life-course persistent and adolescence-limited antisocial pathways among males and females. *Development and Psychopathology, 13*, 355–375.

Moon, M. M., Sundt, J. L., Cullen, F. T., & Wright, J. P. (2000). Is child saving dead? Public support for juvenile rehabilitation. *Crime & Delinquency, 46*, 38–60.

Moore, S. (2009, August 9). Mentally ill offenders strain juvenile justice system. *New York Times*. Retrieved from http://www.nytimes.com/2009/08/10/us/10juvenile.html.

Mordoch, E. (2010). How children understand parental mental illness: "You don't get life insurance. What's life insurance?" *Journal of the Canadian Academy of Child & Adolescent Psychiatry, 19*, 19–25.

Moretti, M. M., Obsuth, I., Odgers, C. L., & Reebye, P. (2006). Exposure to maternal vs. paternal partner violence, PTSD, and aggression in adolescent girls and boys. *Aggressive Behavior, 32*, 385–395.

Murphy, D. (2014, September 27). Texas mom used 7-year-old in cocaine deals. *New York Daily News*. Retrieved from http://www.nydailynews.com/news/national/texas-mom-7-year-old-cocaine-deals-sheriff-article-1.1955235.

Murphy, K. A., & Smith, D. I. (2009). Adolescent girls' responses to warning signs of abuse in romantic relationships: Implications for youth-targeted relationship violence prevention. *Journal of Interpersonal Violence, 25*, 626–647.

National Center on Addiction and Substance Abuse at Columbia University (CASA), & United States of America. (1999). *No safe haven: Children of substance-abusing parents.* Retrieved from http://www.centeronaddiction.org/addiction-research/reports/no-safe-haven-children-substance-abusing-parents.

A New Freedom. (2016). Retrieved from http://www.newfreedomprograms.com/aboutus.php.

Nielsen, L. (2012). *Father–daughter relationships: Contemporary research and issues.* New York: Routledge.

Nielsen, L. (2014). Young adult daughters' relationships with their fathers: Review of recent research. *Marriage & Family Review, 50*, 360–372.

Northern Arizona Regional Behavioral Health Authority. (2014). *Scope of work: Residential treatment services, therapeutic group home services, behavioral health group home services.* Retrieved from http://www.narbha.org/includes/media/docs/CPS-Scope-of-Work—Room—Board—RBHA-costs-rev-7-09-by-CPS-.pdf.

Nunn, K. B. (2002). Race, crime, and the pool of surplus criminality: Or why the war on drugs was a war on Blacks. *Journal of Gender, Race & Justice, 6*, 381–445.

Nurse, A. (2002). *Fatherhood arrested: Parenting from within the juvenile justice system.* Nashville, TN: Vanderbilt University Press.

Odem, M. E. (1995). *Delinquent daughters: Protecting and policing adolescent female sexuality in the United States, 1885–1920.* Chapel Hill, NC: University of North Carolina Press.

Office of Justice Programs. (2015). *Program profile: Multisystemic therapy—psychiatric.* Retrieved from https://www.crimesolutions.gov/ProgramDetails.aspx?ID=176.

O'Keefe, M. (2005). Teen dating violence: A review of risk factors and prevention efforts. *National Electronic Network on Violence Against Women, 1*, 1–5.

Pasko, L. (2010). Damaged daughters: The history of girls' sexuality and the juvenile justice system. *Journal of Criminal Law and Criminology, 100*, 1099–1130.

Pasko, L., & Lopez, V. (2015). The Latina penalty: Juvenile court and correctional attitudes toward the Latina juvenile offender. *Journal of Ethnicity in Criminal Justice, 1–20.* DOI: 10.1080/15377938.2015.1015196.

Pawlby, S. J., Mills, A., & Quinton, D. (1997). Vulnerable adolescent girls: Opposite-sex relationships. *Journal of Child Psychology and Psychiatry, 38,* 909–920.

Peck, J. H., Leiber, M. J., & Brubaker, S. J. (2013). Gender, race, and juvenile court outcomes: An examination of status offenders. *Youth Violence and Juvenile Justice, 12,* 250–267.

Pehlke, T. A., Hennon, C. B., Radina, M. E., & Kuvalanka, K. A. (2009). Does father still know best? An inductive thematic analysis of popular TV sitcoms. *Fathering: A Journal of Theory, Research, and Practice about Men as Fathers, 7,* 114–139.

Pickett, J. T., & Chiricos, T. (2012). Controlling other people's children: Racialized views of delinquency and whites' punitive attitudes toward juvenile offenders. *Criminology, 50,* 673–710.

Pinderhughes, E. E., Nix, R., Foster, E. M., & Jones, D. (2001). Parenting in context: Impact of neighborhood poverty, residential stability, public services, social networks, and danger on parental behaviors. *Journal of Marriage and Family, 63,* 941–953.

Potochnick, S. R., & Perreira, K. M. (2010). Depression and anxiety among first-generation immigrant Latino youth: Key correlates and implications for future research. *Journal of Nervous and Mental Disease, 198,* 470–477.

Potter, H. (2015). *Intersectionality and criminology: Disrupting and revolutionizing studies of crime.* New York: Routledge.

Prado, G., Pantin, H., Schwartz, S., Lupei, N., & Szapocznik, J. (2006). Predictors of engagement and retention in family-centered substance abuse and HIV preventive interventions for Hispanic adolescents. *Journal of Pediatric Psychology, 31,* 874–890.

Provine, D. M. (2008). *Unequal under law: Race in the war on drugs.* Chicago, IL: University of Chicago Press.

Provine, D. M., & Sanchez, G. (2011). Suspecting immigrants: Exploring links between racialised anxieties and expanded police powers in Arizona. *Policing and Society, 21,* 468–479.

Purdie, V., & Downey, G. (2000). Rejection sensitivity and adolescent girls' vulnerability to relationship-centered difficulties. *Child Maltreatment, 5,* 338–349.

Quiroga, S. S., Medina, D. M., & Glick, J. (2014). In the belly of the beast effects of anti-immigration policy on Latino community members. *American Behavioral Scientist, 58,* 1723–1742.

Rabinovitz, L. (1989). Sitcoms and single moms: Representations of feminism on American TV. *Cinema Journal, 29,* 3–19.

Rhodes, T., Bernays, S., & Houmoller, K. (2010). Parents who use drugs: Accounting for damage and its limitation. *Social Science & Medicine, 71,* 1489–1497.

Richter, K. P., & Bammer, G. (2000). A hierarchy of strategies heroin-using mothers employ to reduce harm to their children. *Journal of Substance Abuse Treatment, 19,* 403–413.

Rios, V. M. (2008). The racial politics of youth crime. *Latino Studies, 6,* 97–115.

Rios, V. M. (2011). *Punished: Policing the lives of Black and Latino boys.* New York: New York University Press.

Roberts, D., Coakley, T. M., Washington, T. J., & Kelley, A. (2014). Fathers' perspectives on supports and barriers that affect their fatherhood role. *SAGE Open, 4,* 1–10.

Robinson, J. D., & Skill, T. (2001). Five decades of families on television: From the 1950s through the 1990s. In J. A. Bryant (Ed.), *Television and the American family* (pp. 139–162). New York: Routledge.

Rodriguez, N., Smith, H., & Zatz, M. S. (2009). "Youth is enmeshed in a highly dysfunctional family system": Exploring the relationship among dysfunctional families, parental incarceration, and juvenile court decision making. *Criminology, 47,* 177–208.

Rohner, R. P., & Veneziano, R. A. (2001). The importance of father love: History and contemporary evidence. *Review of General Psychology, 5,* 382–405.

Romero, M. (2011). Constructing Mexican immigrant women as a threat to American families. *International Journal of Sociology of the Family, 27,* 49–68.

Roy, K. M., & Dyson, O. L. (2005). Gatekeeping in context: Babymama drama and the involvement of incarcerated fathers. *Fathering, 3,* 289–310.

Ryder, J. A. (2014). *Girls and violence: Tracing the roots of criminal behavior.* Boulder, CO: Lynne Rienner.

Salisbury, E. J., & Van Voorhis, P. (2009). Gendered pathways: A quantitative investigation of women probationers' paths to incarceration. *Criminal Justice and Behavior, 36,* 541–566.

Sanftner, J. L., Ryan, W. J., & Pierce, P. (2009). Application of a relational model to understanding body image in college women and men. *Journal of College Student Psychotherapy, 23,* 262–280.

Santos, C., & Menjivar, C. (2014). Youths' perspective on Senate Bill 1070 in Arizona: The socio-emotional effects of immigration policy. *Association of Mexican American Educators Journal, 7,* 7–17.

Schaffner, L. (2006). *Girls in trouble with the law.* New Brunswick, NJ: Rutgers University Press.

Schaffner, L. (2008). Latinas in US juvenile detention: Turning adversity to advantage. *Latino Studies, 6,* 116–136.

Schaffner, L. (2014). *Teenage runaways: Broken hearts and "bad attitudes."* New York: Routledge.

Scharf, M., & Mayseless, O. (2008). Late adolescent girls' relationships with parents and romantic partners: The distinct role of mothers and fathers. *Journal of Adolescence, 31,* 837–855.

Scharrer, E. (2001). From wise to foolish: The portrayal of the sitcom father, 1950s–1990s. *Journal of Broadcasting & Electronic Media, 45,* 23–40.

Schmeeckle, M., Giarrusso, R., Feng, D., & Bengtson, V. L. (2006). What makes someone family? Adult children's perceptions of current and former stepparents. *Journal of Marriage and Family, 68,* 595–610.

Sedlak, A. J., & Broadhurst, D. D. (1996). *The national incidence study of child abuse and neglect.* Washington, DC: U.S. Department of Health and Human Services.

Sedlak, A., & McPherson, K. S. (2010). *Survey of youth in residential placement: Youth's needs and services.* Washington, DC: Westat.

Sered, S. S., & Norton-Hawk, M. (2014). *Can't catch a break: Gender, jail, drugs, and the limits of personal responsibility.* Berkeley, CA: University of California Press.

Siegel, J. A. (2011). *Disrupted childhoods: Children of women in prison.* New Brunswick, NJ: Rutgers University Press.

Silver, L. J. (2015). *System kids: Adolescent mothers and the politics of regulation.* Chapel Hill, NC: University of North Carolina Press.

Silverman, A. (2009, December 17). Suicidal tendencies: The Arizona Department of Juvenile Corrections is a bloody mess. *Phoenix New Times*. Retrieved from http://www .phoenixnewtimes.com/news/suicidal-tendencies-the-arizona-department-of-juvenile-corrections-is-a-bloody-mess-6445829.

Silverstein, L. B., & Auerbach, C. F. (1999). Deconstructing the essential father. *American Psychologist, 54*, 397.

Simons, R. L., Wu, C. I., Johnson, C., & Conger, R. D. (1995). A test of various perspectives on the intergenerational transmission of domestic violence. *Criminology, 33*, 141–172.

Skowyra, K. R., & Cocozza, J. J. (2007). *Blueprint for change: A comprehensive model for the identification and treatment of youth with mental health needs in contact with the juvenile justice system*. The National Center for Juvenile Justice and Mental Health Research, Delmar, NY: Policy Research Associates. Retrieved from http://www.ncmhjj.com/ wp-content/uploads/2013/07/2007_Blueprint-for-Change-Full-Report.pdf.

Smetana, J. G., Campione-Barr, N., & Metzger, A. (2006). Adolescent development in interpersonal and societal contexts. *Annual Review of Psychology, 57*, 255–284.

SmithBattle, L. (2007). "I wanna have a good future": Teen mothers' rise in educational aspirations, competing demands, and limited school support. *Youth & Society, 38*, 348–371.

Sterk, C. (1999). *Fast lives: Women who use crack cocaine*. Philadelphia, PA: Temple University Press.

Strauss, S. M., & Falkin, G. P. (2001). Social support systems of women offenders who use drugs: A focus on the mother–daughter relationship. *American Journal of Drug and Alcohol Abuse, 27*, 65–89.

Strom, K. J., Warner, T. D., Tichavsky, L., & Zahn, M. A. (2010). Policing juveniles: Domestic violence arrest policies, gender, and police response to child–parent violence. *Crime & Delinquency, 60*, 427–450.

Suchman, N., Pajulo, M., DeCoste, C., & Mayes, L. (2006). Parenting interventions for drug-dependent mothers and their young children: The case for an attachment-based approach. *Family Relations, 55*, 211–226.

Svensson, R. (2003). Gender differences in adolescent drug use: The impact of parental monitoring and peer deviance. *Youth & Society, 34*, 300–329.

Szapocznik, J., & Coatsworth, J. D. (1999). An ecodevelopmental framework for organizing the influences on drug abuse: A developmental model of risk and protection. In M. Glantz & C. R. Hartel (Eds.), *Drug abuse: Origins and interventions* (pp. 331–366). Washington, DC: American Psychological Association.

Taylor, M., Decker, S., & Katz, C. (2015). Statewide responses to a proposed realignment of juvenile corrections in Arizona. *Criminal Justice Review, 40*, 488–504.

Teplin, L. A., Abram, K. M., McClelland, G. M., Dulcan, M. K., & Mericle, A. A. (2002). Psychiatric disorders in youth in juvenile detention. *Archives of General Psychiatry, 59*, 1133–1143.

Teplin, L. A., Abram, K. M., McClelland, G. M., Washburn, J. J., & Pikus, A. K. (2005). Detecting mental disorder in juvenile detainees: Who receives services. *American Journal of Public Health, 95*, 1773–1780.

Thrane, L. E., Yoder, K. A., & Chen, X. (2011). The influence of running away on the risk of female sexual assault in the subsequent year. *Violence and Victims, 26*, 816–829.

Tolman, D. L. (2009). *Dilemmas of desire: Teenage girls talk about sexuality*. Cambridge, MA: Harvard University Press.

Tosouni, A. (2010). Who's bad? An ethnographic study of incarcerated girls. PhD dissertation, University of California, Irvine, CA.

Tosouni, A. (2014). We're not supposed to have nothing in here: Life in juvenile jail through the voices of incarcerated girls. *Criminology, Criminal Justice, Law & Society, 15*, 60–79.

Tracy, E. M., & Martin, T. C. (2007). Children's roles in the social networks of women in substance abuse treatment. *Journal of Substance Abuse Treatment, 32*, 81–88.

Trinder, L. (2008). Maternal gate closing and gate opening in postdivorce families. *Journal of Family Issues, 29*, 1298–1324.

Tucker, J. S., Edelen, M. O., Ellickson, P. L., & Klein, D. J. (2011). Running away from home: A longitudinal study of adolescent risk factors and young adult outcomes. *Journal of Youth and Adolescence, 40*, 507–518.

Tyler, K. A., Hoyt, D. R., Whitbeck, L. B., & Cauce, A. M. (2001). The impact of childhood sexual abuse on later sexual victimization among runaway youth. *Journal of Research on Adolescence, 11*, 151–176.

Valdez, A. (2007). *Mexican American girls and gang violence: Beyond risk*. New York: Macmillan.

Van Olphen, J., Eliason, M. J., Freudenberg, N., & Barnes, M. (2009). Nowhere to go: How stigma limits the options of female drug users after release from jail. *Substance Abuse Treatment, Prevention, and Policy, 4*, 1–10.

Van Parys, H., & Rober, P. (2013). Trying to comfort the parent: A qualitative study of children dealing with parental depression. *Journal of Marital and Family Therapy, 39*, 330–345.

Van Schaick, K., & Stolberg, A. L. (2001). The impact of paternal involvement and parental divorce on young adults' intimate relationships. *Journal of Divorce & Remarriage, 36*, 99–121.

Walker, S. C., Bishop, A. S., Pullmann, M. D., & Bauer, G. (2015). A research framework for understanding the practical impact of family involvement in the juvenile justice system: The juvenile justice family involvement model. *American Journal of Community Psychology, 56*, 408–421.

Walsh, F. (Ed.). (2012). *Normal family processes: Growing diversity and complexity*. New York: Guilford Press.

Wasserman, G., McReynolds, L., Ko, S., Katz, L., & Carpenter, J. (2005). Gender differences in psychiatric disorders at juvenile probation intake. *American Journal of Public Health, 95*, 131–137.

Wekerle, C., Leung, E., Wall, A. M., MacMillan, H., Boyle, M., Trocme, N., & Waechter, R. (2009). The contribution of childhood emotional abuse to teen dating violence among child protective services-involved youth. *Child Abuse & Neglect, 33*, 45–58.

Wesely, J. K. (2012). *Being female: The continuum of sexualization*. Boulder, CO: Lynne Rienner.

Wessler, S. F. (2011). *Shattered families: The perilous intersection of immigration enforcement and the child welfare system*. Applied Research Center, New York. Retrieved from https://www.raceforward.org/research/reports/shattered-families.

White, C. (2015). Incarcerating youth with mental health problems: A focus on the intersection of race, ethnicity, and mental illness. *Youth Violence and Juvenile Justice, 14,* 426–447.

Wolf, A. M., Graziano, J., & Hartney, C. (2009). The provision and completion of gender-specific services for girls on probation variation by race and ethnicity. *Crime & Delinquency, 55,* 294–312.

Yoshikawa, H., Kholoptseva, J., & Suárez-Orozco, C. (2013). The role of public policies and community-based organizations in the developmental consequences of parent undocumented status. *Social Policy Report, 27,* 1–17.

Young, A. M., & d'Arcy, H. (2005). Older boyfriends of adolescent girls: The cause or a sign of the problem? *Journal of Adolescent Health, 36,* 410–419.

INDEX

abusive relationships, 19, 53–56, 82–103; counterstrategies in, 99–102. *See also* dating violence; domestic violence; sexual abuse

Acoca, Leslie, 82–83

adultification, 46–58, 106, 141

adverse childhood events (ACEs), 17

aftercare services, 155, 176–177, 181–182

Aid to Families with Dependent Children, 25

Aldridge, Judith, and colleagues, 12, 183

anti-family policies, 25, 44, 46, 60–61

anti-immigrant policies, 14–15

Arditti, Joyce, 13, 65, 186; and colleagues, 17

Arizona Department of Juvenile Corrections, 150–151, 204nn3–4

Arroyo Verde Correctional Facility, policies and programs at, 150–155

"bad boys," appeal of, 84

Bammer, Gabriele, 127

Banwell, Cathy, 127

Belknap, Joanne, and colleagues, 12, 103, 107, 167

Blakely, Kiri, 42

Bortner, Margaret, 27

Bottcher, Jean, 47

Burton, Linda, 47

Bush, George W., 25–26

Cady, Bonnie, 167

Cantrell, Brian, 42

Carbone-Lopez, Kristin, 106, 110

child protective services (CPS), 12, 17, 18, 20, 27–28, 39–40, 45, 48, 184

Chin, Gabriel, 13

Cleaver, Hedy, 184

Clinton, Bill, 25

collateral consequences, 13, 126

contextual risk factors, 17

cultural stereotypes, 12, 15–16, 44, 145–146, 182–183, 185

cutting, 104, 204n3

dating violence, 19, 83, 101, 202n1

Dedel, Kellie, 82–83

DeHart, Dana D., 83

DiIulio, John, 146

domestic violence, 19, 39, 41, 45–46, 54, 80, 82–83, 87, 146

drug use: by girls, 2–3, 16–17, 20, 77–78, 92, 104–123, 186–187; legal responses to, 13–14, 187; pathways to, 106–108; by parents, 5–6, 10, 13, 14, 26, 28–29, 33–39, 45, 95, 105, 107, 122, 126–128, 184, 186; types of, 20, 105–106, 108, 117–118, 201n1. *See also under* mother-daughter relationships

dysfunctional families, 6, 17, 18, 22–41; girls' positive memories of, 22–23, 28–32; traditional family norm vs., 23–26, 28, 31–36

ecodevelopmental framework, 7–9, 165

extended families. *See* kinship care

Falkin, Gregory, 128

father-daughter relationships, 19, 62–81, 170, 201n1 (chap. 3); drug abuse bonding in, 77–80, 119; influence on dating choices, 85; maternal interference with, 66–67

fathers: "deadbeat dads," 26, 27, 64; sociocultural views of, 63–64

Feld, Barry, 146

Fine, Michelle, 43

Fineman, Martha, 26

Foshee, Vangie, and colleagues, 83

ABOUT THE AUTHOR

VERA LOPEZ is an associate professor of justice studies in the School of Social Transformation at Arizona State University. She earned her PhD in School Psychology from the University of Texas at Austin.

AVAILABLE TITLES IN THE RUTGERS SERIES
IN CHILDHOOD STUDIES

Printed in the United States
By Bookmasters